IT
NEVER
RAINS IN
TIGER
STADIUM

IT
NEVER
RAINS IN
TIGER
STADIUM

JOHN ED BRADLEY

ISBN: 978-1-933060-33-0

ESPN books are available for special promotions and premiums.
For details contact Michael Rentas, Assistant Director, Inventory
Operations, Hyperion, 77 West 66th Street, 11th floor,
New York, New York 10023, or call 212-456-0133.

FIRST EDITION

10 9 8 7 6 5 4 3 2 1

For Coach Mac

CONTENTS

When I was a child, I spake as a child, I understood as a child, I thought as a child: but when I became a man, I put away childish things.
—1 Corinthians 13:11

Chapter One

LEAVING
THE
TEAM

YOU SHOULD'VE SEEN my father's arms. He didn't lift weights or do push-ups or exercise them in any way, and yet they were packed tight with muscle. When I was a boy and he lifted his high-ball in the evening for a sip, a round knot the size of a softball came up under the skin and slowly flattened out when he lowered the glass back down. I loved his arms so much that I memorized every vein, sinew, and golden hair. I knew the wrinkles of his elbows.

In the summer, when he worked for the city's recreation department, supervising the baseball program at the park, Daddy liked to come home for lunch and a nap. He had lemonade and a BLT, then he had me lie close to him on the sofa, and he draped an arm around me. "One ... two ... three ... " he'd count in a whisper, and then he was out, sleeping that easily.

I lay there wondering if I'd ever have arms like his. I needed both hands to travel the distance around his wrist, the tips of my thumbs and fingers barely touching. I felt the hardness of his forearm. I saw how his wedding band fit him like a strand of barbed wire on a tree whose bark had grown around it. He smelled of the grass and the sun, of green and gold days that started early and ended late.

"Were you a good player?" I asked him once as he was coming awake.

"Was I what?"

"A good player."

"You want to know if I was a good player?"

"Yes, sir."

"What kind of question is that?"

"I don't know. Did they run your name in the paper a lot?"

He looked at me in a way that let me know he wanted my attention. "None of it matters, John Ed. Was I a good teammate? Did I do my best and give everything I had to help the team? These are the questions you need to be asking."

I wondered how to answer them, these questions he found of such importance. Many years would have to pass before I was old enough to join a team. He pulled me close again, as if he'd just remembered something. "John Ed?"

"Yes, sir."

"Always be humble."

The rest of the year he worked as a civics teacher and coach at the high school in town. The town was Opelousas, on the road between Alexandria and Lafayette, and it was just small enough, at about twenty thousand, to be excluded from Louisiana state maps when TV weathermen gave their forecasts in the evening. In the morning, my father left home wearing coach's slacks with sharp creases and a polo shirt with a Tiger emblem and the words OHS FOOTBALL printed in Halloween orange on the left breast, the lettering melted from too much time in the dryer. A whistle hung from a nylon cord around his neck. It was still hanging there when he returned at night and sat down to a cold supper—the same meal Mama had served her children hours earlier. "You don't want me to warm it for you, Johnny?"

"No, baby. That's okay."

Sometimes in the afternoon, Mama drove me out to the school. She parked under the oak tree by the gymnasium, pointed to where she wanted me to go, and I walked out past a gate in a hurricane fence to the field where my father and the other coaches were holding practice. Four years old, I wore the same crew cut that my father wore. I stumbled through tall grass and out past the red clay track that encircled the field. At home, my father didn't raise his voice, but here he seemed to shout with every breath. A team manager took me by the hand and led me to a long pine bench on the sideline. I sat among metal coolers, spare shoulder pads and toolboxes crammed with first aid supplies. I waited until the last drill had ended and the players came one after another to the coolers for water the same temperature as the day, drunk in single gulps from paper cups shaped like cones. The players took turns giving the top of my head a mussing. "You gonna play football when you grow up?"

"I don't know."

"You gonna be a coach like your daddy?"

"I want to."

Already I was certain that no one mattered more than a coach. I would trade any day to come for a chance to be that boy again, understanding for the first time who his father was. Give me August and two-a-days and a group of teenagers who are now old men, their uniforms stained green from the grass and black with Louisiana loam. Give me my father's voice as he shouts to them, pushing them harder than they believe they can go, willing them to be better. Give me my father when practice is over and he walks to where I'm sitting and reaches his arms out to hold me.

I HEARD IT when I was a kid. I still hear it. You run into a former ballplayer and give him a minute, and suddenly he's haranguing you about the deleterious effects of global warming on the game of football, arguing that the sunshine that lit the fields back when he played was more golden than it is today. As a matter of fact, everything was better back then—before the world went all to hell. You played with broken ribs and noses, tonsil and toenail problems, abscessed teeth and even certain gastrointestinal disorders, and instead of steroids and human growth hormones, you fed yourself a diet rich in protein and complex carbohydrates. Want to get bigger and stronger? Take a B12 shot and wash down half a dozen raw eggs with breakfast. For lunch, eat a twenty-ounce sirloin pan-fried in butter. After supper, get a soupspoon and carve a hole in a tub of ice cream.

I suppose it's easy to understand why so many of these old boys come off as a little sour—their prime is past, their future uncertain. And I suppose it's also easy to dismiss them out of hand for being such miserable bores. But then one of them will suddenly stop editorializing and focus on the memory of a teammate. This is when things get interesting. A moment ago, the crusty bear was complaining that no college coach is worth three million dollars a year and that TV timeouts make games drag on too long. Now he's bawling into his hands.

I'm guilty of being confused about a lot of things, but I understand why teammates always get a pass. Once upon a time I played the game, although that might be hard to believe to look at me today, with my hair streaked gray and my neck about as big around as a pencil. I was a center for Louisiana State University in the late 1970s, back when Charles McClendon was coach, and I played with people who were so good to me that I've often wondered if I was somehow ruined by their goodness. Want to know what love feels like? Have a couple of teammates carry you off the field when you're so tired and beaten that you're no longer able to carry yourself. Want to witness firsthand an act of courage that brightens your opinion of your fellow man? Have a fullback step up out of nowhere and pick up the blitzing linebacker that you, anchor of the line, failed to block.

I probably think about my LSU teammates more than I should. No, I'm sure I do. I wonder what they've gone and done with their lives. Do they have grandkids? Have they made money? Are they happy?

On more than a few occasions, while out on the road for a magazine assignment, I've spotted young men who brought old teammates to mind. One might have the same self-assured stride as our top wide receiver, while another has a profile nearly identical to that of a reserve quarterback. Though I'm never tempted to walk up to one of them and humiliate myself by peppering him with questions, I often imagine the conversation we'd have. "You know, you look like a college buddy I had a long time ago. Of course, I haven't seen him in ages. For all I know, he could weigh four hundred pounds and get around in one of those motorized scooters. Or maybe he died. But I swear, you look just like him. You're not related to Leigh Shepard, are you?"

"Who?"

"God, did that boy have potential. If he hadn't worn his knees out and quit the squad to return home to Texas, he surely would've been a great one."

And on and on it goes, my description of Leigh Shepard or whomever else growing more detailed as I ramble on.

This is an odd confession, but until about ten years ago, I could rattle off the entire numerical roster for the 1979 LSU football team, beginning with the lowest digit, Carlos Carson's number 3, and ending with the highest, Mark Ippolito's 99. When I encountered a number on a billboard or highway sign, I automatically associated it with a teammate. Once when I was driving through southern Louisiana, I saw a roadside marker for U.S. 90. Demetri Williams, I thought to myself. What a fine defensive lineman. He had real quick feet coming off the ball and could obliterate you with a swim move if you didn't pop him in the mouth right off the snap. Used to stand in front of a mirror in the locker room after practice combing his hair with a pick, working out the indentations left by the padding of his helmet.

At home at night, I'd watch the weather forecast and hear "thirty-five degrees in Baton Rouge" and find myself saying to the screen, "That's cold. Better wear your winter coat, Rusty Brown."

Yes, Rusty wore number 35.

Crazy, I tell you.

Here's another confession: I still remember the most insignificant things about my teammates, even though I have to concentrate to tell you what I had for dinner last night. I remember how tall they were and how much they weighed—that's easy—but I also remember things that don't matter anymore, that probably never mattered: the kinds of cars they drove, the music they played in the dorm, how many letters they earned, their injuries, their dreams, their girlfriends' favorite lipstick colors, the length of their sideburns, their times in the 40-yard dash.

On the day in spring when scouts from the NFL came to time us, Carlos ran slightly better than 4.3, fastest on the team. I ran a 4.9, not bad for an offensive lineman. The slowest guy? I'll spare him the distinction of being named here, but I can still see the large, fat-padded boy laboring to cover the distance as his teammates stood by in gray T-shirts and purple shorts, whistling and applauding to help him along. He ran it in 6.3. And even at that speed, I knew the coaches who were clocking him had stopped their watches several ticks before he actually crossed the finish line, not wishing to have him forever contemplate a double-digit 40 time.

I remember their voices and how they sounded when we prayed together deep in the stadium before kickoff, and how they sounded later when things were coming apart and they cursed in anger and despair out on the field. I remember how quiet they could be after a road loss on the flight back to Baton Rouge. And I remember how they carried on when we won. Heaven help me, but I remember how they smelled on a Saturday morning in the spring when we scrimmaged in Tiger Stadium and the beer they'd drunk at sorority parties the night before came whispering from their pores like sewer steam from the manhole covers on Dalrymple Drive.

I remember how one of them came to my room in Broussard Hall and told me he was going to kill himself because he was stuck on the scout squad and his girlfriend had left him. I remember how we sat and talked for hours and how he didn't kill himself after all, and how the next time I saw him he pretended I wasn't there and I let him walk right past me.

On the day I turned forty-three years old, I woke up thinking, Whatever happened to Robert DeLee?

DeLee, a tight end from the small town of Clinton in East Feliciana Parish, wore number 43 my last year. When I was a freshman, it had belonged to Jack Clark, a running back. Jack too, I thought to myself. Where on earth has he slipped off to?

I'd seen neither of them in more than two decades.

The truth is I didn't want to see them—Robert or Jack or anyone. Seeing them would only have reminded me of what I'd lost. And so I carefully avoided events where my teammates might've turned up and most of the towns and cities where they came from. If I had to visit suburban Houston to interview a source for a story, my one worry when I saw a highway sign directing me to Friendswood was running into Big Ed Stanton. An offensive tackle and my former roommate, Big Ed had come from Friendswood. The odds surely were against me bumping into him—Big Ed could've been living in Alaska for all I knew—but I never relaxed during my stay. When I took my source out to dinner, I looked for Big Ed at the other tables in the restaurant. When I filled the tank of my rental car, I lowered my head and turned my back to the road in case he happened to drive by.

One day, I was waiting in the checkout line at a store in suburban New Orleans when a man standing behind me called out my name. I recognized the voice and, because I recognized it, I hesitated before turning around. "Did he see me?" I mumbled to my girlfriend, making sure to keep my head down.

"Yes, he saw you. He's looking right at you."

"Are you sure?"

And then the voice called my name again.

It was Charles McDuff, a tackle from Baton Rouge who'd arrived at LSU the same year I had. There had been twenty-nine of us in the 1976 freshman class—all bona fide studs with all-state and all-district patches on the leather sleeves of our high school letter jackets—and Charles was the first of the group I'd seen in fourteen years.

A couple of shoppers stood between us, and I couldn't reach past them to shake his hand. "How are things going?" he asked.

"Things are good, Charlie. How 'bout with you?"

Charles and I had always gotten along well, and yet I was uncomfortable seeing him again. The media guide had listed him at six-foot-six and two hundred and sixty-three pounds, but in actual fact he was a shade taller and his playing weight was closer to two hundred and ninety. Even after all these years, he still looked like a player. He had a bull neck and shoulders thick and cut with muscle. His hair was bleached white from the sun, his complexion a dark reddish-brown. Charles had always liked the beach.

I was paying what I owed when his voice came again. "I own a boat now, John Ed. You and me, we should go fishing sometime."

I looked at him and smiled. "Sure, Charlie. Sounds good, man."

"You'll go with me?"

"What are you talking about? I'd love to go."

He gave me his phone number and asked me to call him and schedule a date. "I've been traveling a lot for *Sports Illustrated*, but as soon as I get a break I'll do it," I said. "We'll fish. Most definitely."

I started to leave, but then for some reason I turned around and faced him again. "Charlie, you ever see anybody anymore?"

"Yeah. Sure, I see them. Some of them. You?"

"Not really."

He nodded as if he understood, and we parted without saying anything more. I never did call him about a fishing trip.

A year went by and then a second, and then one day the phone rang, and it was my sister Donna crying on the other end. Charles McDuff was dead. He'd suffered a pulmonary embolism while vacationing with his family at a resort town on the Alabama Gulf Coast. "How many kids did Charlie have?" I asked.

"Three boys."

"Three boys," I repeated.

"John Ed, I'm so sorry."

I didn't know what to say to that. She was sorry? Sorry for me?

I'd been his teammate once, but how could that matter anymore? It was such a long time ago.

That night I did my best to think about anyone but Charles and anything but LSU football. But the more I tried to will him out of my head, the more he seemed to occupy it. I sat in the dark of the kitchen drinking beer until I emptied out the refrigerator, and late that night, when I should've been sleeping, I let out with a few choice words that probably scared the hell out of my neighbors. It wasn't the first time I'd screamed into an empty house, but I'd never done it at 4 a.m. before.

I wanted to call someone and talk about Charles McDuff, and I knew it had to be one of my teammates, preferably an offensive lineman. I waited until the sun came up, and I called Baton Rouge information and ticked off a few names to the operator, then I ran down Big Ed's number in Texas. But in the end, I didn't call. I didn't do anything but sit there with my empty beer bottles and think about calling.

Toward noon, I surrendered to a sentimental impulse and dragged several cardboard boxes out of a closet. In one there were plaques and framed certificates wrapped in paper, letters tied with kite string, a short stack of souvenir game programs, and a couple of photo albums crowded with news clippings and yellowing images of boys who were actually capable of dying.

If Charles McDuff could die, it occurred to me, we all could die.

At the bottom of a second box I found a gray T-shirt with purple lettering that said NOBODY WORKS HARDER THAN THE OFFENSIVE LINE. It was one of about two dozen shirts Charles had made up for the linemen on the 1979 squad. The year before, we'd lost several great players to graduation, and Charles had hoped the shirts would inspire us to pull together as a unit. We were an undersized bunch and not terribly talented, but we always played as if somebody had forgotten to tell us we weren't the best and toughest collection of linemen in school history. And we always wore Charles's shirts. We wore them to class. We wore them to church on Sunday. We wore them with our game uniforms, the lettering poking out above our shoulder pads. It seems crazy now, but there was a time when I considered stipulating in my will that I be buried in that old dishrag.

I tracked down information about the funeral arrangements, and I got dressed, intending to go. I put on a dark suit and a necktie and my good shoes. I filled up the tank of my truck for the drive to Baton Rouge, and I started down the road, rehearsing what I'd say to his widow and children, and what I'd tell my teammates to explain why I didn't come around anymore. "Forgive me," I planned to say. "This might sound weird, but I truly believe I loved it too much."

I drove almost all the way there before turning around and heading home.

IT ENDS FOR EVERYBODY. It ends for the pro who makes ten million dollars a year and gets his face on magazine covers. It ends for the high school kid who never comes off the bench but to greet his teammates as they leave the field and file past him on their way to the Gatorade bucket.

For me, it ended on December 22, 1979, at the Tangerine Bowl in Orlando. We beat Wake Forest that night, 34-10, in a game that came and went in a chaotic, brightly colored blur, as all games do. When it was over Big Ed Stanton and I grabbed our heroic old coach, hoisted him up on our shoulders, and carried him out to midfield. Newspapers would run photos of Coach Mac's last victory ride, with Big Ed and me, smeared with mud, serving as his chariot. Coach had a hand raised above his head as he waved good-bye to a cleared-out stadium, and it struck me that his expression showed little joy at all. He looked tired and sad, after a just-okay 7–5 season. His career was ending too, after eighteen years as head coach.

We were quiet on the flight back to Baton Rouge. When the plane touched down at Ryan Airport, no cheers went up, and nobody said anything. I spent the next week in Opelousas, trying to catch up on sleep and recover from injuries that didn't want to heal. My sprained left ankle was swollen and the color of plums, and my sprained right shoulder was so sore I couldn't lift my arm above my head. Cuts and abrasions of varying severity peppered both hands. The bridge of my nose featured a purple bump the size of a Milk Dud, and my lower lip was split open like a piece of fruit left in the sun too long.

My worst injury, however, was a jagged, seeping wound at the center of my chest. It stained my shirt red when I went to church on Christmas morning, and I was so sick of the pain and the problems it brought that there were times I wanted to take a pocketknife and carve it out of my chest.

I didn't like having to answer questions about the injury. Talking about it put it front and center in my head. So whenever anyone asked me what had happened, I usually made up a story. "I was shot," I said.

"You were shot?"

"Yes. I was shot while trying to foil a bank robbery."

If they laughed or said anything that expressed doubt, I quoted Marlon Brando in *Apocalypse Now*. "The horror," I said in a rough whisper. "The *horror*."

It started during the winter of my sophomore year, when our team doctor removed a sebaceous cyst the size of a peanut from my chest. Dr. Alvin Stander had closed the incision with three little stitches. The procedure took no more than half an hour. But the day after Doc Stander applied the suture, I busted it open while working out in the weight room. Rather than report to the training room for medical attention, I walked back to my locker, stood before a mirror, and plucked the stitches out with my fingers.

During spring practice in April, the small scar where the cyst had been became raw and sore when the hard foam liner on the breast-plates of my shoulder pads rubbed against it. I could have exchanged the pads for a pair that didn't dig into my chest, but I was superstitious about every article of clothing that made up my uniform. I'd played well while wearing those shoulder pads—well enough to be named to the Southeastern Conference's All-Rookie Team in 1976 and to become the first offensive lineman in the modern era of LSU football to win a varsity letter his freshman year. Way more important, though, was the fact that those shoul-der pads had helped us win games. And so I convinced myself that it was my obligation to the team to keep wearing them.

I could imagine my conversation with Coach Mac if we suddenly started losing. "Buddy, do you know why Tulane just beat us for only the second time in thirty years?"

"My shoulder pads?"

"That's right, my boy. *Your shoulder pads!*"

By the summer of my senior year, I had a pretty nasty scar on my chest. In August, Doc Stander removed the plug of tissue and gave me one more set of stitches. Because I still refused to replace the pads, team trainers shaved my upper torso with disposable razors and wrapped it each day before practice with Ace bandages hold-ing a square of sponge over the incision. It took only a few days for me to rip open the new sutures, and this time I refused to have the wound repaired. In one game late in the year, I lost so much blood that the bottom half of my jersey was soaking wet. "Hey, Bradley, somebody stab you in the chest?" one of the game officials asked.

"No, sir. I got shot trying to foil a bank robbery."

He pulled me out of the huddle by the back of my shoulder pads and ordered me to the sideline for medical attention.

Trainers cleaned me up and shot the area around the wound with a painkiller, team managers gave me a fresh jersey, and I missed only one offensive series and played the rest of the game. By the end of the season, however, I had a hole in the middle of my chest three inches long and an inch wide. It looked like a crater on the moon.

AFTER THE TANGERINE BOWL, I went home for what remained of the Christmas holidays and spent the first few days in the small room at the end of the hall that I shared with my kid brothers, Bobby and Brent. I woke from long naps not knowing where I was or how I'd gotten there. On Christmas Eve, I woke up in the afternoon and bolted for the door, afraid that I'd missed the bus to the stadium for a game. At night, I had vivid dreams, and I tumbled out of them in a sweat. I suppose you could call them nightmares, but they didn't carry the usual images of failed final exams or plane crashes or Boo Radley hiding behind the bedroom door. My dreams had me jumping offside, or muffing the center-quarterback exchange. They had me snapping the ball over the punter's head. Somebody from the other team always recovered the ball and raced toward the goal line, with me in pursuit but never able to catch up.

One afternoon, I emerged from a three-hour nap aware that I was not alone in the room. I cracked my eyes open and absorbed the fuzzy, indistinct forms of nine-year-old Brent and several of his friends. Huddled together by the door, they were watching me past the gloom. A couple of them, I noticed, were wearing LSU jerseys. "John Ed, want to come outside and play with us?"

"I'm not feeling so great today, Boo. Can we do it tomorrow?"

"You can be all-time quarterback. All you have to do is throw the ball. You don't have to run or tackle or anything."

"I'm not myself today, Boo. I don't think I can do it."

"Please," he said. And the other boys joined in: "Come on, John Ed. Please. *Please* come play with us."

I swung my legs over the side of the bed, and the boys let out a chorus of yelps as they scrambled down the hall and filed into the yard. I sat on the edge of the mattress, trying to get my bearings. A few minutes passed before I was able to stand without having to place a hand on the wall for support.

I spent a lot of time that week in front of the bathroom mirror, studying the messy business at the center of my chest. This one day, my father came in and stood behind me. I watched him in the glass over the lavatory as he got a close look at the meaty gash. I could tell he didn't like it. My chest was beginning to scab, and this made it itch, and the itching was driving me to scratch the scab in my sleep. Blood caked the hair on my chest and belly and formed black crescents under my fingernails.

"What do you think?" I said.

My father's approach to injury was always to will it away. Don't acknowledge it and it doesn't hurt, and if it doesn't hurt then it doesn't count. That kind of logic can get you killed, I realized, but it was how I'd dealt with every pain I'd ever known, and it was going to carry me past this one. "Pretty bad, huh?"

He shrugged. "Give it some time. You'll heal."

I wanted him to tell me that I should be proud to wear that scar, a badge of courage fiercely won, and evidence that I had played for LSU. But my father wasn't the kind of man to say a whole lot. He watched me in the mirror until the silence embarrassed us both. "Was it worth it?"

"It was the best time of my life."

"But was it worth it?"

"Yes, sir. It was worth it."

"Then clean yourself up and don't pick at that scab again." He reached up and gave my shoulder a squeeze. "No more hanging your lip, okay? Your mother's worried about you, and your brothers and sisters need to see you happy to finally be home."

I REMEMBER HOW GOOD it felt when the people I cared about said they were proud of me, back in the days when I was still young enough for people to talk about me in such terms. LSU fans from my hometown who never missed a game told my parents they stood and cheered when my name was announced. It was a wonderful thing to hear the name of an Opelousas boy broadcast in Tiger Stadium, they said. And when folks in the seats behind them told them to sit down and stop blocking the view, the hometown fans remained on their feet and made even more noise. After games, when I left the locker room, they were stationed outside the stadium to cheer and shout my name. Little boys held out souvenir programs for autographs. I always signed mine with curlicues, then added, "Number 56 in your program, Number 1 in your heart," disgracing myself for all eternity.

I was the only scholarship player from our town, and I hadn't been home since August when I left for the beginning of two-a-days. Over the course of the year, my parents had received letters

16

from fans saying nice things about how well I played. Mom displayed them on the kitchen counter. "Did you see Mr. Dubuisson's letter?" she said. "You remember Mr. Dubuisson, don't you, John Ed?"

"Sure, I know Mr. Dubuisson."

She handed me a card, and I read the handwritten note in silence: *My dear friends, I know you are proud of John Ed, as is all of Opelousas for his athletic achievements. But more importantly I know you are prouder for the fine young man that he is. I make this statement from what I have heard of him from others–mainly from my son and those of his friends whose evaluations I respect. Congratulations.*

I still visit this picture when things are hard and I struggle to write or to pay my bills or to keep the black cloud of depression at a distance. The details are so clear that I can shut my eyes and pretend I'm right back in the warmth of my mother's kitchen. The past and the present become so close in step that they are one step, and I visit the rooms where five children never endured a bad day alone, where my father is still a coach and my mother's days are endless expressions of kindness to everyone she encounters. I can provide the smell of a meal baking in an oven that broke down and was replaced seventeen years ago.

On Christmas day, we left for Our Lady Queen of Angels as a family, everybody dressed up, the girls wearing perfume, us boys awash in aftershave. My mother led the way to a pew in front, and after the Mass I shook almost as many hands as I did at the stadium after games. Men and boys who loved LSU, schoolteachers and offshore oil-field workers and insurance agents, young girls carrying prayer books who sidled up to me and asked if I had a girlfriend. What did people do when the real stars turned up? I wondered. I am a lineman. How do fans treat our quarterbacks?

We opened gifts in the living room. I gave my mother a souvenir game ball signed by my teammates, the names piled on top of each other, THANKS FOR ALL THE SUPPORT painted in white lettering on the side. Mama put the ball on a shelf among framed photos of dead relatives and her prized collection of dime store clocks that incessantly chirped and chimed.

Brent handed me a gift wrapped in red foil. I peeled the paper away and found a scrapbook filled with newspaper clippings chronicling the season. One page included a note to my parents from Coach Mac. "Mr. and Mrs. Bradley," it said, "I'm so pleased that the squad chose John Ed to be one of their captains. He's the best thing that has happened to me." Another letter from Mac, fixed under a transparent sleeve on the next page, was addressed to my father. "Hello John—Words can't express my feelings toward your son. He's a prize." The last page of the scrapbook included a small photo from the Opelousas *Daily World* showing me with my helmet tucked under one arm. The pocket of flesh under my left eye was puffy and bruised. Under the picture, Brent had added letters cut from purple and gold cardboard paper. "Darn," it said, "that's the end."

He sat on the sofa surrounded by gifts and wrapping, watching me, waiting for a reaction. "I really love my book."

"Mama helped me."

"You did a good job, little brother."

My parents gave me a first-edition copy of Ernest Hemingway's *A Moveable Feast*. "It's about his years in Paris when he was a young writer," my mother said.

"I'm going to live in Paris one day," I announced.

"I know you will, John Ed."

"And I'm going to write books every bit as good as Hemingway's."

"We know it," she said with a smile.

They'd sent you out in the world with a dream attached and the dream was LSU football. Over time, everyone else might forget how you looked under the lights in the purple-and-gold uniform, but your family would never forget.

A WEEK LATER, I returned to the stadium to clean out my locker. I parked across from the entrance to Tiger Den, went inside, and made my way down the long, narrow hall past the equipment room. There were four locker rooms in the rabbit warren that filled the space beneath the stadium's north end zone, and my locker was in the first of them, the room reserved for veteran players.

I'd brought along an Army-issue duffel bag, and I began filling it with the locker's contents: thigh and knee pads, gym shorts, T-shirts, a mesh practice jersey, a dozen pairs of shoes for a dozen different playing surfaces. I had a clutter of toiletries and old game programs in the cabinet at the top of the locker, and I used an arm to sweep them all into a trash can. My name tag was next. It was held in place in a metal slot, and I slid the card out and sat for a minute studying the purple stenciling against the gold matte board. "Trample the dead, hurdle the weak," someone had scribbled in the corner. One of our graduate assistants, Jim Klaczak, always yelled those words when we ran out on the field, and it came to serve as a rallying cry, especially for my 'mates on the offensive line. When the score was going the other way, or when we needed a spark to play harder, someone inevitably shouted, "Trample the dead," and received a chorus of "Hurdle the weak" in response. Somehow it took the sting out of being beaten, and it made winning feel better.

I owned two helmets, and I packed them next: the one I'd

received as a freshman and cracked my senior year in the game against Florida State and the replacement I'd worn to finish out the season. I was less attached to the new helmet than to the old one, but there was no chance I'd leave either behind. The back and sides of the cracked helmet were plastered with the small, round Tiger stickers the coaches gave out for big plays. Recover a fumble, they gave you a sticker. Pancake a nose guard, you got another one. I ran my fingertips over the surface, feeling the scars in the hard plastic crown. The crack looked like a lightning bolt, running from the top of the face mask all the way to the back of the skull. I wish I could say a single fantastic blow had fractured the helmet, but the truth is I have no memory of how it happened. I could've plowed my head into the sternum of a mike 'backer or struck a return man smack in the mouth as he was receiving a punt. But it's also possible that I had let the helmet drop to the ground too hard when I returned to the sideline and had a seat on the bench.

When I finished packing, I walked down the chute that led to the playing field. I pushed the big, metal door open and squinted against a sudden blast of sunlight. The stadium was quiet against a blue winter sky. As I glanced around, I could point to virtually any spot on the field and tell you about some incident that had happened there. I knew where teammates had dropped passes, made key blocks and tackles, threw interceptions, and recovered game-saving fumbles. I knew where they had suffered career-ending injuries. I could point out the spot where Scott Sulik blew out a knee in a collision with Charles Alexander, our All-America running back. It had happened in spring practice, and Scott, a strong safety, never played again.

The year before, as a junior, I'd dated a cheerleader named Missy Crews, and now I let myself imagine her on the sideline, her right leg kicked high above her head, the left one planted in grass painted purple and gold. She was wearing a uniform, the skirt so short you could see the hard, smooth curves where her hamstrings met her buttocks. "Hi, Miss," I said whenever I came off the field after a touchdown. "Way to go, kid," she answered, flashing her pom-poms against the stadium lights.

I was only twenty-one years old, and yet I was afraid that nothing I did for the rest of my life would equal those days when I played for LSU. I might have a satisfying career and earn a lot of money, I might marry a beautiful woman like Missy and fill a house with perfect kids, I might make a mark of some significance in the world. But what if I never had it better than when I ran out under the goalposts on Saturday night, the crowd on its feet, my team-mates all around?

It's true that some men never recover from the loss of a game they played when they were boys. It's also true that I was deter-mined not to be one of them. You weren't going to catch me twenty years later boasting about the cheers I'd heard when I was a kid. I knew the type who couldn't give it up, and I refused to be him. He kept going to games and reminding anyone who'd listen how things used to be. His wife and kids rolled their eyes as he described big plays, quoted from halftime speeches, and embel-lished a "career" that no one else remembered. To listen to him, he'd never blown a snap count or busted an assignment or had a coach chew him out for dogging it or getting beat. In his mind, he was forever young, forever strong, forever golden.

Standing there in Tiger Stadium, I squeezed my eyes closed and lowered my head. Then I wept.

"Hell, no," I said. "That is not going to be me."

I LEFT THE STADIUM carrying the bag and headed for Broussard Hall, the athletic dorm, which had been my home ever since I'd arrived on campus three and a half years earlier. It was time to clear out of there, too.

Some players hated dorm life, and most of the seniors had elected to move out before the Tangerine Bowl; at least one of them was so excited by the prospect of being set free that he stuck his arm out the window and shot the bird at the stately old building as he was motoring away. My sentiments were different. The dorm had been home. And I hated to have to give it up. Rather than surrender the room before our trip to Orlando, I left my possessions behind on the odd chance that some miracle happened and the NCAA extended the eligibility limit to five years.

There wasn't much to pack: the paperback novels assigned in lit and writing classes, a portable record player and a small collection of albums, an ancient black-and-white TV set that didn't work any-more, the few changes of clothes I owned. It took only a few trips to haul everything down the stairs to the parking lot where I had left my dad's old Chevy Impala with the trunk cocked open.

My first roommate in Broussard, defensive end John Adams, married his high school sweetheart and left the dorm after our jun-ior year, and I moved down the hall and claimed the open bunk in Big Ed's room. Because we both played on the offensive line, Big Ed and I sometimes carried a projector home from the stadium after practice and watched film. We didn't have a screen, so we played it against the wall over Big Ed's bunk. We took turns han-dling the clicker, reviewing plays over and over. Each weakness we discovered helped our chances, and we studied with a level of con-centration that I never mustered for my classes. Sometimes a player outweighed you by fifty pounds and had muscles in his eyelids, but on film you saw that he was vulnerable to chop blocks, so you knew how to beat him when a pass play was called. Or maybe he didn't have good hands, got tied up easily at the point of attack, and couldn't shuck his blocker on running plays, and then you knew how to handle him when the quarterback called for a dive up the middle. Even the greatest player had his Achilles' heel, and the film revealed it if you watched long enough.

I usually began to fade after a couple of hours, but Big Ed kept studying well past midnight. He took notes, scribbling on a yellow tablet by the light from the projector. "You see what he's doing there, John Ed?" he said more than once, snapping me awake. I looked across the room at the fuzzy image burning on the wall, and there next to it stood Big Ed, hopping with excitement, his finger pointing out a detail that was certain to make us winners that week.

He wore glasses with brown plastic rims, a pencil behind his right ear. In his plaid button-down shirt, khaki pants, and boring shoes, you might've taken him for an engineering student with an overactive thyroid, but I once watched in awe as he lifted a three-hundred-pound defensive lineman off his feet, drove him back ten yards, and planted his backside in the sod. We had some real talent on that team. Had they all wanted it as much as Big Ed, we never would've lost a game.

We were scholarship athletes and campus celebrities, so students and faculty generally assumed we were living in luxury. In fact, Broussard's accommodations weren't much better than those in any other dorm. Each room came equipped with a pair of platform beds, built-in closets and desks, and a small sink with a medicine cabinet. The bathroom was down the hall—a community affair with a single, trough-shaped urinal, a clutter of sinks and toilets, and a large, open shower room. The best thing about Broussard—and no doubt the reason students in other dorms envied us so—was the deep pile carpet that covered the floors. It was a dark purple accented with yellow flecks, and the simple act of walking on it in your bare feet was enough to inspire the true believer to break into a warbled rendition of the Tiger fight song.

I knew one player who got married for the sole reason of being excused from having to live in Broussard. Residency there was otherwise mandatory. When I asked him if his wife knew what had really led him to the altar, he shook his head and said, "Nope, and I hope to God you don't tell her, John Ed. She's a romantic sort of gal—there are yellow butterflies on our shower curtain—and I don't think she'd understand."

During the season we had an 11 p.m. curfew every night of the week but Saturday, when coaches let us stay out until 2 a.m. Curfew was strictly enforced, usually by dorm monitors, but also by graduate assistants assigned to the football team who burst into your room without fail minutes after the deadline like a SWAT team storming a drug den. If you were late returning, coaches made you run extra conditioning drills after practice. You ran until you collapsed. If you missed three curfews, you were automatically kicked off the team.

"Fellas, what are you going to tell Mama and Daddy when all of a sudden you show up on their doorstep?" Coach Mac said. He held a thumb out at us. "What are you going to tell the people in your hometown who were so proud to have you playing for LSU? It'll be in the newspaper, front-page news: LSU PLAYER DISMISSED FOR BREAKING TEAM RULES."

He let us think about it for a moment, then he lowered his voice. "Priorities, fellas. Always remember your priorities."

There was rarely a private moment for residents of Broussard. When we weren't tolerating curfew checks or unannounced visits from coaches who wanted to make sure we were studying, team trainers were barging into our rooms in search of prescription meds from the training room. Players lived year-round with injuries that required antibiotics, painkillers, and other drugs, and the trainers made sweeps to make sure we weren't stockpiling the stuff and flirting with addiction. The sweeps came only a couple of times a year, but they were reminders that our lives were not our own.

Drug stockpiles weren't the only things forbidden in your room. Mac wouldn't let us have women in there either. In fact, women weren't allowed past the sitting area in the lobby. Get caught with one and you were gone from the team, your scholarship revoked, your name forever sullied. It took only one incident and you were banished. "I don't care if it's your mother," Coach Mac warned us. Up went his thumb again. "Please don't test me, fellas."

One night, I got up late and staggered down the hall to the bathroom. A naked coed was sitting on the middle toilet, her long hair hanging in a tangled mess in front of her face and covering her breasts. The overhead lights were off, but I could see her in the moonlight pouring through windows made of mottled glass. I recognized her as one of the regulars who hung around the stadium after games, hoping to catch our attention. The guys called them groupies, but I'd been calling them regulars ever since I mentioned the breed in front of my father and he gave me a look. I stood before the urinal and fiddled with the slit in my boxers. There was nothing doing. I decided to go back to my room and pee in the sink.

"They catch you with him and he's off the team," I said to the girl.

She reached for the roll of toilet paper on the floor between her feet. "He doesn't get off the bench anyway. Wouldn't matter none."

With my belongings safely stowed in the car, I returned to the room to scrub the sink and sweep the floor before turning the key over to the proctor. The room was already spic-and-span—Big Ed had made sure of that before he left—but I performed the chores one more time, still not ready to let the place go. Several underclassmen came by to wish me luck, and I hugged a few of them and promised to keep in touch. I was removing hardened toothpaste deposits from the sink when I heard Marty Dufrene out in the hall. Marty was my backup at center, an able one at that. I pulled the door open and yelled for him to come over. "It's all yours," I told him.

"I'll do my best to make you proud, John Ed."

"You'll do great. I'm already proud."

Marty was lean and powerfully built. He stood six-foot-two, two hundred and thirty-five pounds, about average for a center in those days. On the field, he played with a kind of swagger, as if he was certain he could handle any opponent, and this swagger, I noticed, extended to Marty's life outside the game. The boy had no doubts about his place in the world. His Cajun accent immediately identified him as pure Louisiana thoroughbred, and no one was more impressed with his stellar bloodline than Marty himself. Football schools from the Midwest featured humongous linemen brought up on corn, potatoes, and prime beef. LSU always had guys like Marty, raised on crawfish from the mudflats and seafood from the Gulf of Mexico. They might not be as big as players from other parts of the country, but they hit every bit as hard and showed their class by helping you back to your feet after they knocked you down. The son of an offshore oil-field worker, Marty was a 4A All-State center in 1976. He'd vacillated on committing to West Point or LSU before he realized there really was only one choice for him.

The only problem I ever had with the guy was that we played the same position and he wanted my job. Going into my senior year, I was listed on the first team, Marty on the second. One day after practice, he told me he was going to beat me out. I couldn't believe his nerve. "I want to play pro ball," he said.

I shook my head and laughed. "Pro ball?" I mumbled under my breath as I wheeled around and started to walk away. "To hell with that, Dufrene. I'm going to see to it that you don't even play in *college*."

I now realized that without Marty pushing me, I might've been a bust. His chutzpah had so infuriated me that I'd wanted to punch him out, but over time, it had pushed me to work harder than I would have otherwise. I remember summer days when I ran wind sprints on the track at my old high school to finish off a conditioning routine that had started hours earlier. It was late in the afternoon, and the tartan surface was so hot it bubbled in spots, like gumbo left on the fire too long. I ran until my whole body was ablaze, and then I collapsed in the infield clover with my arms out on either side, chest pumping for air. Come the fall, I'd be facing nose guards and linebackers for USC and Alabama, the best teams in the country. I should've been focused on those players. Instead I was thinking about Marty, that sonofabitchin' Marty. Who the hell did he think he was, saying he was going to take my job?

"When we kick Bear Bryant's ass next year," he told me that last afternoon in the dorm, "I want you to come celebrate with me in the locker room after the game."

"I'll be there, Marty. I promise."

I dropped the key off and headed to the parking lot, trying to pretend it was just another day. As I pulled away from the building, I threw a wave out the window, although I'm not sure anybody was looking. In the rearview mirror, I watched Broussard get smaller and smaller.

They'll never see me again, I thought to myself.

Chapter Two

SAVAGE
PRIDE

BEFORE WE LEFT for the Tangerine Bowl, I signed a lease for an inexpensive two-bedroom apartment in a poor but colorful neighborhood several miles from campus. Rather than move in with a teammate, I decided to further accentuate my break from football by recruiting a writer friend to share the place with me.

Although he had the tall, athletic build of a wide receiver, Larry Henry was an ex-Marine with no connection to the LSU football program and only a marginal interest in the game. He'd spent two years in the Corps, one of them stationed at Okinawa, and now he was pursuing a bachelor's degree in creative writing. Like me, Larry wanted to be a novelist, and he was constantly quoting lines from obscure poems and stories that he'd memorized. When he discovered new material that struck him as particularly moving or profound, he was quick to let me know about it. "God*damn*," he'd shout, then remove his glasses and wipe fake tears from his eyes.

One night he opened a window, stuck his head out, and started howling like a wolf—all because he'd read something he liked. Another time, I watched him throw a copy of Flannery O'Connor's *Wise Blood* at the living room couch. It hit a pillow and fell to the floor, bending the paper cover. "Sonofa*bitch*," he said, rubbing the goose bumps on his arms.

Larry called me Pride, and I called him Savage, names meant to illustrate the kind of people we were. When a writing instructor opened the semester by asking why we'd enrolled in his class, you didn't catch Larry or me raising a hand to say, "Because I want to learn more about myself." Larry and I didn't care about that; we already knew too much. We wanted to write books so good that readers threw them against the furniture.

He wasn't like Big Ed or any of the other guys on the team, and maybe that's what drew me to him. I'd dreamed about being a writer since I was a kid, but until my sophomore year at LSU, this was an ambition I'd kept to myself because I didn't want my team-mates to think something was wrong with me. Where I come from, big-time jocks didn't write thank-you notes, let alone poems and stories, and most didn't contemplate reading a book, much less writing one. A good number of the boys I grew up with went from college to white-collar professions, but more found work as rough-necks on off-shore oil rigs, joined the military service, or fell into landscaping businesses that had them cutting grass all day. Finding one who'd admit to wanting to become an artist was about as easy as finding an ivory-billed woodpecker in a nearby swamp. I'd declared zoology/pre-med as my major when I first reported to LSU. During my freshman year, however, I'd made the varsity, and football was eating up study time. I missed classes, and my grades suffered. To boost my grade point average, I started taking writing courses that I figured I could pass with ease. I turned in each assignment with the name John Bradley typed under the title on the upper left corner of the first page. In a story class my sophomore year, the instructor read one of my longer efforts out loud. It took him most of the hour, and when he was done he said, "Are you the John Bradley who plays football?"

"Yes, sir."

"But the roster says your name is John Ed Bradley."

"It's a lot to say," I answered, not wishing to add any more.

He seemed to understand. He looked at me and nodded. The next week I changed my major to English.

THE YEAR BEFORE we rented the apartment together, Larry and I drove to Mexico to see if bullfights were indeed as Hemingway had described them in *The Sun Also Rises*. We went in Larry's Toyota Celica, leaving hours after I finished spring practice with a good performance in our annual intrasquad game. We drove as far south as Monterrey and a hotel on a hilltop with sweeping views of the city. That night we sat out on the balcony drinking whiskey, smoking cigars, and talking about everything but football. Bats flew up from the scrubby canyon below, and lights from the hotel terrace made them look like stars shooting in reverse. In the morning we got up late and drove to a village called Cadereyta and watched as amateur fighters slaughtered one bull after another on the dirt floor of a *plaza de toros* that looked like a badly constructed miniature of Tiger Stadium. The fights were bloody and hard to stomach, and after only the first of them, I turned to Larry and said, "Maybe he could write his ass off, but when it came to bullfights, Hemingway was full of shit."

Sickened by what we had seen, Larry and I spent most of the afternoon flirting with girls and tossing pocket change at kids who fought over the coins like pigeons chasing sunflower seeds. The more we flirted, the more girls appeared to receive our attention, and the more money we threw, the more kids circled around us with hands out. One was selling homemade popsicles, and Larry ate half a dozen of them, despite my warnings about Montezuma's revenge. As we arrived at the hotel, his face went white, and he dropped to his haunches. His shirt was soaked with sweat. "Must've been the popsicles," he said.

Because he was too sick to drive, I got behind the wheel and started for the border, stopping only for bathroom breaks at cantinas and gas stations and for naps on the side of the road. At night, we lay on the hood with our backs against the bug-smeared windshield, staring up at a moon that looked not a bit different from the one we knew back home in Louisiana. This was the first time I'd ever left my country, and the first time since I was a toddler that I'd gone an entire week without gripping the strings of a football.

I liked how I felt, and I liked the picture of the future I was building for myself. You might have to travel far to find them, but there were places on this earth where LSU football wasn't being discussed when you walked into a café in the morning and asked for a booth in the back.

There on the side of the road, in a place far from home, I felt a freedom I'd never known, and I knew it would be gone as soon as we saw the signs directing us to Louisiana. A truck filled with farmhands clattered by, the dusty men gazing at us and pointing. Larry went back inside the car and slept sitting upright in the seat, and I dug around in the trunk until I found a screwdriver. I wanted to be prepared in case bandits showed up and asked for our wallets.

I dreaded having to return to the team's off-season conditioning program, and the thought of classes and final exams made me even more miserable. However, a couple of surprising things happened when I got back to campus. My teammates couldn't get enough of my stories about the Monterrey whorehouses where I claimed to have spent the week, having my way with one smoldering beauty after another, and I couldn't enter Allen Hall without creative writing students approaching me with questions about my journey of self-discovery across the hostile terrain of old Mexico. They'd never expressed a whit of interest in my role on the football team, even on those days when I showed up for class with my head shaved, wearing bowl rings and watches and my purple letter jacket with the big roll collar. Suddenly I was every bit as tragic and heroic as Hemingway's Jake Barnes, and damn if I didn't still have my manhood intact. "You don't want to see what I've seen," I told them, borrowing a line from old war movies.

The trip proved that Larry and I were different from the other students. Or so I argued. They were effete intellectuals who'd gone to Florida for spring break. Their idea of adventure was bathing on the beach without sunscreen, while ours was to toe the abyss and gaze out at the immortal darkness. We were men—men who conveniently avoided any mention of how popsicles had brought Larry to his knees or how I'd demonstrated grace under pressure by brandishing a screwdriver to protect myself from the natives.

MY FIRST WEEK in the new apartment, I found myself in the back bedroom unpacking bags and boxes stuffed with football loot and still struggling to absorb the fact that it was really over. Football had been so demanding that I'd fallen behind and now needed two semesters to graduate. My typewriter sat on the old saloon table I used as my desk, a ream of paper next to it. There were no curtains or blinds on the windows, so I covered them with sheets I'd stolen from the dorm, both stamped with warnings against removing them from Broussard Hall. From my window, I could see trash bins, abandoned barbecue kettles, and a rusty, three-wire clothesline holding clothes clips that spun like whirligigs in the breeze. I plugged in the radio I'd received for playing in the 1978 Liberty Bowl and gave the dial a spin. On WJBO, the big local station that broadcast our games, somebody was talking about Bo Rein, the young coach from North Carolina State who had replaced Coach Mac. It didn't take long to figure out that this wasn't a sports story. Rein's plane had crashed at sea, killing him and the pilot. He had been returning to Baton Rouge from a recruiting trip to Shreveport when his scheduled forty-minute flight drifted east over Virginia and went down in the Atlantic Ocean. Military jets had successfully intercepted the plane, but the pilots were unable to detect signs of life in the cockpit. Rein's plane had reached an altitude of almost eight miles, much higher than it should've been flying, then came down after exhausting its fuel supply. Both the pilot and the coach had likely been rendered unconscious by a sudden loss of cabin pressure.

I'd never met the man, and the only time I'd ever seen him was the day I cleaned out my locker. He had been entering the football office as I exited the stadium for the last time. He paused and looked at me, probably because I was wearing my letter jacket and toting a bag packed with gear. Did he recognize the sadness in my face? Rein had been a player once himself, so he had to understand.

I should have said something to him—wished him luck or told him that he was in for the time of his life, getting to coach the home team in Tiger Stadium. He must've felt like he was living a dream, every moment until the last one.

The next day, a reporter called to ask me if I'd heard anything about a replacement. "What do you mean?" I said.

"You know, who the next coach might be."

"The man just died, and you're asking me that?"

I didn't want to be rude, but some people leave you no choice. I put the receiver down.

TWO WEEKS LATER, I flew to Alabama with Coach Mac to attend the Birmingham Touchdown Club's banquet honoring the player of the year in the Southeastern Conference. Each school in the ten-member league had nominated a player for the award, and I was LSU's unlikely choice for 1979: a physically unimposing lineman who'd started full-time only as a senior. I'd decided that it was either a miracle or rigged ballots that had put my name on several postseason all-star teams—the All-Louisiana team, the Academic All-SEC team, and the All-SEC team. Actually, I was the second-team center, behind Alabama's magnificent Dwight Stephenson, who would go on to become a star with the Miami Dolphins and a member of the Pro Football Hall of Fame. I'd seen enough film of him to know that I was nowhere in his league. On the flight to Birmingham, I asked Coach Mac why I'd been selected to represent LSU at the banquet. I wasn't fishing for a compliment. I'd had a fine year by any standard and had graded out higher than any other player on the offense, but I still wondered if my performance on the field was equal to the award. Every time I indulged the notion that I was something special, I heard a familiar voice whisper in my ear. "Always be humble," it said.

We were flying first class, sharing a console that held apple juice in cocktail glasses and more bags of peanuts than we could ever eat. Coach Mac reached over and grabbed the back of my hand. "You earned it, John Ed, that's why. Don't let me catch you thinking you didn't." He leaned back in the seat and pulled at his neck-tie, making sure it covered the buttons of his shirt. "There wasn't anyone who meant more to us this year on or off the field. And that's what this award is about. Your teammates counted on you, and you never let them down. Your coaches voted you this award. No one is more deserving."

I leaned back in my own seat, turned, and watched him sleep. I'd idolized the man since I was a boy, but the truth is, not everyone saw in him what I did. In November of 1978, the school's Board of Supervisors had voted to give Coach Mac only a one-year exten-sion on his contract, effectively firing him after the 1979 season. In my time as a player, we'd put up winning records every season, including two eight-win seasons, and earned invitations to three bowl games—strong results for most programs, but not for LSU.

Detractors said Mac couldn't win big games, and while they never seemed to consider that he'd had only one losing season since he replaced Paul Dietzel in 1962, they were quick to point out that he'd succeeded in beating Bear Bryant and Alabama only twice in sixteen meetings. Few teams managed to beat Bryant in those years, but LSU fans expected us to. And close didn't cut it. On November 10, 1979, we lost 3-0 to the Crimson Tide at home. They went on to rout Southwest Conference champ Arkansas in the Sugar Bowl and finish number one in the final AP poll. We went on to see our coaches summarily dismissed. Rather than seek jobs with other schools, most of them were so disillusioned that they started searching for careers in other fields: public relations, insurance sales, fund-raising. At age fifty-six, Mac was too old to land a head coaching job with another major program, so he was moving on to serve as executive director of the Tangerine Bowl.

Like most of my teammates, I wasn't sure how much I was respon-sible for Mac's demise, but it did gnaw at me that his last season as a football coach coincided with mine as a player. My exit was a natural one, prescribed by the NCAA's eligibility standards, while he was facing the humiliation of not being wanted any longer. I might've felt less guilty had I not been one of his last captains.

And yet, we never once heard him complain. To the contrary, he continued to work at the job with drive and enthusiasm, proudly reminding us at every opportunity how blessed we were to be at LSU. Mac wasn't the kind of man who'd admit to living by a code, if only because his code didn't allow for the depth of self-examination that would lead him to codify his conduct. But if you observed him long enough, you understood that self-pity had no place in his life. You could feel all you wanted, but you should never feel sorry for yourself. And you should never give up.

I recall sitting several rows behind him one day on a team bus as we drove through campus. We passed Fraternity Row on Dalrymple Drive, and there, hanging from an upstairs window in one of the houses, was a sheet with a clumsily painted message: HELP MAC PACK. Similar signs were displayed on other school buildings, including Tiger Stadium. You learned to ignore them, along with fans who shouted their displeasure with Mac when they saw him in public. But every man on the bus that day was thinking the same thing: He wanted to scale a drainpipe to the second floor and pull the sign down. Better still, he wanted to light a match and set the whole building on fire.

Mac merely bunched his lips in what might've been a smile before looking away. Turn the other cheek, the Bible said. Mac had a real gift for showing us how it was done.

In Birmingham, he and I had cocktails in the hotel lounge before the banquet. I was uneasy drinking whiskey in front of him, even when he ordered and paid for it. I was about to ask the bartender for a Coke when Bear Bryant entered the room and walked over to us. I'd seen him up close only once before: knocked to the ground on the Alabama sideline, I'd looked up to find him staring down at me, his epic face and houndstooth hat backlit by the stadium lights. "Okay, so you're Bradley," he said after Mac introduced us. He ordered me another whiskey even though I hadn't sipped the first one yet.

Mac and Bryant both grew up in rural Arkansas, and Mac had played for Bryant at Kentucky before serving for a couple of years as an assistant on his staff. Even though the men had competed hard against each other for decades, it was nice to see their easy alliance tonight. This was a revelation to me, because Mac had always seemed more charged up for our games with Alabama than for those against teams the sportswriters would have you believe were our real rivals, Ole Miss and Tulane. As Bryant stood stoically sipping at his glass, a foot resting on the bar rail, Mac grew more animated in the presence of his mentor, his laughter reaching heights I'd never heard from him before, hands fluttering like a bird.

If a man coached you when you were a boy, it occurred to me, he was your coach until the day you died. We lingered at the bar in our tuxedos until the emcee called for everyone to be seated, and then we moved among big, round tables dressed in white linen, searching for our name cards.

It was no surprise when Alabama quarterback Steadman Shealy was named the conference's best player. I received a handsome trophy identical to the ones given to the eight other also-rans, and when I took the elevator up to my room, I cradled it in my right arm the way a running back is taught to cradle a football. The room faced the downtown business district, and I sat up by the big picture window gazing out at the city until morning, my hand on the wooden base of the trophy. I never turned back the bedspread, and I didn't change out of my tuxedo until minutes before I was scheduled to meet Mac in the lobby for the drive to the airport.

Once we landed, he gave me a lift to Convention Street and parked by the curb in front of my apartment house. "You live here now?" he said, staring out with a peculiar expression on his face.

"Yes, sir."

"You couldn't find anything else?"

"To be honest, Coach, it was the only place I looked at."

"I bet you miss the dorm food."

"I do, I miss it a lot. I guess I need to learn how to cook like Li'l Bit." One of the cooks at Broussard, Li'l Bit was so named because she was frugal in spooning out our meals. "Could you give me just a li'l bit more, please?" we begged.

"You shouldn't call her Li'l Bit, son. She never liked that."

"You're right, Coach. Sorry."

He extended his hand for me to shake. "Buddy, I so enjoyed being your coach. You ever need anything, you call me, you hear?"

I got out of the car and walked with my tuxedo and trophy through weeds and large patches of brown spots to the front door. When I looked back, he was still parked there, bent forward in his seat, watching me through the glass.

MY CHEST WOULDN'T STOP hurting. I had to be careful about what I wore. T-shirts were fine, but only baggy ones made of cotton. My scar wouldn't tolerate polyester. And it didn't like certain detergents. Buttons hurt too, and I couldn't wear polo shirts because the vent at the neck ground against my flesh and made me want to scratch and claw the wound out.

I met with Doc Stander and asked for help, and he sent me to a plastic surgeon who handled special cases for the team. The surgeon took me into a room and instructed me to remove my shirt and lie on a table. He shot my chest with anesthesia, and I watched in the lenses of his eyeglasses as he removed the fatty wad of tissue that was the scar and applied a tight row of stitches.

"How many?" I asked when he was done.

"I didn't keep count."

"How many would you guess?"

"I'd say more than fifty, inside and out."

I started taking pain pills. They didn't help. My chest hurt worse than any broken bone or high ankle sprain I'd suffered in the past, worse than the time I was speared in the groin during a nationally televised game and threw up on myself, and worse than the few times I'd been knocked unconscious, and worse than the countless stingers that had so taxed the nerves in the back of my head that I still don't feel a thing when you touch me there.

I doubled up on the pills and consumed my whole supply in a few days. Rather than call the doctor for more, I drank from Larry's stash of whiskey until I reached the desired effect. I'd never been much of a drinker, and I'd rarely ever been drunk. What I learned about whiskey was that it really didn't numb the pain, but it did numb the one in pain—until he blacked out, which was the next best thing.

Alone in my room, I lay in bed on sheets stained brown from blood and said every prayer my mother had ever taught me—the Hail Mary, the Act of Contrition, the Lord's Prayer, the Glory Be. Classes were in full swing, but I skipped them and stayed home, WRKF playing Dixieland jazz and classical music on my Liberty Bowl radio, used paperbacks I'd bought at yard sales piled up in bed around me.

Only weeks before, skipping class would've meant inviting Coach Mac's wrath and a suspension from the team, but no one came to check on me. For the first time since eighth grade, I was facing 3 p.m. on a winter day with no obligation to be in a weight room working out.

Larry poked his head in from time to time. "You okay, Pride?"

"Fine, Savage."

But I was not fine. Long after the pain left my chest and the doctor took the stitches out, I did not want to leave my room.

I WOKE TO THE SMELL of cigarette smoke. Beyond my open door, I could see in the living room the cherry tip of a cigarette flare in the darkness. "That you, Savage?" I called out.

There was no answer, so I got out of bed, put on a robe, and shuffled out to see who it was. Larry's door at the opposite end of the hall was closed.

A woman was sitting on the couch. She didn't get up when I walked in and asked what she was doing there. Instead she removed her shoes and shoved them one after the other under the coffee table, using the big toe of her right foot to guide them until they were standing side by side. She pulled her legs up beneath her and let out a sigh as she settled deeper into the cushions.

"Are you the roommate?" she asked, taking another drag. She didn't bother to turn her head away when she blew the smoke out.

"What's that?"

"He told me his roommate was a player."

I stood in the middle of the room staring at her. I suppose I was still half asleep, because my inclination was to defend myself against the heretical suggestion that I was anything but a writer. Then, in my confusion, I felt a bump of fear at the prospect of being caught with a girl in my room.

41

"My ex had season tickets," the woman said in a peckerwood drawl more commonly heard in the wilds of neighboring Mississippi. "We used to go to the games." She pumped a fist in the air. "Go Tigers. Man, we raised us some hell pulling for them boys. Nothing like Tiger Stadium on a Saturday night, huh, sugah?"

I was starting to wake up. "How do you know my roommate?"

"I don't know him—not really, anyway. I met him earlier tonight at Murphy's."

"Why is his bedroom door closed?"

"He said he didn't feel well. He put me out and locked it." She blew more smoke. "My car's parked at the bar, and somebody's going to have to drive me back there to git it." She pumped her fist in the air again, and though they didn't issue a sound, her lips repeated the words "Go Tigers." "What's your name?" she asked.

I told her, chewing the damned thing as I'm wont to do, saying Jah Ned rather than John Ed.

"Jah what? Tell me again, honey."

But I'd already said it one time too many.

I walked to Larry's room and banged on the door. I gave it a shove and jiggled the knob, but he'd locked the door from the inside. "I really, desperately need your help here, Savage," I said.

He never answered.

I returned to my room and got back in bed. The red tip of her cigarette flared one more time, then went out, and I heard the woman's bare feet on the floor. She was standing in the doorway. I turned on the lamp next to the bed. The green glass shade didn't allow much light, but I saw her expression change as she absorbed the contents of the room. Covering the bed was a purple wool blanket with a gold letter L sewn in the center and gold piping around the edges. The school had given me the blanket when I earned my second letter, and in one corner my name was stitched in gold thread. Hanging on the back of a chair was my letter jacket. Jewelry I'd received for playing in bowl games was displayed on the top shelf of a bookcase. On the floor at the foot of the bed was a group of trophies I'd taken home from the team banquet in December.

"You old tomcat, you. You really did play."

I shrugged and practiced what I'd planned to say to anyone who asked me about my past in the game: "Yes. But that was another life."

"Can I ask you what happened to your chest?"

The top of my robe had pulled open. I quickly closed it again.

She shuffled over and sat on the edge of the bed. She reeked of wet rayon and fried bar food, and a thin scum of lipstick formed a halo around her mouth, hinting at a time when she and Larry had gotten along better. "That is so nasty," she said and let out a breath. She reached over to open the robe. I pushed her hand away. "I like a scar on a man," she said. "It means he ain't wasting his life sitting at home in the Barcalounger."

"Let me get dressed and I'll drive you back to your car."

"Can't I stay here with you tonight, sugah? What's wrong, Jah? You played football for LSU so you're too good for me? Is that it?"

"I didn't say I'm too good. I just need to take you back to the bar."

"Y'all weren't worth a shit anyway," she said, pushing by me. "Always lost the big ones. Mac never could beat the Bear, could he now?"

She was still beating me up twenty minutes later when I dropped her off. Her car was in worse shape than the Impala, and the Impala had more than two hundred thousand miles on it, a faded paint job, bald tires, and a vinyl soft top peeling like bark from a sycamore tree. "Losers. That's all you boys ever were."

There was a world outside of football that I knew nothing about, and in it there were people whose destinies were governed by random encounters in barrooms late on a Friday night.

When I returned to Convention Street, the sun was coming up and coloring the trunks of the pecan trees that lined the street. Larry was still locked in his room. I started a pot of coffee going and sprayed disinfectant on the couch. Then I went to my room and carefully arranged my LSU blanket and letter jacket in a plastic pillow bag. I put the jewelry and other things in boxes and stacked them in back of the closet. Some of the trophies were too tall for boxes, so I stood them on the floor, next to the duffel bag containing my helmets.

Finally, I took a couple of sheets and covered the pile. I made sure you couldn't see anything.

EVERY DAY for nearly four years, I'd stepped on a scale and recorded my weight on a chart for the coaches. It was the first thing you did when you arrived at the stadium for practice. I never saw a coach look at the chart, but the assumption was that you were being closely monitored in this regard as in all others. The official 1979 roster listed me at six-foot-three and two hundred and thirty-four pounds, but those measurements were taken in the spring, when I was recovering from the flu. By the fall, I'd grown an inch and had added close to eleven pounds. I more accurately came to six-four and two forty-five. In less than a decade, the game would have quarterbacks bigger than that.

Without Li'l Bit and the dorm cafeteria to sustain me, I began to lose weight. Larry's favorite meal was Hamburger Helper and canned okra with stewed tomatoes, and we ate it three or four nights a week, usually as we read in silence at the kitchen table.

My specialty was cornbread sprinkled with sugar, topped with cold milk, and served in a shallow bowl. I dropped twenty pounds in my first month out of football. I surely would have lost more if not for my discovery of microwave burritos at a nearby 7-Eleven—meals I usually consumed after midnight while sitting on the curb out front with my back against the ice machine. People no longer noticed me when I stopped by the convenience store and walked the aisles looking for the big, orange sale stickers. Nor did they look when I went to the mall or to church or to a movie. I generated no interest when I strolled across campus between classes. Before, there'd been enthusiastic greetings from students who yelled out questions that I usually answered with a grunt. One time as I walking down a campus street, a beautiful coed in a convertible pulled up beside me, honked the horn, and asked if I needed a lift. When I told her no, she said, "What about a back rub? Think you might need one of those?"

Now I seemed to be growing less visible by the minute. Back in August, at the start of two-a-days, my neck had measured better than nineteen inches. By April, it was down to sixteen. My clothes hung on me like a tent with poles placed too close together.

"What are you going to do about it?" I said out loud one night after yet another awful meal with Larry. I was at the kitchen sink washing a pile of dirty dishes. This was our arrangement: The cook cooked; the one who didn't cook washed dishes.

Larry was in the living room. He put his book down. "You say something, Pride?"

"No, man. Nothing."

"I thought I heard you say something."

"No, Savage. Not me."

I was relieved that he hadn't heard me. But the question was an honest one. What was I going to do about not having football anymore? I was deep into the spring semester, moving along like a cheap clock that needed to have its batteries changed. Classes ended for the day, and there was nowhere to go, nothing to do. No meetings with coaches to attend, no film to watch, no workouts to complete, no practices to endure, no reporters to talk to, no autographs to sign. I didn't have to visit the training room for whirlpool or hot-wax baths or ultrasound treatments or massages or traction or complicated ankle tapings or shots to kill whatever pain had sprung from whatever injury.

I didn't have the dorm, I didn't have the food, I didn't have my teammates, I didn't have the life. My mother encouraged me to look for the good in things, and I'd managed to come up with only a few noteworthy items. For one, I didn't have to stay up late and get up early to shoehorn study time into my day. I slept a lot now. And keeping up with class assignments, once an impossible task, suddenly had become a breeze. I was carrying twenty-one credit hours and making straight A's even though I was barely trying.

One day you're on the team, the next you're a guy with a pile of memories and a feeling in his gut that he is seriously done.

THIS AFTERNOON I spent several hours in the library working on a poem for one of my classes. I called it "See Rock City," and although I wasn't sure what it was about, I was confident that my classmates would be able to tell me tomorrow when I read it out loud to them. I was sitting on a bench in the Quadrangle with about an hour to burn before I left campus and returned to Convention Street. Without football, time management had taken on an altogether different meaning. I now managed time by killing it in great, heaping chunks. I enjoyed watching the late

AmericanAirlines® oneworld

BOARDING PASS AmericanAirlines®

PASSENGER NAME
KREAGER/MICHAEL

FROM:
MINNEAPOLIS-ST PAU

TO:
DALLAS/FORT WORTH

FIRST

FREQUENT FLYER # 8JD5778PLT
RECORD LOCATOR GMUYEA

FLIGHT AA549   CLASS X   DATE 12SEP   DEPARTS 915A

GATE E14   BOARDING TIME 845A   SEAT 6F

ELECTRONIC 001707516619O

BOARDING PASS
KREAGER/MICHAEL

FROM:
MINNEAPOLIS-ST PAU

TO:
DALLAS/FORT WORTH

FLIGHT AA 549   SEAT 6F

FIRST

DATE 12SEP   CLASS X   DEPARTS 915A

winter light redden the terra-cotta rooftops of the old classroom buildings. Even more satisfying was the parade of girls in faded jeans and cashmere sweaters who moved across the Quad, books held like nursing babies at their chests. On rainy days, I scrutinized the shelf of literary criticism in the student union bookstore and played a game of finding the title with the deepest layer of dust on top. It was usually good for an hour. Next I visited the natural science museum in Foster Hall, where stuffed animals were displayed in large glass cases. One of these cases held a snake whose tail rattled when you stepped on a platform. I hated snakes. But it was a real joy to wait in the room until some unsuspecting visitor walked in, then watch his reaction when he got close to the reptile display and I stepped on the platform.

I was sitting on my favorite bench, wondering how to nudge the day forward, when David Woodley, a teammate until a few months ago, came striding over. David seemed happy to see me again, but he still made an effort to greet me with his well-practiced reserve, giving a limp handshake rather than the bear hug I might've expected from any other member of our class. "What have you been doing with your life, Bradley Boy?"

"Typing. What about you?"

"Working out for NFL teams. I hope one of them drafts me."

Surely you're dreaming, I thought. A Shreveport native, David had split time at quarterback with Steve Ensminger of Baton Rouge. And though he was a gifted athlete with sprinter's speed and a powerful throwing arm, he had never quite lived up to his potential, never enjoyed the full support of the fans the way the hometown favorite had. When we played together in the Louisiana High School All-Star Game the summer before our freshman year, I was certain that David would develop into the finest and most loved quarterback to play at LSU since Bert Jones. Instead his inconsistent play and aloof demeanor sometimes had fans booing him when he ran out on the field. By the spring of our senior year, David had grown estranged from most of our teammates. Coach Mac once gave me a dorm-house key and sent me to the room David shared with Charles McDuff. As a team captain, one of my duties was to try to talk sense to players who seemed hell-bent on being kicked out of the program. David had stopped showing up for workouts at the stadium, and he was avoiding Mac's phone calls. "Go find him," Mac had told me. "I'm sure you'll have an easier time getting through to him than I have." David was sitting in bed with a litter of crushed beer cans on the floor. Cigarette smoke clouded the lights overhead. He'd opened the windows, no doubt to clear the air before a dorm monitor busted him, and a ninety-degree draft was pouring into the room. "You all right, Bones? Hey, man, talk to me."

His hair was a frizzy nest, and he was as pale as the sheets wrapped around his legs, but he seemed relieved that it was me checking up on him instead of a coach. He took a sip from a can, then let it drop to the floor with the others. "Leave me alone, Bradley Boy." He fell over on his side.

Later, when I saw Coach Mac, I told him David wasn't feeling well. "You sure it's a virus?" he said.

"Pretty sure, Coach."

"Then why doesn't he come down to the training room and see a doctor?"

"I had it too. You can hardly lift your head off the pillow."

On the Quad, David looked nothing like the drunken shut-in of a year ago. He had trimmed his hair and gotten some sun on his face. For years he'd been so skinny you could see the bones of his rib cage, but now he'd put on weight and looked thick in his clothes. He exuded confidence—just what the NFL wanted to see in a prospect.

"You're not working out for any teams?" he said.

"Nah."

"How come?"

"Don't want to."

"Why wouldn't you want to?"

"I've already lost thirty pounds. Besides, I don't think I'm good enough. I'm ready to leave football behind, Bones. I'm a writer now. As a matter of fact, I wrote a poem today that I'd like to read to you if you have a few minutes to spare."

He smiled the way I'd hoped he would and glanced at his watch. "Sorry, I'm already late for class."

"Don't let me keep you."

We spent a long while looking at each other. And for the first time since I'd met him, I had the vague sense that he gave half a damn about me. "I used to walk by your door in the dorm and hear you typing," he said. "Everybody else was playing music, watching TV, or talking on the phone. You were typing."

"It drove my roommates crazy."

"Good luck, John Ed."

Hearing him say my name—my real name—stirred up something deep down in my throat, and for a moment I could barely breathe. "Same to you, David," I said, calling him by his real name for the first time in years.

I FIRST MET Jerry Stovall when I was in high school and he came with three other assistants to pitch me on signing with LSU. It was after a home game late in the season, and the four men formed a tight circle around me in the locker room, making it impossible for me to ignore them. Except for the towel hanging around my waist,

I had nothing on, and I wished they'd waited at least until I could have gotten into my shorts. As soon as he started to speak, I knew why Coach Stovall had such a big reputation as a recruiter. He could've made a fortune leading tent revivals or taking prayer requests for donations from international television audiences. He owned you with the power and sincerity of his voice and the intensity of his focus. At the time, he was in charge of the running backs, but everyone knew him as one of the greatest football players the state had ever produced. He was the Heisman Trophy runner-up at LSU in 1962 and later became an All-Pro defensive back with the St. Louis Cardinals. When we were kids, my brother Bobby and I had a hard time pronouncing his name, so we called him Snowball. That he played for an NFL team with red jerseys served to further emphasize the uniqueness of his name. We let out wild screams whenever he appeared in televised games: "Cherry Snowball!"

"John Ed," he was telling me now, "I'd like to offer you a position as a graduate assistant, working with our offensive linemen and coaching the JV team."

I was sitting across from him in his new office—the same office that Coach Mac had occupied before surrendering it to Bo Rein. In Mac's day, the walls had held photos of his family and friends and plaques honoring his achievements. Now they were empty but for nails poking out from the wood.

"Have you considered a career in coaching, John Ed?"

"No, sir, I can't say I have."

"Your dad was a coach."

"Yes, sir, he was. But it's been my dream for a long time to be a writer. I want to be a novelist, Coach."

"I've never had a player sit across from me and tell me that."

I hated to have to turn him down. I hated to turn down anyone who was kind enough to offer me a job at this point in my life. I wondered if he'd heard reports that I'd taken to napping on the benches in the Quadrangle and eating burritos on the ground in front of a convenience store.

For several uncomfortable moments, I sat there looking down at the hands folded in my lap, searching for the words to reject the offer. "It's awfully good of you to think I could contribute to what you want to do here, Coach. You have to know I take that as a great compliment. I love LSU as much as anyone, I think you know that. And I never doubted that playing football here was a privilege. But I also know that if I don't break from it now, I'll never break from it. I want to finish school, then go out and see the world, Coach. All I've ever known is football. I don't mean to be disrespectful, but there's got to be more. And while I'm sure that most people who come from the state of Louisiana would disagree with me, LSU football can't be all there is."

He quietly chuckled to himself as he walked around the desk and leaned back against it. He brought his arms up and crossed them at his chest. "I understand your feelings, John Ed. But I think you'd make a fine coach. You understand the game, you already have the respect of the players, and I know you'd be an asset to the program and represent the school well. We'd love to have you. Look, why don't you go home tonight and think about it? I'll give you 'til morning to make up your mind."

I left the office and drifted across the street in the general direction of the cage that housed the team mascot, Mike IV, a five-hundred-pound Bengal tiger. If you caught him at the right time, he'd come out unprompted and let you hear it.

"Mike," I said with an ease that suggested we were old friends. "Hey, man. You in there?"

I stood as close to the cage as you could get, but he wasn't outside in the sun, where he usually spent his time, and I couldn't see

him back in the shade of his den. Even though I'd visited the stadium almost every day for four years, I had bothered to walk across
the street and have a look at Mike in his cage only a dozen times.
I should've felt guilty about that. Instead I was worried about how
to impress on Coach Stovall that I was determined to be a writer.
"Hey, brother. Long time no see. Come out and let me talk to you."

During games, they wheeled Mike out into the stadium in a gilded
cage barely big enough to hold him. Cheerleaders rode on top of
the cage, caught his roars with a microphone, and sent them out
over the intercom system. It always made me a little sad to hear
him. But Mike's roars terrified opposing players. "What's the deal
with the tiger?" a nose guard for USC asked me after Mike erupted
with a particularly heartfelt growl. The player's eyes were huge and
unblinking. "Mike's here tonight in case we can't handle you by
ourselves," I told him.

Mike's name appeared in purple on the roof of his cage, the Roman
numeral IV clearly painted over a Roman numeral III. I couldn't tell
you the life expectancy of a tiger, but I figured it had to be longer than
the career of a football coach. My father had lasted fifteen years in the
profession, all but two of them as a high school assistant, and he
barely made enough money to feed and clothe his family and drop a
fistful of cash in the collection basket at church on Sunday. How long
could a guy without his heart in it last? I never aspired to be LSU
Coach V or VI or VII or VIII. Let somebody else have the job. Me?
All I ever wanted was to leave a pretty piece of writing behind.

"You think I'd make a good coach, Mike?" I asked now, even
though there was still no sign of him. "Hey, Mike, what's the problem, old boy? Why don't you come help me?"

I glanced around to make sure I was alone. The wind was starting to pick up and blow clouds of baby flowers that looked like
pink dust from the crepe myrtles.

It was the strangest thing, but when that defensive lineman asked me about Mike, I wanted to punch him. I wanted to drive my fist into the eyehole of his face mask. It was okay for people to talk about me. It didn't even bother me when, there on the line before I snapped the ball, they defamed my mother. But Mike was different. It wasn't his fault he was stuck in a cage and harassed until he let out a roar. Mike was beautiful. Better yet, he was innocent.

"Mike, if you think I should become a football coach, I want you to step out now and growl for me. I really want you to let me hear it."

But Mike stayed out of view, hidden in his den.

I walked back to the stadium and entered the football office. Coach Stovall's secretary greeted me with a smile, a sad one. She seemed to understand why I'd returned so quickly. "Think Coach would let me have another minute?"

She made the call, and he came through the door and met me in the outer office.

"Coach, I appreciate it and all, I really do. You can't know how much I appreciate your confidence in me. But I don't need until tomorrow to give you my answer. Coach, it's my destiny to be a writer, it just is. I don't know why I have to do it, but I know I have to try. If I don't, nothing will ever seem right to me for as long as I live."

Except for a couple of my instructors, I'd never known a real writer before. But I'd known dozens of coaches. I grew up with them. And I knew that at the heart of every one, there was a little boy who stayed in the game because he didn't want it to end.

Coach Stovall stepped up and put his arms around me. "Never forget us," he said.

Chapter Three

THE
CHUTE

YOU ENTERED THE CHUTE across from the equipment cage and the surface of the floor changed from industrial carpet to a tan-colored cork that kept you from slipping when you had cleats on. You walked past the weight scales and the padded tables where the trainers wrapped ankles, and then past a large room on your right that everybody called the torture chamber. For most of the year, it was used for storing equipment—practice dummies, field cones, kickers' nets, bags of spare balls. But in the offseason we trained there. The coaches killed the air conditioning or raised the heat, and we wrestled and did floor exercises and other odd maneuvers they seemed to invent on the fly. Most of the drills were meant to improve our quickness and endurance and test our will. One of them, for instance, had us lying on our backs five men across until a whistle blew, then sprinting to the other end of the room and breaking down in front of the wall. To break down meant to stop suddenly and run in place, and you ran in place by pumping your arms and legs as fast as you could, and your feet made a noise like drums beating, and because the door was closed, the sound, with nowhere to go, echoed in the room. Then came a second whistle and you slapped your open hands against the wall, and the coaches liked it when everybody hit the wall at the same time, because it made a sharp report that suggested teamwork and discipline. I once slapped the wall so hard I fractured my wrist and ended up in a cast for six weeks.

So you passed the torture chamber and came to the bottom of the chute. The door straight in front of you led to the playing field, and the one on your right led to the weight room. And that was where I found myself one day in the spring of my sophomore year. I was doing butterflies on a Nautilus machine, deep into my second set, when Coach Mac appeared at the door, a look of urgency on his face. It was so strange to see him in the weight room that I stopped before I was finished, as did most of the other players. Coach Mac coached football, and he left this part of our education to the strength coach.

"This ain't good," I heard someone whisper.

I knew Mac was there for me.

He moved past the squat racks and everyone drew closer, as if to protect against what he had to say. A voice that might've been my own shouted in my head, *"Run, boy. Run away from here. Run."* Mac's eyes shifted from one player to the next. "Where's John Ed?" he said.

No one responded—they refused to rat me out—but Mac seemed to sense that I was behind him. He wheeled around. "I walked right past you," he said. He grabbed my shirt and gave it a tug. "Come."

I followed him out into the chute, and he put an arm around me. "I'm sorry, but I have to tell you this." He held me with his eyes, and somehow I knew what it was before he said it. "Buddy, your father had a heart attack."

I ran a hand through my hair and wiped my mouth with the only dry spot left on my shirt. Then I moved around to make sure my back was turned to the weight room. If I began to cry, I didn't want my teammates to see me. "Is he dead, Coach?"

"No, but he's in the hospital in intensive care. So you need to go on home. Take care of your business, look after your family, and come back when you're ready."

"My dad's only forty-five years old, Coach."

He shook his head as if to say it didn't make a bit of sense to him, either.

One of my sister Donna's friends was waiting outside when I left the stadium. She'd volunteered to drive me to Opelousas. I folded my body into the passenger seat and sat slumped against the door. She didn't have any more information than I did, and yet she spoke as if she knew with certainty that Daddy was going to be okay. I wanted to tell her to please be quiet, to please please please be quiet, to shut up goddammit, but somehow I managed to hold my tongue. She only meant to make me feel better. I hadn't showered, and I could feel the sweat on my skin starting to cool beneath my clothes. I hadn't trained well that day, and I was glad to be out of the weight room and away from the strength coach who'd ridden me hard for any number of monumental screwups and unforgivable sins. Now I wondered if God was punishing me for praying to get out of the workout. He'd let me out, all right.

I hadn't cooled down properly and my hamstrings were beginning to cramp. My mouth was parched and tasted of old pennies and probably smelled worse. By now my teammates were finishing up. They were heading to the showers or to the training room for treatment. Soon they'd all be heading back to Broussard Hall for supper and laughs in the cafeteria. That would show me what to pray for.

Donna's friend drove faster as we crossed an elevated roadway over the Atchafalaya Spillway. The heart attack was my fault, I decided. What kind of God gives your father a heart attack as a way of letting you out of a workout? I didn't know how I was going to explain myself to my mother if he didn't make it.

They were all there in the emergency waiting room—Mama, my brothers and sisters, my grandmother, aunts and uncles and cousins, friends from town. The automatic doors swept open, and I stepped into grief so heavy it seemed to hop up on my chest like an animal. Outside there were people who worked with my father at the school board and a couple of men he'd coached years before. My mother walked up and put her arms around me. "How is he?" I asked.

"He wants to see you. He's been asking for you."

"He isn't going to die, is he, Mama?"

"No. And don't say that. Don't ever say that." She reached up and put her fingertips over my mouth.

A nurse led the way. He was lying on a gurney, hooked to machines. A canula ran in his nose, and the ward's fluorescent lights gave his skin a yellow cast. His eyes, when he opened them, were shot red around the hazel irises. He began to tear up, and the tears ran down into the hair at his temples. I put my hand in his on the side of the bed, felt the fingers as thick as pipes, the palm a strong, hard slab. "Take care of your mother and your little brothers," he said. "I want you to promise me."

"Why should I have to take care of them? That's your job."

He swallowed as best he could. It seemed to give him pain.

"What about Gina and Donna?" I said. "Don't you want me to take care of them, too?"

58

"They're grown. Just help your mama with the boys. Promise."

They let him out a few days later, and when I returned to Opelousas and saw him again, I didn't ask him about our talk, the vow he'd extracted from me that day in the hospital or the tears he'd let fall from his eyes. Instead we talked about football. I'd never get used to seeing him measure out his pills at night as he lay on his side on the old comforter that covered his and my mother's bed. That he took them was his only admission that anything was wrong. At odd times over the years, when we were all together as a family, celebrating Christmas or Easter or the birth of another grandchild, I'd have to fight off a sudden urge to say to him, "You must've thought you were going to die, to say those things to me." But I never did speak those words, never once brought up the episode that nearly killed him. To mention the possibility of his dying would be to invite the possibility that he might.

The other thing that always stopped me was the memory of my mother's hand on my mouth, her fingertips keeping my lips closed, fears unspoken.

I WAS DOOMED from the start. If not an LSU football player, what else might I have become? Daddy was so devoted to the team that in the fall he weighed the merits of each week based on whether the Tigers won or lost on Saturday night. My mother wasn't much better. When she went to Tiger Stadium, she wore corsages made of giant chrysanthemums. At the center of each flower, purple pipe cleaners spelled out *L S U*. A little metal football and a collection of satin ribbons completed the arrangement. During the season, our refrigerator typically held more than milk and eggs; Mama's football corsages lined the shelves in varying states of decay. She seemed loath to throw them away, especially those she'd worn to Tiger victories.

I know nothing about astrology or astronomy—I'm not sure I could explain the difference between the two—but I am sure the stars contributed to how I turned out. The year of my birth, 1958, was the year LSU won its first and only outright national championship, and August, when I made my arrival, was when the two-a-day practices began. My father could be as thoughtful and philosophical as any other high school coach when his own team lost, but he was so devoted to LSU that he was far less understanding when the Tigers from Baton Rouge did. How many times did he leave the house late in a televised game, unable to watch another play? If it looked like the Tigers were going to lose a close one, he was especially long in returning. "Where have you been?" we'd yell at him, when he finally came back inside.

"Nowhere," he'd say. "What happened?"

In those days, LSU games rarely appeared on television more than a couple of times a year. And so we were dedicated listeners to the radio broadcasts and play-by-play announcer John Ferguson. We listened while my mother made potato salad in the kitchen and Daddy barbecued outside on the patio. He'd sit there in a lawn chair, lost in concentration as his chicken burned, a purple-and-gold cap tipped back on his head. His arms, legs, and neck glistened with mosquito repellant, and he sipped from a can of beer wrapped in a foam hugger advertising a local insurance agency. Not far away from his smoldering pit, on a narrow piece of finely manicured St. Augustine, I acted the game out with neighborhood friends, some of us dressed in Little Tiger uniforms. We played until somebody ran into a ligustrum hedge or got clotheslined by a real clothesline, and my father called for an end to the rough-and-tumble and sat me down next to him.

"Settle down now," he'd say. "LSU's on."

In his mind, the football team represented the entire state of Louisiana, and the way the team performed gave the rest of the nation a snapshot of what kind of people we were. Notre Dame's boys might be bigger and stronger than ours, but we weren't afraid to line up against them and see who wanted it more. USC might have better talent—okay, he'd concede that—but you needed more than talent to beat LSU. The Tigers often were underdogs, just like the state of Louisiana. Our players scrapped and hustled and always showed good sportsmanship, never more so than when they lost. On defense, they fought off larger opponents, swarmed to the ball, and made spirited gang tackles, and on offense, everyone gave a second effort, including the quarterback, who wasn't afraid to lower his shoulder and block a player twice his size if that was what it took to win.

Daddy had no use for showboats and loudmouths. He believed that humility was equivalent to class in a man, and nothing pleased him more than to hear a player deflect the praise he'd earned and credit his teammates instead. Players who danced in the end zone after scoring were buffoons. Those who calmly handed the ball to an official were to be admired.

Opelousas produced few athletes who went on to play in Baton Rouge. Those who did carried a large part of my father's identity with them. I remember when John Weinstein and Skip Cormier played on LSU's defensive line in the early 1970s. Both made big hits in important TV games that we watched as a family. Every time the announcers mentioned either Weinstein's or Cormier's name, Daddy turned in his seat and faced his children. "He's from here," he said.

When Jeff Sandoz, a football and track star at Opelousas High, signed a scholarship with LSU, my father drove me to his house one day after school and parked by the curb in front. We sat there a minute looking at the place, even though we'd seen it a thousand times before. I didn't have to ask him why we had stopped there. When we returned home, he had me go inside and get a football. We spent the rest of the afternoon throwing passes in the yard.

There were great Americans who came from Opelousas, but in my father's mind, none were greater than the town's football players. Alamo hero Jim Bowie, for instance, spent a large part of his childhood in Opelousas. He invented a knife that was good for gutting wild game, but remembering him would've been easier had he played on Saturday in Baton Rouge. Rod Milburn, the track star who won a gold medal in the 110 meter hurdles at the 1972 Munich Olympics, grew up in Opelousas and returned home for a parade in his honor. Daddy enjoyed watching Milburn run, but I'm sure he'd have liked him even more had Milburn used his speed to haul in long passes from quarterbacks in yellow helmets. Paul Prudhomme, the Cajun chef, was another Opelousas boy. In the 1980s, Prudhomme's signature creation, blackened redfish, became so popular that the redfish population in the Gulf of Mexico was threatened with annihilation, prompting the state of Louisiana to impose limits on harvesting it. Prudhomme was a student at Opelousas High when my father was coaching there. One day I asked Daddy what he remembered about the man, and he said, "Well, he wasn't a cook then. And he wasn't a man. Everybody called him Gene."

"That's what you remember? That he wasn't a cook or a man and his name was Gene?"

He shrugged. "What do you want me to tell you?"

"What kind of person was he? What was he like?"

"Like any teenager. I don't know—he was a young kid."

"So he was Gene, a young kid who wasn't a cook or a man yet.

That's what you remember?"

"Don't get smart with me, boy."

There was another Prudhomme from Opelousas who went on and made everybody proud. He was Paul's cousin, Remi Prudhomme. At LSU in the early 1960s, Remi earned three letters as an offensive guard. He later played with the Kansas City Chiefs and the Buffalo Bills. In 1970, when the Chiefs faced the Minnesota Vikings in Super Bowl IV, my father pointed out Prudhomme with a finger as he lined up to cover on a kick. I kept one of my own fingers on Prudhomme as he ran down the field trying to make a hit on the return man. When I removed my finger, there was a thin trail in the dust moving west to east, perfectly bisecting the TV screen.

The next time the Chiefs kicked off, we watched as the Vikings' returner fumbled the ball and Prudhomme fell on it. I gave a shout and danced around the room, but my father showed no emotion. The recovery had set up good field position for the Chiefs, who later would score. "He's from here," I said.

"Yes, he is," Daddy answered, failing to register that I was being smart with him.

"Went to the high school."

He got it finally and flicked a finger against the top of my skull.

A year or two later I rode with him one Saturday afternoon to pick up something at Jimmy's Cash Store on the Old Sunset Road. You crossed some railroad tracks and the little package store was there on your left, directly across the blacktop from where Mr. Alfred Lagrange had his yam kiln. Parked out on the white shell lot in front of Jimmy's was a shiny new car growing less shiny by the minute. Every time a vehicle passed down the road, dust rolled up and tumbled over in a cloud. It was fine for my father's truck to get dirty—it was a 1963 GMC with rust holes in the bed and dents in the hood—but it was hard to watch it happen to something as pretty as that car.

I waited outside. The store had plate glass windows plastered with white butcher's paper advertising sale items in black and red ink: pork chops, boudin, hogshead cheese, a four-roll package of toilet paper, a box of twelve-gauge shotgun shells. Tired of waiting, I let myself out of the truck and went in. I could hear my father's voice coming from the rear of the store, back near the beer cooler. I found him talking to a huge, muscle-bound man wearing a black shirt and blue slacks. "John Ed, come over here. I want you to meet somebody."

It was Remi Prudhomme. He had dark, curly hair kept in place with Brylcreem or some other such product, and his face was burned by the sun and showing black stubble that tracked downward to the bottom of his neck and upward to within an inch of his eyeballs. Daddy told me to step closer and have a look at his Super Bowl ring. Remi Prudhomme held his hand out. "You want to try it on? Here. See how it fits."

It was a gaudy thing that sparkled and flashed when you moved it under the ceiling lights. He pulled it off and handed it to me. I could've slipped two fingers into the ring. "You gonna play football when you get older?"

"Yes, sir."

"Who you gonna play for?"

"LSU Tigers."

And then he did what they all seemed to do. He gave the top of my head a shake.

I got another look at Prudhomme as he was leaving the store. He was carrying a flat of beer with one hand up by his shoulder, the way a waiter carries a tray. He slid the case into the front seat of the sedan then got behind the wheel and started the engine. I watched as he lit a cigarette and took a long drag that boiled in his lungs awhile before issuing from his nostrils in fast-moving parallel streams.

"I thought you said football players weren't supposed to smoke?" I said to my father. We were heading home now.

"They're not. Cigarette smoke cuts your wind. Come the fourth quarter, your lungs feel like they're about to explode."

"How about beer? What does that do?"

"Nothing good, either." He seemed to anticipate my next question. "Remi's not thinking straight today, John Ed. He's got a lot of God-given ability, but he must've left his thinking cap back in Kansas City."

We went down the road a ways, headed for Delmas Street. "I don't really like the Chiefs," I said.

"You don't like Lenny Dawson?"

"He's all right, but I don't want to play for Kansas City."

"I don't blame you." He shook his head. "What did you think of Remi's Super Bowl ring?"

"I don't like jewelry, either," I answered.

"Neither do I," said my father, "especially on a man."

THE EARLIEST INDICATION that I might have a future as a college football player came in the spring of my sophomore year at Opelousas High. The fantasy had long been there, of course, but so few boys from my school received scholarship offers that I was certain I'd never get one. This belief was based on many factors, not the least of which was a strong personal conviction that I wasn't any good.

At six-foot-two and a hundred and eighty-seven pounds, I was hardly the bulky Neanderthal recruiters envision for the center position, and I didn't run particularly well, either. The year before, in a postseason bowl game with a small school from the parish, I replaced the starting center at the beginning of the second half and promptly gave up two sacks. That I gave up no more the rest of the afternoon had nothing to do with my ability to rebound from adversity. Desperate to neutralize a nose guard who threatened to single-handedly wreck our chances to win, head coach Mickey Guidry schemed to have both guards help me out in passing situations. When our quarterback dropped back to throw, three of us were assigned to block one man, and while this left the lanes on either side of me open for blitzing linebackers to exploit, the defense was committed to dropping back to protect against the pass. I got a lucky break that day. Had the other team seized the opportunity and rushed its linebackers, I would've given up more sacks in one half than the average lineman does in his entire high school career.

At season's end, I decided I wanted to be the kind of lineman who blows people off the ball. To gain body mass, I put myself on a diet of my own invention and began to consume carbohydrates in vast quantities—pasta, bread, rice, and more pasta, bread, and rice. Each night at supper, my mother let me eat as much as I wanted, but the staple of my diet was ice cream. At the K & B drugstore in town, you could buy a half-gallon carton for a dollar. Occasionally the store sold two for the price of one. On those days, I arrived early and loaded a shopping cart with the cube-shaped cartons. I paid for this haul with money I'd saved from cutting grass, picking pecans, and other odd jobs. Peeling back the paper carton like a banana and munching from one end to the other, I often ate an entire half gallon in a single sitting.

I once ate four cartons in twelve hours and never picked up a spoon. "You're gross," my sisters told me.

By spring, I'd grown an inch taller, had gained twenty pounds, and had become more competitive at practice, often in view of the visiting recruiters who watched every move from behind Ray-Bans and the bills of low-riding baseball caps. Our offensive line coach, Madison Firman, liked to put us through a drill called Bull in the Ring. Six players formed a circle around a single man, positioning themselves five yards away. Firman assigned each player on the ring a number then called out the number of the man he wanted to attack the bull. The objective was to drive the bull out of the ring or, in the case of the bull, hold your ground.

Firman occasionally called the numbers of the players standing directly behind the bull. He did this because it was important for a lineman to keep his head on a swivel. The bull ran in place at the center of the ring, pivoting from side to side in anticipation of the next assault. Rarely more than a few seconds separated one strike from the next. The bull took a beating, even when he managed to remain in the ring.

Whenever Firman assigned me the bull position, I concentrated on using the first few hits to send a message to the guys on the ring. I knew better than to rely on just a shoulder or a forearm; that got you nowhere. Instead, I braced my neck and speared the charging player under the chin with my helmet. This snapped his head back and took away his bearings. I completed the strike by thrusting forward from my hips and lower body, which was often enough to put the invader out of commission.

Firman liked to send the toughest players after the bull at the end of the drill, and by the time they came running at me, I'd reached a murderous state. Even after all the players in the ring had been vanquished, I continued to run in place, challenging Firman to send more. I moved my body in a tight pivot, ready for any challenge he had to offer. "Who's next?" I yelled, still wearing my mouthpiece. "Send him. Come on, Coach. Send somebody."

By then, I'd learned how to let my mind go, how to escape the practice field, and even as I was handing out and receiving hits, I was at home in an air-conditioned room eating a cube of ice cream in front of the TV. Or at a movie with Denise Landreneau, holding her hand in the dark theater and stealing kisses whenever the action slowed.

Firman had yet one more exercise to test our toughness: a long chute made of iron pipes, standing slightly more than four feet tall and running for a distance of ten yards. Every day Firman had us run from one end of the narrow tunnel to the other. The object was to train yourself to keep your body low to the ground, to strike with more power than you would if you ran tall. Everybody hated the chute. If you lifted your head, you banged your helmet against one of the pipes on the ceiling. The blow knocked you senseless. To make the drill even more difficult, Firman placed boards end to end on the ground to make us widen our stances. Linemen who blocked with their feet too close together had poor balance and virtually no punching power. The boards forced us to keep them shoulder-width apart, which gave us a better base from which to operate.

Players with low centers of gravity had no problem running the chute, but tall guys struggled to keep their balance. I can still feel the *clap clap clap* of my helmet clipping the pipes as I ran, *clap clap clap* as I raced to the opening. Sometimes, for sport, Firman ordered a player to greet you on the other end. The moment you cleared the last pipe, a defensive lineman uncoiled from a four-point stance. You took blows coming and going—the first to your face, the second from a pipe to the back of your head.

Firman liked to hear us growl when we ran drills: Like scores of other state high school teams that wished to emulate LSU, we were nicknamed the Tigers. "Growl," Firman shouted. "Come on. Let me hear you." But it was hard to growl like a Siamese kitten, much less a Bengal tiger, on a muggy Louisiana day when you were exhausted and struggling to breathe, and one afternoon our growls must've sounded puny and insincere. They'd put him in a mood. "Growl for me. Growl, I'm telling you. *Growl!*"

I growled as loud as I could, but as I was leaving the chute Firman cocked a forearm and slammed it against my shoulder. "I told you to growl. That's not growling."

A former college lineman, Firman had maintained a massive upper body, arms dense with muscle, and lean, well-defined legs into his early thirties. He didn't hit me as hard as he could have, but the blow packed enough power to lift me out of one of my shoes. "Hey, son, you growl when I tell you to growl. Let's go."

I looked at him with all the fury I could muster. It was a look meant to communicate a barely controlled desire to kill him and every member of his family.

I slipped my shoe back on and started to run past him when suddenly he grabbed the back of my jersey and pulled me toward him. "Don't look at me like that."

"How did I look at you, Coach?"

He hooked a finger on the bottom rung of my facemask and pulled me closer still. "Don't talk back to me, either. You know better than to talk back to me, John Ed."

"Coach, I didn't mean—"

"What did I just tell you?"

"But Coach—"

The recruiters were watching from under a goalpost about thirty yards away. Worse, my father had witnessed the incident. He was standing on the other side of the chain link fence that separated the field from a campus parking lot. You've shamed him, I thought.

Daddy had left coaching several years before to become a school principal, but he still showed up for most practices, drawn less by my role with the team than by habit. Twenty-five years before, he'd been the starting center at Opelousas High. Now that job belonged to me. He'd also played linebacker on defense, as I did. Who'd have thought that Johnny Bradley—*Coach* Bradley—would raise a son who got smart and talked back to authority?

Firman blew his whistle, ending the exercise. He ordered us to break the line in half and moved players to the defensive end of the chute. I joined this group, aware that it was an opportunity to unload on someone and redeem myself. I nailed a couple of guys as they left the chute, hitting them with such force that I could feel the air exit their lungs and their weight shift downward when their knees gave out. I glanced over at my father to see his reaction. He gave none. The recruiters didn't seem impressed either.

We were scheduled to move to the main field for a scrimmage, but Firman shouted for us to stay where we were. "Big Hamm," he called out. "Get over there." He was pointing to the chute exit, where I had just been. "John Ed," and now he motioned for me to stand at the entrance.

I considered throwing my helmet at him and sprinting for the showers, even as my teammates began to applaud and pound my shoulder pads. Donald Hammond wasn't like the rest of us. For starters, he was so heavy he eclipsed the three-hundred-and-fifty-pound weight limit on the locker room scale. Players joked that the only way to get the correct reading was to take him to the feed store on Railroad Avenue and put him on a scale used to weigh sacks of beans and corn. When Guidry couldn't find a helmet big enough to fit Hamm, he ordered a shell without any padding from a manufacturer that supplied equipment to the NFL. Even that helmet didn't fit. Big Hamm's face poked out and pressed up flush against the birdcage.

Big Hamm was a nose guard, and it was impossible to move him off the line of scrimmage, even when we double- and triple-teamed him. He lifted guards and centers off their feet and drove them into quarterbacks, then drove the quarterbacks into running backs, then drove the whole pile into the ground. He might've rated as the finest defensive lineman in the history of high school football if only he were effective for more than ten plays a game. He was so big he usually lost his wind after a few series of downs, and after that his night was over. Simply jogging from the sideline to the defensive huddle was enough to exhaust him. He spent the rest of the game recuperating on the bench, an oxygen mask held to his face.

Big Hamm was a hard worker, but Guidry and Firman let him coast through most practices. And Firman inserted him into drills only sparingly, not wishing to hurt anyone, including Hamm himself, who suffered the effects of the weather more than the rest of us. To my recollection, Firman had never put Big Hamm in the defensive position at the end of the chute. It meant suicide for the charging player. I was going to my death, and I knew it as well as everyone else.

"You scared, John Ed?" Firman said.

"I'm not scared."

"What did you say?"

"I'm not scared, *Coach*." I added a growl to prove it.

"He says he's not scared of you, Big Hamm."

Big Hamm smiled and buttoned his chinstrap, and then he lowered himself to a four-point stance. I hesitated a moment before getting in position. By now my teammates, standing all around me, had reached a near-hysterical state. They screamed and laughed and threw fists at each other's pads. Players and coaches came running from other parts of the field, many of them letting out war cries. I glanced at the recruiters then over at my father. They stared back with the unflinching stoicism you see on the faces of pall-bearers at a military funeral.

"Go on my count," Firman said. "On two ... " He held an invisible football in front of him, imitating a quarterback under center. "Blue seventy-eight," he called. "Blue seventy-eight. Hut *hut—*"

I came blasting out of my stance and hurtling down the chute as fast as I could run, taking short, choppy steps to keep from catching my cleats on the boards and growling with such ferocity that I surely would have impressed a real tiger. My helmet smacked a pipe on the ceiling and gave my neck a jolt, but I continued forward, gaining speed and momentum. Then suddenly I was in the cool and the dark of a movie theater with Denise Landreneau, sharing popcorn and a Coke as we watched Robert Redford and Barbra Streisand in *The Way We Were.* Hubbell Gardner was the name of Redford's character, and I recalled how much I disliked my own name, and of course I made a mental note to ask my parents why on earth I had to be called what I'm called when they could've gone with Hubbell, and then the movie screen went black as I cleared the last pipe and Big Hamm exploded into me.

He came up from down low and caught me in the exact spot where I myself aimed when I wanted to hurt people—the chin. It seemed he'd crushed my jaw and shattered my teeth even though I was wearing a mouthpiece. The second blow came from behind me, and it was every bit as devastating. Big Hamm had me pinned against the pipes. He pushed through me as he'd been taught to do, aiming his helmet at a spot just behind me. The chute came up off the ground. When I finally came to, half a minute later, it was to the cheers of my teammates.

Firman lifted me off the ground, and I registered the look of surprise and admiration on his face. Each player took a turn slapping my helmet. This was their way of congratulating me, but each slap sent an electric shock from the top of my skull into my left shoulder. The last player to slap my helmet was Big Hamm himself. I dropped to the sod again.

The scrimmage was out of the question. Somebody hoisted me up and walked me to the locker room carrying a good share of my weight. I was deposited on a padded table and our team trainer, Colonel Dudley Tatman, put an ice pack on my tender, stinging neck. When practice ended and the rest of the squad joined me, I was sitting on a metal folding chair in front of my locker, naked but for a jockstrap and the Ace bandages that kept the ice pack in place. I noticed the recruiters watching me from across the room.

My teammates later told me that the collision with Big Hamm sounded like a shotgun blast. I snapped his head back and he staggered a step in reverse before recovering and making his kill.

"You're a brave man," one said. "I want you to remember what I'm telling you today. Are you listening?"

"Yes, I'm listening."

"You're going to play for LSU."

"Get out of here."

"Hey, just remember what I'm telling you."

I was the last player to leave. I'd missed a ride home with my neighbor Timmy Miller, a receiver on the team. Guidry offered to drop me off, but when we walked outside, I saw my father's pickup waiting under a streetlight in the parking lot. He himself was leaning against the old heap as a cloud of insects flew in the hot, yellow air above him. Cold water from the ice pack drained down my back and settled in the seat of my pants as I limped to the passenger side and let myself in.

"Thank you, Mickey," my father called out.

"Good to see you again, Coach."

Each gave the other a wave, and Guidry secured the locker room door. I was looking back at Coach in the side-view mirror, waiting for my father to start for home, when he cupped his mouth with his hands. "Hey, Coach Bradley," he shouted.

My father wheeled around and brought a hand to his ear.

"John Ed's going to be one hell of a football player."

We started down Judson Walsh Drive, passing under the heavy branches of pine and oak trees that lined the road and formed a tunnel, each of us holding an arm out his open window. The air smelled of evergreen mixed with honeysuckle and gardenia from the old Humble Village neighborhood that had been abandoned decades before and now stood black and overgrown, a ghost town on the side of the road. I wanted to go to my room, get in bed, and hide under the covers until I was so old that the day had been erased from the memories of everyone who witnessed it. My father hooked a right onto Old Sunset Road. He started working through the gears, and by the time he reached third I couldn't keep a lid on it anymore. "I hate it," I said, stuff leaking in a torrent from my nose. "I hate it, I tell you. I hate it, I hate it ... "

There was a smile on his face. He reached over and felt the ice pack to make sure it was still cold. "You hate it? You hate football?"

"Yes, I hate football."

He was quiet for a time, and I looked at him in the light of the dashboard. "You want to quit?" he asked.

"Yes, sir."

He nodded, keeping his eyes on the road. "Well, if that's what you want, you can call Coach Guidry and Coach Firman in the morning and let them know. When we get home, you can tell your mother. You can tell your brothers and sisters, too."

"I didn't say I was going to quit. I said I *wanted* to quit."

"Then I'm mistaken?"

"Yes, sir."

"You won't need to call your coaches?"

"No."

"No, what?"

"No, sir."

He parked in front of the house and killed the engine. I could see Mama at the kitchen window and behind her Donna on the phone. A year ahead of me at school, Donna was a cheerleader and one of the most popular girls in her class. No one was prouder than she of my place on the team. Now Bobby entered the picture, standing on his tiptoes to look out the window and see who'd pulled up out front. He vanished, and a few seconds later I spotted him at the door, waiting to find out how practice went, to check my arms and legs for new cuts and bruises, evidence of collisions with teammates.

At that moment I understood something that I was sure my father had realized long ago. There comes a time when quitting stops being an option, when quitting means quitting on those who are counting on you and quitting on your destiny, and although I was still groggy from Big Hamm's hit, I understood this with absolute clarity. It was too late now to quit the team. It would always be too late.

My father never wore a hat in the house. He took his cap off. "I don't want to make you think you have to play," he said. "Everybody gets knocked down. Not everybody gets up, though. Today you got up."

"You don't need to tell me that. It would be better if you didn't say anything." I pushed the door open and stepped outside. "What'd Mama cook for supper?"

"Mixed meat and rice and gravy."

"I hate mixed meat."

"When you're done eating, you're going to thank her and tell her how good it was. You hear me, boy?"

"Yes, sir."

He took his time walking around to my side of the truck, and together we started under the pine trees for the house. I wasn't feeling any better, so he held me by the elbow and made sure I didn't drift.

THE FIRST RECRUITER met me in the gymnasium between classes. From Tulane University in New Orleans, he wore a green shirt with an emblem of a cresting wave embroidered on the left breast. He said he'd been in one of the football offices watching game film from the year before, and he liked my aggressiveness and quickness off the ball. While describing Tulane's new home field, the Superdome, as "the most spectacular stadium ever built in the history of mankind," he paused in mid-sentence and reached for my hand. "By God, that isn't a hand. What you have there, John, is a mitt. How big are your feet?"

"Pretty big, Coach."

"I'm sure they are, son. But what size shoe do you wear?"

"Thirteen. Twelve-and-a-halves fit me better, but they're hard to find, and twelves are too small." I looked down at my Chuck Taylor All Stars, wondering if he intended to woo me with a new pair of shoes.

"You've got a good foundation there," he said.

"That's nice of you, Coach. I really appreciate that."

I was relieved when he suddenly lost interest in further discussion about my feet. His expression grew serious, almost grave. "I think you're a very special talent, I want you to know that. We'd

away, figuring he'd have more time alone with me if he caught me after I said hello to the others. The one who arrived last took the position closest to the door and thus had only a brief moment to make an impression. An average Thursday produced five recruiters. A good one attracted seven or eight. Some of the coaches talked to other seniors on the team—quarterback Thibodeaux, offensive guard Glyn Rogers, and cornerback Darrel Toussaint, all of whom would go on to play college football. Even though the recruiters made an effort to keep their distance from each other, they all seemed to get along well. The ones from the smallest schools approached with the most enthusiasm, using the force of their personalities to charm me. Those from the big schools were more reserved; they saw no point in having to make a sales pitch for a program as wonderful as theirs.

I walked from one to the next wishing them well in their games on Saturday. On a few occasions, I wished a coach well in a game against the coach next in line. I wished that coach well, too. It always embarrassed me to hear what they had to say in response.

"I tell you what, John, our chances this weekend would be greatly improved if you were suiting up with us."

"They've got a lot of talent, while we're still in a rebuilding mode. You could be a part of something really special. If we sign you, I'm sure the ripple effect will be tremendous. Other recruits will follow, all because of what you started. Let me ask you something, John Ed: Do you want to be responsible for a revolution?"

"You're the finest offensive center in the state this year—not only among high school players, but I'd argue among college players as well. Why don't you schedule an official visit with us? We'll have a private plane pick you up and take you back, and I promise our girls are a whole lot prettier than any you'll find anywhere else in this country."

"You want a challenge, son? Come on up to Natchitoches. We'll give you all

the challenge you can handle and then some. By the way, we'll let you play on the baseball team, too. What jersey number do you want?"

They came wearing navy, powder blue, black, crimson, yellow, white, orange, maroon, and green polo shirts. No purple-and-gold. As I left the locker room each Thursday, those were the colors I searched for, and always, it seemed, the only colors not on display.

After practice, my teammates and I liked to stop by the Phil-A-Sak for big glass jugs of Gatorade that we drank while seated on tailgates in the parking lot. When I arrived home, I could always count on spotting an unfamiliar car parked on the street in front—generic company sedans with mud caked in the wheel wells from traveling the Louisiana back roads in pursuit of football talent. I entered the house one night, and there at the kitchen table sat coaches from three different colleges talking in animated tones with my father about famous coaches they'd known and famous games they'd been a part of, while Mama served them heaping plates of round steak, rice and gravy, and macaroni salad. I pulled up a chair and joined them. Other times, I'd offer a polite wave and slip quietly past with my schoolbooks and gym bag, headed down the hall to my room. It wasn't uncommon for Mama to have to come remind me that the coach was a guest in our home and there to see me, not her and my father. She warned me about forgetting my manners and being disrespectful. "But I don't feel like hearing it tonight," I complained.

"Then just smile. Just stand there and smile at the man." She showed me how to do it.

"I don't want to waste his time, Mom."

"Well, if that's how you feel, maybe it's time to let him know it. Spare him the trouble and spare yourself."

She was less insistent that I speak to them when they called me on the phone. Holding the receiver to her ear, she let me know who was calling by mouthing the name of the recruiter and his school. Weeks of calls had honed her ability to read my mood for conversation with a single glance, and then she'd either hand me the line or provide interference without discouraging them from calling back. "Listen, Coach," I heard her say, "we are so flattered that you called John Ed tonight, but he has exams in the morning, and I'm sure you'll understand if he can't come to the phone right now. Think you could try him another time?"

My reason for not wishing to talk was more complicated than my mother knew. Although there might be homework to do, the truth was I couldn't bear to hear the coaches telling me how good I was when I knew for a fact that I couldn't be worth much if LSU didn't want me. That summer my name appeared on every list of blue-chip recruits published in the state, in some cases as a member of the Top 10, and this year I was destined to make All-Parish, All-District, and All-State in Louisiana's largest school classification. And yet LSU couldn't mail me a measly form letter and questionnaire. Boosters from other schools were writing me notes with lunch invitations. I wondered if folks down the road in Baton Rouge even bothered with lunch. The situation put me in bad form. On a visit to one Louisiana school, a booster drove me around a city block that had a Chevrolet dealership. He went around so many times that I finally told him he was making me carsick. "You don't like the new Camaro?" he said. I didn't answer and he gave up and took me back to my hotel.

Arkansas wrote to me again. The letter's return address included an impression of a red boar. I might have been more impressed had they got my name right. The envelope was addressed to Jim Ed Bradley, even though the recruiter referred to me as John Ed in the salutation. I threw the letter in the trash. "Ain't going there," I said.

"But that's a great school," said one of my friends on the team.

"Must not want me that bad if they call me Jim Ed."

"Listen to yourself. Your ego is out of control."

"How can that be, if LSU isn't even recruiting me?"

I whittled my list of favorites and scheduled trips for the first few weeks of the season. My earliest visit was to Mississippi State in Starkville, a town some four hundred miles away. Rather than have me drive the distance, the university sent a small private plane to pick me up at the Opelousas airport. It was the first time I'd ever flown, and the pilot insisted I join him in the cockpit.

An assistant coach met me on the tarmac and drove me to a hotel in the town where two girls were waiting for us in the lobby. One, a petite brunette in a petite dress, had been assigned to show me around for the weekend. I could smell her perfume from twenty yards away as I stood at the registration desk and filled out a card. I'd heard stories about recruits who were offered more than grants-in-aid on their official visits, and I wondered if my escort had anything in mind for me. That question might've been answered a short time later when the girl was driving me around campus on a tour of landmarks she seemed to find important. "I'm going to call you later tonight to see if you need anything. Do you think you'll need anything?"

"I doubt it. I packed my suitcase pretty good."

"Don't be surprised when the phone rings."

I shrugged. "Some shampoo maybe."

The phone rang as I was getting ready for bed, but I didn't answer it. I was not ready for college girls who required that much perfume. Even more important, I was not sold on the Bulldog football program. The athletic dorm and facilities were state-of-the-art, just as the recruiter had promised, but I needed all of ten minutes to conclude that I was not a good fit for the place. Most of the players had accents that I could barely make out, a problem compounded by the fact that not a few of them have chaws of tobacco and dips of snuff in their mouths. My mother taught me never to say "Huh?" in conversation with anyone I meant to impress. But in Starkville, I must have said "Huh?" to every other person I met.

When I asked players what they liked about the school, they all said, the girls. When I asked what they didn't like, they all said the town was dry, meaning it had strict laws prohibiting the sale and consumption of alcohol. To get a beer, you had to drive to a honky-tonk across the county line. "My advice to you is this," said one. "Don't come here if you like to have a drink every now and then. If drinking isn't important to you, then you might like it all right."

Head coach Bob Tyler was sitting by himself at the top of the stadium the next day, watching his team practice on the field below. I climbed the long run of cement steps and took a seat next to him. Tyler was wearing sunglasses that covered most of his face. He immediately asked me if LSU, a league rival, was recruiting me yet, and when I said no, he grew quiet and seemed ready to abort the conversation. Maybe he was the kind of coach who only wanted to sign out-of-state recruits he couldn't have, or maybe, after sizing me up, he didn't like the way I looked. But something had turned him off. I was trying to figure out what it was when he removed his glasses and looked off at the sky. He used the flat of his hand to shield the sun. A silver speck was moving against the vast blue expanse. "Spy plane," Tyler muttered.

"What's that, Coach?"

"Spy plane." He was more excited now. "Can you read the numbers?"

"Can I do what?"

He started bellowing at the field, and in no time one of the student managers came bounding up the stairs, his face bright red with the effort. "Can you read the numbers on that airplane?" Tyler was pointing now, but the speck had vanished.

"Coach, what's a spy plane?" I asked

"Certain schools have been known to send out a plane to fly over a football field when an opponent is practicing. They take pictures from up there."

"Oh."

He put his glasses back on. "They're trying to get offensive and defensive formations, anything that will give them an edge. It's cheating." He looked at the sky. "The SEC office is going to hear about this."

That night, the phone rang again in my hotel room. Perhaps because I was feeling depressed, wondering if I'd have to spend my college days at a place where I couldn't understand anyone and the coach saw spy planes at practice, I went ahead and answered it. "Do you need anything?" a girl's voice asked.

"Yes, I do, as a matter of fact. I need you to not call here again."

The next morning, they drove me to the airport and sent me home. I never heard from Mississippi State again.

I VISITED MORE SCHOOLS, all of them in-state. None felt right. I liked the coaches at the University of Southwestern Louisiana, only about twenty miles south of Opelousas, and I put the Cajuns at the top of my list, although I wasn't ready to make a commitment yet. My parents had received their undergraduate educations from the school, and I had plenty of family who lived in Lafayette. USL's recruiter, Sam Robertson, was one of the few coaches I enjoyed talking to on the phone at night. The head coach, Augie Tammariello, almost had me convinced that I was the one player who could win his team a championship. On the Sunday afternoon of my official visit, he made an impassioned plea for me to commit. "I can't commit today, Coach. Sorry about that."

"But all you have to do is say yes." He stared at me from across his desk. "Say yes, John Ed. Yes. Yes. Say *yes*. Come on ... *yes!*"

"Coach, I'll say maybe. That's the best I can do right now."

There was a chalkboard in the room. He stood up and wrote *Yes* on the dusty surface then underlined the word several times and added a run of exclamation points.

"Maybe, Coach. Look, all I can give you today is a maybe."

But I was seriously tempted to pledge my services and get the whole ordeal over with. The pressure to decide was keeping me up nights, and I was having a hard time focusing in class. I wished the coaches would leave me alone, but at the same time, I didn't want to disappoint them. Suppose I ruled a school out and then changed my mind? Would it still want me? Better to keep my options open, even if that meant losing my mind.

Some of the recruiters had convinced me that their jobs depended on getting my name on a scholarship form. If I went somewhere else, their wives and children would have to uproot and move to another town. I didn't want that to happen, did I?

"No, Coach. That would be terrible."

"Then you're telling me you're ready to commit?"

"Coach, I meant I didn't want to see you lose your job and all."

"Do you have any idea what it's like for kids to start all over at a new school and have to make new friends? You really need to think about this, when you're weighing your decision. Where you elect to go to college will affect more than you alone. You have the fate of a lot of good people in your hands. Now isn't the time to be selfish."

"You're right, Coach."

"Then you're coming?"

"Not yet, Coach. I apologize, but I can't say that yet."

Signing day was a couple of weeks before Christmas. By the end of September, I was so stressed out I wanted to hide under my bed every time the phone rang. The world was riding on my shoulders, and a bunch of college football coaches had put it there.

One day during my lunch break, I stopped by the gymnasium to seek advice from Guidry, but his office door was closed and an assistant told me he was tied up in a meeting. "He's in there with Charles Pevey," he said and pointed to the door.

"Charles Pevey? Charles Pevey from LSU?"

The assistant was reading a newspaper at his desk. He lifted it high enough to keep me from seeing the smile on his face.

DAYS LATER, I was in Grace Goudeau's English class, working on a theme paper about *Romeo and Juliet*, when a student messenger from the principal's office opened the door and stuck his head in. Shakespeare's tale of benighted love was lightweight fare compared to the tragedy I was enduring as a recruit, and if for no other reason, I enjoyed the play because it reminded me that other people had problems too. "Mrs. Goudeau, can John Ed come to Mr. Ortego's office for a telephone call?"

"Everything all right?" she asked.

The boy seemed agitated. He shook his head. "He really needs to come."

Who died? I wondered.

I ran all the way to the office.

"John Ed," said a vaguely familiar voice on the phone, "it's Coach McClendon over at LSU. How're you doing today?"

"Doing fine, Coach. How about you?"

"Mighty fine, thank you for asking. But I'd sure be a whole lot better if I knew you were going to be joining us in Baton Rouge next year. John Ed," he said now and laughed, "did they announce over the intercom at your school that it was old Coach Mac calling? I always like it when they do that."

"No, sir. A kid from the office came to get me."

"Well, in that case I guess I'll just have to call you back tomorrow and try again."

I returned to Mrs. Goudeau's class and everyone stared as I walked down an aisle to my desk. Did Cholly Mac just offer me a scholarship to play football at LSU? I couldn't say for sure, but the look on my face let my classmates know that everything was okay. "Nobody died, huh?" one of them whispered.

I didn't tell anyone at home about the call. I was superstitious enough to believe that by mentioning it, I'd risk the possibility that it was a mistake on Coach Mac's part. Perhaps he was trying to reach another high school player named John Ed and he'd inadvertently called Opelousas High. Crazier things had happened. But, no, the coach called again the next day, and this time the front office didn't bother to send a messenger.

The voice of one of the ladies who worked in the office came sputtering over the intercom. "John Ed Bradley, please report to the principal's office."

I got up and moved toward the door and the woman's voice sounded again. "John Ed Bradley, Coach Mac at LSU needs to speak to you on the telephone."

As I started down the hall headed to the front of the building, classroom doors pulled open and kids came out to congratulate me. We slapped hands and traded high fives, and then one of my teachers stepped out and applauded with his physics manual tucked under an arm.

"Did they announce it?" Coach Mac asked when I reached the phone at last.

"Yes, sir, they announced it to the whole school."

"Oh, I'm glad. One of these days you're going to look back and be grateful to your old coach for doing that."

Chapter Four

NOBODY WORKS HARDER

WHEN IT WAS OVER, I raised a fist and beat the ground until Big Ed put his arms around me and helped me to my feet. I could've kept punching the turf all night, but it wasn't going to change anything. Back in high school, Coach Guidry had told me never to walk off a football field unless I was physically unable to run, so I buckled my chinstrap and started for the locker room, jogging in the weary way of a man who didn't have a play left in him. As I passed under the goalpost, a group of kids began yelling at me from the seats at field level. I removed an elbow pad and tossed it to them, adding the other one and my hand pads when more kids showed up to beg for souvenirs. I'd have given them everything and walked into the locker room naked, but the equipment manager, I knew, wouldn't have taken kindly to my largesse. At the metal door that led to the chute, I stopped and spoke to a student trainer about my chest. There was blood on my jersey and he wanted to know how I'd made out. "I did fine," I lied. Then I turned and had another look at Tiger Stadium.

Thousands of fans were still at their seats, beating their heels against the aluminum bleachers and cheering us on, even though our game with top-ranked USC had ended. We'd lost 17-12 when the Trojans scored with only thirty-two seconds left on the clock, ruining our dream of pulling off the biggest upset in school history. Somebody needed to tell the fans that the wrong team had won and it was time to put away their whiskey flasks and go home. "What are y'all doing?" I said under my breath.

Maybe I imagined it, but no sooner had I asked the question than the crowd erupted with more noise. You like to make the home folks happy, but you typically don't do that unless you win. Going back to my days as quarterback of the Opelousas Junior High Cavaliers, I couldn't recall any fan who ever stood and cheered for me when I left the field a loser. Tonight had changed my under-standing of what it meant to win.

In the days leading up to the game, even local oddsmakers had predicted that USC would beat us by twelve points. The Trojans, widely advertised as the finest collection of football talent ever assembled on a college team, had All-Americans and future pro stars on both sides of the ball. In fact, the 1979 Trojans had twelve future NFL first-round draft choices and thirty-one overall picks.

Charles White and Marcus Allen were the team's running backs; they each would win the Heisman Trophy before graduating to the NFL. Tackle Anthony Muñoz would become an eleven-time Pro Bowl selection with the Cincinnati Bengals and a member, in 1998, of the Pro Football Hall of Fame. Guard Brad Budde would win the Lombardi Award and play for the Kansas City Chiefs. Dennis Johnson, a future Minnesota Viking, was the Trojans' best line-backer, and Dennis Smith and Ronnie Lott played in the secondary. Smith was a ferocious hitter, but Lott, a junior, was the most physical defensive back the college game had ever seen. He'd spend fourteen seasons in the NFL, most of them with the San Francisco 49ers, where he would play on four winning Super Bowl teams and become famous for punishing licks that forced fumbles and knocked out lights.

By contrast, no one had heard of our guys outside of Louisiana towns like Plaquemine, Baker, Bossier City, and Ville Platte. So how could we have played USC so close? I had no trouble with that one: We had Mac.

LSU had been fielding football teams since 1893 and playing games at Tiger Stadium since the first phase of construction was completed in 1924. Fans for the home team had witnessed Billy Cannon's Halloween night punt return for eighty-nine yards and a touchdown against Ole Miss in 1959, and they'd watched as Bert Jones passed to Brad Davis in the end zone with time expired to beat the Rebels in 1972. They'd seen Tiger greats like Steve Van Buren and Y.A. Tittle, Jimmy Taylor and Tommy Casanova. Now they had the USC game to remember.

The game hinged on a face-mask penalty against Benjy Thibodeaux, one of our defensive tackles, who, from my vantage point on the sideline, looked wholly innocent of the crime. We were leading 12-10 with about two minutes left to play, and USC's final drive to the end zone would've ended if not for the call. Schooled since infancy on the consequences of displaying "unsportsmanlike conduct," I was never one to blame losses on the officiating, but tonight I felt ripped off.

I left the field and went inside the stadium, where everything was quiet but for the clatter of shoulder pads dropped into open lockers and the occasional profanity shouted by a teammate who'd wanted things to end differently. I stood at my own locker and undressed, all the while resisting an impulse to run out on the field again and yell for the other side to come back for more. "Let's play a fifth quarter and see who wins this time," I wanted to say. "Come on, damn you. Show us what you're made of."

I wrapped my middle with a towel, walked back to the chute, and stood on a scale. I was down to two hundred and twenty-two pounds, twenty-one lighter than when I'd suited up four hours earlier. That was nearly a tenth of my body weight, lost in the time it took to watch a couple of movies. It was also sixty pounds lighter than one of the USC nose guards.

I pulled on a T-shirt that said LSU FOOTBALL and stepped into a pair of gym trunks and flip-flops, and then I reported to the weight room where reporters were interviewing players and coaches. "I've been going to ballgames since I was in school here," one of the older newspapermen told me, "and it ranks up there with the greatest ever played in Tiger Stadium. It surely was the loudest. They'll never forget this one."

The man looked to be about seventy, although it was always hard for me to judge a sportswriter's age as they all seemed to come in the same threadbare vintage. If he'd attended games dating that far back, it occurred to me, he might've been present for those played in the stadium when it was first built. I waited until he was finished writing in his notebook. "But we lost tonight," I said. "The other guys won."

"Tell those people that." And now he pointed a pen upward, indicating the fans still beating their feet against the metal seats above us in the stadium.

More than anything, we'd wanted to win it for Coach Mac. Refusing to acknowledge the many other factors that had led to his ouster, we'd had it in our heads that a victory over the country's most celebrated team might be enough to prompt the Board of Supervisors to extend his contract another five years, or at least until he reached a more suitable retirement age. If we could humble the Trojans, I'd told the guys at practice that week, how could the school let him go? Now, with the loss, I felt as if we'd let him down.

"I guess it wasn't meant to be," Big Ed said later in the dorm.

"I guess God wanted something else for us," I answered, even as I lay on my bunk and wondered if God really played a role in the outcome of football games, including those as big as ours with USC.

Unable to sleep, I staggered out in the hall and waited with some of my teammates for curfew check. They were sitting on the carpeted floor in a loose arrangement with their backs against the walls, some with ice packs on their knees and shoulders, others wrapped in bandages. A few had deep, open cuts on their arms and abrasions decorating their chins and foreheads. Like me, they'd been unable to get their bodies to shut down, and they knew that to sleep meant to wake up tomorrow with the game result freshly printed in the newspaper, thus making it irreversible. At this moment it still seemed that if we held on to the night, we held on to the possibility that our fate could be overturned. Benjy wouldn't get the call, the Trojans wouldn't punch it in, Coach Mac wouldn't lose his job after twenty-seven years. If there was any fairness in the world, we'd get what we earned rather than what was dealt.

At half past two, a dorm monitor came by and announced that Mac had suspended curfew for the night, as a gift to us. I hopped to my feet and walked from room to room, knocking on doors and shouting "No curfew, no curfew tonight." Only a couple of the players took me at my word. They came out, pulling on their jeans and shoes and stumbling toward the exits. The rest told me to go away.

Toward dawn I found myself seated in the grass of the levee with a girl I knew. I positioned my body sideways at the crest so that I could view both the Mississippi River to my left and the Ponderosa to my right. I hadn't brushed my teeth since before the game, so I didn't dare kiss her. It was enough to hold her hand and hear her voice. The river was beautiful with lights from the bridge and the far bank shining on it. Still and all, I preferred the view of the practice fields, quiet now in the dark, the well-groomed turtlebacks never so peaceful.

As the sun came up I got to my feet and started down the grade to the Impala parked on a River Road turnaround. The girl, following close behind, stopped about halfway down and slapped her legs. "Mosquitoes 'bout to eat me alive," she said.

Somehow I knew I'd never recover.

EVERY SUNDAY after dinner we met in a large basement room in the dorm and reviewed game film as a team. Coach Mac worked the projector, and his assistants bombed us with criticism when we did things wrong and shouted out praise when we did them right. On any given play, a coach on one side of the room was ripping a kid to pieces in terms too graphic to record here, while on the other side another was screaming about somebody else's performance in language so fat with hyperbole that you wondered if the coach was sweet on the player. We weren't permitted to speak during film sessions, so for nearly three hours we sat grouped by position and listened to the coaches pick apart our every move. One day a player nodded off to sleep in his chair, and a coach, standing fifteen feet away, threw a chalkboard eraser at him. The black missile sailed hard left, in the trajectory of a curveball, and banked against the player's head. He never fell asleep in another meeting. Neither did I.

Each player who saw action the night before was handed a grade sheet in the moments before the film review began. It was a strip of paper two inches wide and eleven inches long that listed every play in which you'd participated, along with a positive or a negative score next to the play. You could get a minus on a play for something as minor as holding your rear end too low when you got in your stance at the line of scrimmage. A lowered backside let the defense know you were likely to drop back in pass protection once the ball was snapped, just as a butt raised too high signaled that a running play was coming. The final score, always circled in colored pencil at the bottom of the sheet, was your overall percentage of success. My grade for the USC game was ninety-three.

I'd entered the meeting certain that I deserved a grade closer to fifty. Rather than gloat, I reminded myself that the mark was purely subjective, determined by offensive coaches who were predisposed to sympathetic grading as a way to honor us for having fought hard against a superior opponent. As the film moved from one reel to the next, I counted plays that got me pluses instead of minuses, and I didn't like it. We had eight regular-season games left. How was I supposed to improve next week against Florida if the coaches were taking it easy on me?

I considered complaining to Mac but feared he'd think I was trying to show off, to prove I wanted to win more than everyone else. Besides, I never would've asked one of my English teachers to reconsider after going soft on me when he graded an exam. I finally accepted the score by recalling the times when I'd been given negatives instead of the positives I thought I deserved.

"Proud of you," Mac said at the end of the session. Actually he only mouthed the words, as he was depositing the last of the film reels into a metal canister. I flashed an uncertain smile then folded my grade sheet and shoved it in the pocket of my jeans.

I SAW HIM AGAIN the next day as I was waiting in line for lunch. He shuffled up behind me, grabbed my arm, and pulled me over by the door to the cafeteria manager's office. He glanced around to make sure no one was listening. Satisfied that I had his attention, he put a hand up to his mouth as if to share a secret. I leaned in close to hear it.

"The pro scouts really liked what they saw from you Saturday," Coach Mac said, whispering. "I just met with several of them in my office."

"The pro scouts?"

"They see you playing in the NFL. Question is," and now he laughed, "do you see yourself playing there?"

We each took a tray and moved down the line. I removed a soufflé cup holding two pills from an aluminum shelf, popped the pills in my mouth and swallowed them without a drink. No coach or trainer had ever told me exactly what the pills were. I assumed one of them was a multivitamin, but the second was a mystery. Some players said it was saltpeter to keep our libidos in check, but more likely it was a highly concentrated salt tablet to help us ward off muscle cramps. I once saw a player remove the alleged saltpeter from the cup and swallow only the vitamin. "What girl would want to fool around with you, anyway?" I'd asked him, to which he'd replied, "Well, your two gorgeous sisters immediately come to mind, if you really want to know." The response was more thoughtful than the perennial favorite that singled out the family matriarch, so I let him have his victory.

Mondays in Broussard Hall meant red beans and rice. I instructed Li'l Bit to give me as much of everything as she could. She ignored me and gave me the same amount she'd given everybody else.

"You project as an outsider linebacker or a tight end," Mac said now. He reached for a slab of apple pie and placed it on his tray.

"I'm a center, Coach."

"Not in the NFL you won't be," he said, then headed off for the table where his assistants were sitting.

I'd been guzzling store-bought water from gallon jugs and eating even when I wasn't hungry in an effort to get my weight up. Like other linemen on the team, I tried to consume at least six thousand calories a day. For breakfast I'd had scrambled eggs, buttered grits, fried ham, biscuits, and orange juice. Between classes I'd run by Der Wienerschnitzel for three chili cheese dogs. The thought of having to eat again held no appeal, but I understood that surviving to the season's end depended on it. Next time I stepped on the scale, I needed more weight.

I put the conversation with Mac out of my head, and I might've forgotten it for good had I not encountered a scout with the Oakland Raiders when I arrived at the stadium after lunch. He stood watching over my shoulder as I stepped on a scale and recorded my weight. I was up to two hundred and thirty-one pounds, still twelve pounds shy of where I needed to be if I hoped to play strong against the Gators.

There were three large laundry bins near the door to the locker rooms—one held freshly laundered T-shirts, the second jockstraps, the third socks. I fished out still-warm articles from each bin and went to my locker to get undressed. Wearing only a jock, I started for the training room to have my chest wrapped for practice when I spotted the scout again. He was watching me in a way that might've made me uncomfortable in any other setting. Football players know little modesty; having your body constantly appraised goes with the territory. Piped-in music was streaming from speakers in the ceiling—Bob Seger, Bruce Springsteen, or some other late-1970s rock 'n' roll balladeer—and I did a little dance from one end of the equipment cage to the other. Did I think

I should demonstrate that snapping a football wasn't my only talent? God knows what was in my head. But I succeeded in getting the scout to smile, and I took this as an invitation to introduce myself. "I know who you are," he said. "That was one fine game you played Saturday."

"We lost," I replied.

"You didn't lose, son. Good luck with the rest of your season."

I didn't think about pro ball again until later in the year, when Coach Mac summoned me to his office and gave me a stack of mail bound together with an ink-stained rubber band. It was from NFL teams, twelve in all. I recalled the day when my high school coach had presented me with letters from recruiters. As I'd done then, I took a seat and flipped through the stash. Not all of the mail was recent. Perhaps Mac hadn't wanted to distract me with the thought of pro scouts watching my every move, or perhaps he'd simply forgotten to deliver them, but most of the letters had postmarks dating back to the beginning of the season. There was mail from the Miami Dolphins, the New England Patriots, the Seattle Seahawks, and the Dallas Cowboys, to name some of the more prominent clubs. Would they hold it against me for not answering? I didn't really care.

In the picture of the future I'd built for myself, I was the author of books that put me on best-seller lists, made a lot of money, and got me dates with beautiful women, and I worried that book editors, literary critics, and others in publishing wouldn't take my writing seriously if I played pro ball.

I'd read somewhere that the average pay for an NFL center that year was around forty thousand dollars. I liked to fantasize about how to spend such a fortune, the used paperbacks and typewriter ribbons I could buy. But I couldn't square the fantasy with the act of suiting up again in any uniform other than LSU's. "You don't even want to try?" my father asked me.

I could've yelled at him for that, but there was genuine compassion in his voice. He and my mother were losing something too.

"It's over," I told him.

I left Mac's office and dropped the letters from the NFL teams in a trash can outside the stadium. We'd won more games than we lost this season, but we'd entered every game after USC feeling a little punch-drunk, as if our vision had been impaired. After such a night, there was an anticlimactic quality to having to face teams like Kentucky and Mississippi State, and by December coaches and players were ready to finish the year and move on. It was true that I'd never forget the hard-fought USC and Alabama games and the final one with Wake Forest in the Tangerine Bowl. It was also true that our humiliating loss to Tulane in the Superdome to close out the regular season would stick with me just as much. Time would enlarge our gutsy performances in the minds of LSU fans. But for me time would also make our failures seem even bigger.

They were letting Mac go. You could never make me believe that my teammates and I weren't the main reason why.

I DECIDED TO HAVE a look at my helmets again. I pulled them out of the closet and placed them side by side on my bed.

If you added up the stickers from both, I probably finished the 1979 season with as many as anyone on the team. I was furious when I cracked the first helmet, in no small part because the stickers I'd earned up until then were not transferable. That is to say, I had to start all over again when the equipment manager issued me a new helmet. Maybe the coaches had a limited number of stickers and were hoarding them as a precaution against running out, but I never could understand why they didn't put fifteen stickers on your new helmet if that was how many you had on your old helmet when you broke it. The way I saw it, they should've awarded you a sticker for cracking the damned thing. But to complain would've been selfish, and in the world I inhabited there was nothing more reprehensible than a selfish ball player. When you saw your position coach talking to your father outside Tiger Stadium after a game, you hoped he was telling him what a team player you were. A team player didn't care about losing his stickers.

And yet, as I sat examining the helmets now, I felt compelled to unite the stickers on one of them—the new one—if not for my immediate gratification, then for the sake of posterity. Wouldn't my grandson take pride in seeing Paw Paw's college helmet plastered with stickers from ear hole to ear hole? But when I tried to peel a sticker off, it tore in half, and I realized I'd just have to learn to live with the situation.

If the lad really needed to know how great Paw Paw was, I could always take him out in the yard and drill a hole in his chest with a punt snap.

MADISON FIRMAN REACHED ME by phone one day in Baton Rouge and invited me to come see him the next time I was in Opelousas. He said he was proud of all I'd accomplished and he wanted to take me out for a steak and a baked potato and fix me up with a blind date. It seemed a strange proposal, coming from a man I'd long regarded as being wholly devoid of sentimentality, but I was touched by his invitation, and I let him know it. "Look, Coach, what if we got together this weekend? Are you free then?"

He lived in a place called Rosa, about twenty minutes north of Opelousas. It was less a town than a smattering of ranch houses on the edge of a cow pasture, and Firman's place, set close to rural Highway 71, would have been easier to find if there were more outdoor lights or signs to guide me. I missed his driveway and had to turn around.

He stepped outside as I was crossing the lawn. It was dark outside, and against the porch light's yellow blossom, his form was a squared-off block quite a bit larger than my own. We were both built like refrigerators, but that night I was a narrow model with a sleek facade while he was an old-time deep freezer bulging with forgotten venison and beefalo. We started to shake hands before deciding a hug was more in order. I didn't embrace him with much enthusiasm, and I sensed that he took my reticence as a slight when I was only trying to protect my chest wound.

He led me into the house and his wife greeted me with a kiss. She was a world-class beauty with a quiet demeanor and the soft, beguiling voice of an old-fashioned movie star. She always struck me as an odd match for the dark, brutish line coach, and I wondered how a woman of such obvious refinement and sensitivity came to share her life with a man who earned his keep teaching teenage boys how best to knock each other down.

Candles burned in the living room, releasing a spicy perfume. A platter of baby vegetables rested on a coffee table. The little carrots and broccoli spears suggested a delicacy that I never would've assigned to the coach, who once, when he was trying to shed a few pounds, sent me to Burger King to pick up his lunch: a Double Whopper and a small diet drink. His wife, it occurred to me, was a miracle worker.

Four years had passed since Firman had coached me, and I should've felt more comfortable in his presence tonight, but I was as intimidated as ever. Yes, my father had encouraged him to be hard on me, but I still resented him for turning my high school football experience into such a misery. I sat on a cushion and dunked cauliflower into a ramekin filled with creamy ranch dressing. "I brought you something, Coach," I said between bites. "Give me a minute. I'll be right back."

I stepped outside. The breeze coming off the pasture was cool and scented with a sharp aroma of horse manure. Above me the sky was a blanket of stars so white the whiteness seemed to cover every spot in the universe. It was good to be out in the country, even on a night when I probably should've stayed home.

I recalled now how Firman punished me once for talking back to him by making me run in place after practice. Each time he blew his whistle, I had to fall to the ground on my chest and quickly bounce back up. The exercise might've been easier had the gym floor been carpeted or made of wood rather than tile on cement, and it might've been less humiliating had cheerleaders not been in the building hanging posters and banners for that week's pep rally. "But, Coach ... " I'd dared to say to him again, and for this Denise Landreneau, my sister Donna, and the rest of the squad got to watch me run in place until I could no longer lift my shoes off the floor. I'd stood there quivering from rage and exhaustion, falling on command, and growling, of course, always growling.

I still had it in for Firman, I realized now. And as I stood outside in the cold, looking off at the winter sky, it occurred to me that he hadn't made me tough enough. Had he succeeded in his mission, I wouldn't have been there tonight.

After a few minutes, I went back in the house. Firman had mixed a drink for me—bourbon and 7-Up on the rocks—and placed it on a table next to a chair in the living room. "I'd like to give you something," I said.

"What's that?"

He walked toward me. "It's for all you did for me."

"That's your helmet, John Ed."

"I want you to have it, Coach. The way I see it, I owe you this and more. I never would've gotten a scholarship to LSU if not for you."

"Are you really giving me your helmet?"

I nodded and placed the new helmet in his hands, forcing him to accept it. Why was I rewarding him with something of such enormous personal value? He himself seemed at a loss to answer the question. "Come on, now. That's your helmet, John Ed. You sure you want to do this?"

"Yes, sir. I want you to have it."

My parents would've wept had I presented it to them. Mickey Guidry would've had a strong emotional response too. Firman briefly inspected the helmet before tossing it at the sofa. It landed with a plop. "John Ed gave me his helmet," he said, then turned and left the room. I assumed he was talking to his wife, but she was nowhere to be seen.

"What about you?" Firman called now from the kitchen.

"You say something, Coach?"

"Ready for another drink?"

I glanced at the helmet as I started in his direction. "Sure, Coach. Fix me another one."

Somewhere on the road to Bunkie, where my date lived, I began to feel sick. Firman pulled the car over on the side of the road, and I tumbled out in a weed-choked ditch. False alarm, as it turned out. "I only had three drinks," I said to Firman.

"Big guy like you." He shook his head.

"That's what I mean."

Sentimental sap. I didn't know why I'd expected a different response from him. He was a coach, and to most coaches a helmet wasn't a symbol representing years of hard work and sacrifice, and it certainly wasn't your heart. It was nothing more than a tool used to strike an opponent and get him to the ground. That it protected brain matter was a secondary function. I had walked into Firman's house and given him something he saw by the hundred every day. Something that hung from hooks in foul-smelling lockers. Would a master plumber be excited about receiving a pipe wrench from a former apprentice after the boy finished trade school?

In the car after dinner, I started to feel bad again. My date reached over the seat and tapped Firman on the shoulder. He glanced in the rearview mirror and applied the brakes with such force that we fishtailed in the dirt and gravel on the side of the road. I stumbled out from the car, a cloak of red from the taillights lighting my way. The spasms came with such violence that I worried I'd toss up my heart along with everything else.

Firman put the emergency lights on and walked to where I'd positioned myself over a ditch. I could hear his shoes crunch the gravel, the sound getting louder as he came closer. I half expected him to shout for me to get up and act like a man. I half expected some form of physical punishment, like the kind he used to hand out in school. But he crouched down beside me and placed his hand on the back of my neck. It was a small gesture, and yet he did it with such gentleness that I suddenly understood and forgave him our entire past together. It was fine that he'd been so hard on me in school. I never should've looked at him wrong or talked back to him. I'd had it coming. And I was right to believe that without him I never would've landed at LSU. Giving him my helmet was long overdue. I should've added my jersey and shoulder pads while I was at it.

"I'm so embarrassed," I said.

"Nothing to be embarrassed about, son."

"I don't want you to see me like this."

He looked back at the car. "It's okay. I'll just wait here with you."

"You don't have to, Coach."

"No," and he crouched down next to me. I felt his hand on my neck again. "I don't want you to be sick alone."

His wife made coffee when we returned to the farm, but I fell asleep in a chair in the living room before it had finished brewing. Hours later I woke up feeling fine, as if nothing had happened. I had slept sitting up, and my head was clear now, my stomach back in order. I had no memory of returning my date to her house. The poor girl, I thought.

A floor lamp was on, and somewhere a clock ticked. It seemed everyone had gone to bed.

My helmet remained on the sofa where Firman had left it. I looked at it a long time, wishing I hadn't cracked the other one so all my stickers were together in one place. What would the coach have said then? With the surface completely covered, each sticker symbolizing a moment of superior individual effort? Would he have been more impressed? Would he have tossed it aside with such indifference?

It occurred to me that every kid who ever played the game was driven by a desire to prove himself to somebody who once had made him feel worthless. And yet, even as I sat there, listening to the clock, I kept remembering how Firman's hand had felt on the back of my neck. I might've left with the helmet and explained to him later that I'd changed my mind. I might've left with it and given him no explanation. But he didn't want me to be sick alone. And so I left it there, tipped back on the sofa, his to keep.

BY THE FALL, I was down to a hundred and eighty-nine pounds. Without money for new clothes, I cut holes in my belts to keep my pants up.

Each week as a scholarship athlete, I'd received fifteen dollars from the university in laundry money. On Saturday morning when I reported to the cafeteria at 10 a.m. for breakfast, an assistant coach, seated at a table near the serving line, gave me a small manila envelope holding a ten- and a five-dollar bill. I never knew anyone who actually used the money to do his laundry. Mothers, sisters, wives, and girlfriends usually took care of that. So to most of us the money was lagniappe and it went to other necessities such as restaurant meals and barroom tabs. Because I almost always tail-gated with my family, I was able to put the money toward clothes and school supplies.

I didn't appreciate the importance of laundry money until I stopped receiving it and had to make up for the shortfall. I could've always cut grass, but I didn't have the funds to invest in a mower. Besides, as an ex-LSU football player still living in Baton Rouge, I had an obligation to at least give an appearance of being on top of the world. A desire to keep up appearances also kept me from seeking a job at a local restaurant or department store. I'd been a four-year letterman in the best conference in all of college football, and four-year lettermen didn't hand over sacks of burgers at the Frostop or stock shelves at Godchaux's.

Desperate to raise cash, I reported to a plasma center after spotting a sign on the building that promised generous payments to donors.

The center occupied a former convenience store, which meant the front was a wall of glass—an architectural detail that let anyone look in from the street. It took me half an hour to build up the courage to leave the Impala and join the collection of struggling students and down-and-out types waiting inside. "How much do you pay for a pint?" I asked the receptionist.

"Twelve dollars."

"That's it?"

"That's it? That's a lot."

I considered telling her that only a few months ago I was all-SEC and captain of the offense, but then I came up with a different approach. "I'm a large man in top physical condition. Can you take two pints out of me?"

She gave me a quick appraisal. "You're not so large."

"I used to be large."

"Sorry, only one pint a visit." She slid a form across the desk.

I debated whether to tell her about the time a couple of years ago when a wealthy booster, hospitalized in Baton Rouge, negotiated with Coach Mac to receive blood from the team. The man had offered thirty-five dollars for each pint, and it didn't matter if you were a starter or a backup. It was spring, months away from the season when sharing our blood would've been as bad as sharing our game plans with rival SEC teams, and the man's offer was nearly three times the going rate. Mac agreed to let us donate, and we all went to the hospital and patiently stood in line.

I would never again hear a fan say the blood in his veins ran purple and gold without thinking about that patient.

To keep from staring at my compatriots waiting their turn, I read the morning paper, holding it high in front of me, as much to block my view of them as theirs of me. But even the most incredible crime stories didn't hold my attention for long. One is given a larger window to the human condition at a blood joint. Perhaps too large a window.

I put the paper down, stretched and yawned, then walked out and burned a few minutes on the sidewalk. I wanted my fellow bleeders to think I needed air. Now I tapped my shirt pocket, pretending to search for cigarettes. Where were my Winstons? I tapped the seat of my pants. Not there, either. Did I leave them in the car?

I slipped behind the wheel and checked the visor. Nope. I ran a hand under the floor mat. Well, my heavens. I leaned over and popped the glove compartment open. Not in there either.

Was anyone still watching? Had I lost their interest this easily? I looked past the glass. Some read, others napped with their heads pitched forward. What a selfish, insensitive lot. Not a one seemed to care that I couldn't find my smokes.

Maybe I owed money to every utility company in town, and maybe my rent was past due, but my blood had value. I was one of Mac's boys.

I left planks of tire rubber in the parking lot on my way out.

LARRY HENRY GRADUATED and left Baton Rouge, and I moved closer to campus. At night, I stayed up late working on a novel about a former college football star who, try as he might, couldn't get the game out of his head. When the words weren't coming, I drove to a hospital downtown and waited outside for the nursing students to end their shift at 11 p.m. I was sort of dating one of them, and she liked to leave the building and find me reading a book by flashlight in the front seat of the Impala.

We drove to Phil Brady's on Government Street and had beer and microwave pizzas at the bar. When it closed, we took long drives around town, often until dawn, when it was time for me to get ready for class. We stopped every now and then in front of big houses where rich people lived and studied them in jealous admiration. I couldn't imagine ever owning a garden shed, much less a house. LSU football had made me think I could achieve anything if I worked hard and believed in myself, but civilian life had become a constant recognition that my days of infinite possibilities were over.

Some nights we parked in a copse of mimosa trees in a vacant lot and made out until our lips were sore and bruised. We pulled at each other until our hair stood up on our scalps and our shirts lost buttons. She didn't let me get very far, but that didn't stop me from reaching for the drawstring on her scrubs every time she let her guard down. Afterward, we drove to Louie's near campus and sat at the counter and had biscuits and cups of coffee. We scrounged used copies of the *Morning Advocate* from tables that had not yet been cleaned. I made a point to avoid the sports section and steered clear of anything else that triggered memories of football.

But then John Adams, my old roomie, came home from Oakland and invited me to a game at Tiger Stadium. John was a rookie with the Raiders, and, next to Big Ed, he'd been my closest friend on the team. I'd confided a lot to John over the years, and I thought I could use his help now. Somebody had to tell me how to get over it.

The Raiders were off this week, and John and his wife, Linda, had come home to Louisiana to visit family and friends. The prospect of entering the stadium as a spectator was terrifying, but I thought it might be just the thing to lift me out of my funk. By facing the place, maybe I could finally reason with my memory of it. Our seats were in the north end zone about halfway up, in a crowd of fans who didn't seem to recognize us.

It was only the third time in my life that I'd sat in the stands. I'd gone to the stadium as the nine-year-old guest of a friend, and then as a seventeen-year-old recruit. Like John, I'd suited up for every game since my freshman year. Neither of us had redshirted. We didn't know how to be fans. And so we sat there looking lost, zombies from another planet.

Moments before kickoff, I spotted a pair of small boys wearing purple shirts and waving Tiger pennants. Their expressions held a mix of wide-eyed awe and reverence, and I wondered if I'd looked like them the first time I went to an LSU game and watched a dream unfold. Tiger Stadium, it occurred to me, wasn't just a place where teams met to play football. It was where people went to worship.

Because he was still playing, John wasn't as anxious about being back as I was. He thumbed through a program and then offered to let me have a look. "No, thanks," I said. I should've been on my feet cheering. Better yet, I should've tried to talk to John about what I'd been feeling. Who better to trust my troubles with than him? He would've understood. And he would've known what to say to me. Instead, I sulked and kept quiet. I didn't even watch the game.

At halftime, I told John I was ready to leave. He offered no argument. The radio in his truck was tuned to the game. John turned it off as soon as he started the engine, and I was grateful for the silence.

In three years together as roommates, John and I had often stayed up late talking in the dark, sharing dreams and secrets, and I was in his wedding. But after this night I wouldn't see him again for more than twenty years. He parked by the door to my apartment with the engine running, headlights splashing against the building. I had to squint to see that he was offering me his hand to shake. "John Ed, you keep in touch," he said.

"You, too," I answered.

MY FATHER, ever the pragmatist, worried about my future more than I did. "What use can you make of an English degree?" he asked. "Do you hope to write for the Opelousas paper when you get out of school?" He knew some of the reporters and editors at the *Daily World*, and they were talented people who earned too little money for their long hours of work. They're worse off than teachers, he said, "worse off than Mama and me." Did I want to teach? Without a degree in education, and lacking certification, I wasn't qualified. "You should go to law school," he told me.

"I'm going to be a novelist."

"But how do you become a novelist?"

"You write a novel."

"Have you written one yet?"

"No, sir."

"How do you get it published when you do?"

"I don't know."

"You don't know." He sounded thoroughly defeated.

"The good writing finds its way," I said.

"It does *what*?" He shook his head and left the room.

I'd graduated weeks ago—graduated with the highest grade point average of any player in my class—but a lot of good the degree and high marks were doing me now. Daddy found me occasional work as a substitute teacher. This meant I babysat rooms filled with teenagers for twenty-five dollars a day, while wearing a necktie. "Weren't you the one that played football?" students asked me.

"You mean wasn't I the one *who* played football?"

"Well, were you him?"

"Were you *he*?"

Anything to avoid the subject. No matter what I answered, they always followed with the same question: "What was it like?"

"What was what like?"

"What was it like to play for LSU?"

After a few weeks, I'd had enough. When principals called and asked me to substitute, I told them I was suffering from a contagious disease—strep throat, usually—and then I uncorked a phlegmy cough before putting the phone down.

WITHOUT FIRST NOTIFYING ME about his intentions, my father called in a favor and arranged for me to interview with a bank in Opelousas. Because of my experience as an LSU football player, he thought they might find a position for me in the P.R. department, speaking at charity luncheons and playing golf with important clients, and generally providing a familiar face to a hometown business that was being led by out-of-town corporate types.

I arrived an hour early, assuming I'd have my audience with the bank vice president as soon as I introduced myself to his secretary. "Why don't you have a seat?" she said and glanced at her wristwatch.

I could see the man through a glass office wall. He sat forward in his chair, reading a newspaper. When he finished, he sorted through mail, tossing some items in the trash, putting others in a wire basket. Next he made a phone call. Leaning back in his chair until he was almost parallel to the ground, he rested the heels of his shoes on the edge of his desk.

More than an hour passed before the secretary ushered me into his office. He apologized for the wait, but he said he had had some important documents to review. My father had dropped off my resume the day before. The man studied it now, unimpressed. "What is this you majored in?"

"English."

He laughed. "Is that some kind of thing they let ball players take to keep them academically eligible?"

He was funny. I laughed too.

He looked up at me, the smile gone from his face. "I always wondered something. Do LSU football players have to go to class like everybody else?"

"What do you mean?" He didn't answer. "I'll have you know I never missed a class. Coach Mac didn't tolerate absences."

"I was glad when they finally got rid of Mac. He could never win the big one."

"We won plenty of big ones."

"You lost more of them than you won."

"No, that's not correct. I played in three bowl games, and in all my years at LSU I was never on a losing team."

He put the résumé down and leaned forward on his desk. "Okay, here's what I can do for you. We just opened the Jim Bowie branch on South Union Street, and I got a teller's position open. Basically you sit at the drive-thru taking deposits and cashing checks, this kind of thing."

"You're offering me a job as a teller?"

"I know it can't be what you're expecting, being an LSU man and all, but you have to start somewhere."

"Give me that résumé."

"What's that?"

"Give it ... " I reached over and yanked it out from under his forearms.

As I crossed the Mississippi River Bridge, driving east from Port Allen to Baton Rouge, I glanced to my right at Tiger Stadium nestled among the trees. There was a time when the sight of the old gray ghost next to the fat, slow-moving river had been enough to give me goosebumps. But today I couldn't bear the sight. I turned my head instead to the State Capitol and the petrochemical plants blowing smoke into the white afternoon. I had half a mind to crush my résumé into a ball and toss it out the window.

Nothing against tellers, but I played football for LSU.

WHAT WAS IT LIKE?

"I'm the teacher here today. I'll be asking the questions."

But what was it like?

"It was wonderful, if you really have to know."

What was so wonderful about it?

"Well, a lot of things. Being on the team for a school like LSU made you feel real good about yourself. Let's start right there. You had tremendous self-confidence. I almost hate to admit this, but you felt slightly superior to everyone else, especially people your own age. We walked between the raindrops. Ever hear that expression? Whoever came up with it must've had us in mind, because it pretty well describes how we thought about ourselves. Nothing could touch us, including the rain. And of course it was amazing how people treated you out in public. Ask the waiter at a restaurant to bring the check, and he politely bows at the waist and tells you it's all been taken care of. 'Who took care of it?' you ask. And he nods his head at some man sitting nearby with his wife, and they're smiling at you with such obvious admiration, so you walk over to them to say thanks. 'No, thank *you*, young man,' they tell you. 'Thank you for all the pleasure you've given us.' And I was just a lineman. I mean, you have to admit that's wonderful, right?"

What else?

"Oh, I don't know, plenty of things. Like how chartered planes took us to away games—Southern Airways, usually. We were all big guys, so everybody wanted an aisle seat to stretch out their legs. You got to meet a lot of pretty girls. I should mention that. You had a scholarship, so you didn't have to pay for your education. Your food, your books—paid for."

Uh-huh.

"I remember one night in Broussard I somehow got my hands on a house key, and I broke into the cafeteria hours after it had closed and there was a freezer with a big box full of ice cream sandwiches, and I ate about twelve of them, sitting in the dark. I was afraid I'd get caught, but nothing ever happened. I felt bad about it, though. I felt so bad I confessed it to a priest, and I could hear him laughing on the other side of the screen. For my penance he told me to beat Ole Miss next week."

Can I go to bathroom?

"No, you may not. Read the pages I assigned you. Or put your head on your desk and go to sleep."

What else was it like?

"I've told you everything."

Did you ever see anybody get killed in a game?

"No, but I once hit Wes Chandler so hard on a punt return that I knocked him out. He didn't move for five minutes."

Who is Wes Chandler?

"Guy who played for Florida and then the Saints."

You knocked him out? You really knocked him out?

"I think he was knocked out. Maybe he was just groggy and pretending to be knocked out. Or maybe I made that story up. Read your assignment."

It was rough, though, wasn't it?

"Yes, it was. One time one of my teammates got hit so hard he had a fit of some kind and swallowed his tongue. We were playing in Tiger Stadium, and this happened on the field right in front of our sideline. He was shaking like an epileptic having a seizure, and they couldn't get him to stop, and Mr. Ladd—Tracy Ladd, he was the head trainer ... Mr. Ladd shoves his hand in Willie's mouth and grabs his tongue and pulls it out. There was this white foam all over Willie's face."

Willie? Willie who?

"Doesn't matter. It mattered then, but it doesn't matter now. You asked me what it was like, and I'm trying to tell you."

Did you think Willie was going to die?

"You don't think about dying. You're too young to think about dying."

You ever get hurt like Willie?

"My senior year we played Colorado up in Boulder. In the second quarter, I took a knee to the back of my helmet and blacked out. I ended up playing the rest of the game, even though I didn't know I was playing. What I'm trying to say is, I kept playing even though I was in another world—la-la land. My body did what it was supposed to do, but my mind had gone somewhere else, and I wasn't recording a single moment. Hours later we're flying into Baton Rouge. I can see the runway lights. I turn to John Adams, who's sitting next to me, and say, 'Did we win, John?' He looks at me like I've lost my mind. 'What do you mean, did we win? We won 44-0.' I have a look out the window, and right at that moment the plane touches down, and all the players and coaches start cheering."

It was like that, wasn't it?

"Yes, it was. It was just like that. You had it made and believed you'd always have it made."

Never thought you'd be a substitute teacher, did you?

"No. A real teacher, maybe. But never a substitute."

I TRIED TO LAND a job with the morning and afternoon papers in Baton Rouge. Neither wanted me. I asked for freelance assignments. The sports editor at the *State Times*, Dan Hardesty, offered me twenty-five dollars to write an eighteen-inch story about the LSU women's gymnastics team. That amounted to seven hundred and twenty words—hardly enough room to clear my throat, let alone sing. And of course, I hated to waste my talent writing about sports. I stayed up all night working on the story, hammering away until it read like a prose poem to the uneven bars. In the morning, Hardesty took the first page in hand and glanced at it. "Your lede is too long," he said. "You wrote three sentences instead of one."

He read no further. He handed the copy back to me and told me to rewrite it, and I made a sizable display of tearing the pages into pieces and throwing them into a trash can en route to the elevator.

I did not get paid. More freelance work was not forthcoming.

I contacted the local alternative paper, a weekly tabloid called *Gris Gris*. Editors there ignored my entreaties. I wrote to a Baton Rouge advertising firm, offering my services as a copywriter. No one responded. Answering a want ad, I applied for a position in LSU's Sports Information Department. My résumé wasn't acknowledged.

I was home one afternoon, napping, when the mail arrived, falling through a slot in the door. A letter from a producer at ABC-TV in New York informed me that I was a candidate for a job as color analyst for the network's college football telecasts. ABC was conducting a national search, and someone in the LSU football office had recommended me. Would I consent to a phone interview?

A man called a week later and asked if this was a good time to talk. "Of course," I said, "I don't have any appointments. Is this the interview for the job doing college games?"

"Yes. And I have only one question."

I waited.

"What would you say if you were covering a game and late in the fourth quarter you saw two players from the same team fighting on the sideline next to the bench?"

"The players are teammates? These are teammates who are fighting?"

"Yes. They are teammates. What is your answer?" He sounded like the moderator of a television game show.

In the seconds before I responded, I calculated the risk of giving the wrong answer. The producer, I was certain, had heard the same response from all the other candidates. I needed to be original. "I'd say it's a good thing," I told him.

"It's a good thing?"

"One of them is showing the other that he won't accept anything but his best effort. And he's making an example of him in front of his teammates. Get with the program, he's saying, or get your ass whipped. It's your choice."

"Interesting."

A letter arrived four days later informing me that I'd failed to make the list of finalists. I wrote the producer a long, profanity-filled reply, warning that if he ever called me again, I was going to personally have him prosecuted for harassment; he needed to watch his back when he left his office at the end of the day. I asked him why he'd chosen to pick on me of all people when all I'd been doing was quietly going about my business, not hurting anyone, working every day on poems and stories that would never be completed let alone published, still saying "Yes, sir" and "No, sir" to adults as I'd been taught to do, opening doors for women, giving them my umbrella when it was raining outside, and pretty well keeping my pants on despite many opportunities to take them off.

Why did he say "interesting" and encourage me if he thought I gave a stupid response to his stupid question? Was my answer the problem? Or did I sound too much like a Louisiana hick who didn't deserve a job except as a player or a coach?

I didn't mail the letter.

I read the classifieds instead, including the ads that promised I could earn millions without ever leaving home. The state school for the blind needed someone to live in a dorm on campus and monitor the students. I mailed my résumé with a cover letter and a picture clipped from an LSU souvenir program showing me in uniform. The head of the school invited me over for an interview. "Let me ask you," he said in his office, "why do you want this job?"

"I guess because I always liked young people."

"You like young people, do you?"

"Yes, sir."

It was clear he didn't know what to make of me. Did I get hit too hard in the Tangerine Bowl? Had performance-enhancing drugs rotted out my brain stem? "When I put that ad in the newspaper," he said, "John Ed Bradley's the last person I ever imagined applying for the position. I thought we'd get a bunch of lonely retired people, ladies primarily." He looked down at my résumé. "A little more than a year ago you were playing for Cholly Mac in Tiger Stadium. You were an excellent student, made Who's Who and Mortar Board and all that." He tapped the paper with a finger. "By God, son, you won all these honors."

"Would I get a room where I can live without having to pay rent?"

"Yes, you would."

"Would I get to eat here without having to pay?"

"You would, yes."

"And all I'd have to do is look after the students at night?"

"It's not as easy as you think. It can be extremely demanding, as a matter of fact. And there's not much money in it, hardly any at all."

"But during the day I'm free to write?"

"Seems to me there are easier ways to buy some writing time. Look, nobody but you has answered the ad. The job is yours if you want it. If I don't hear back from you in a couple of days, I'll figure you reconsidered and found something else."

At home later it occurred to me that, if I truly meant to make an adventure of my life, I should also consider joining the Peace Corps. But then I recalled somebody telling me that the Peace Corps didn't want any more liberal arts graduates. It wanted people with practical trades—electricians who could bring light to a jungle village. Not people who could deep-snap a ball half the length of a football field.

As the day wore on, I considered following the lead of generations of males from the Bradley clan and enlisting in the United States Marine Corps. I must have mentioned the service as a career possibility in a phone conversation with Donna, because the next morning my father was knocking at my apartment door. He'd skipped work and driven all the way from Opelousas. The man was always fastidiously put together, his shirts and pants pressed, his tie knot perfectly centered below his Adam's apple. But this morning he was a crooked, rumpled parody of himself. His eyes shone with fatigue. A cowlick stood up at the back of his head.

Even more surprising was the fact that he'd come with a gift. He pressed it against my chest as I stepped back to let him in. It was a white button-down dress shirt—still wrapped. He'd never given me a present before. Always they'd come from my mother and him, and she'd picked them out. "Here's this shirt I bought you." He pivoted on a heel and looked at me. "Have you done it yet?"

"Done what?"

He didn't say anything, and then I assumed he'd somehow heard about the position at the blind school.

"I told the man I'd give him my answer today."

"Your mother is very upset, and so are your sisters. Donna's been crying since last night."

"Really?"

He walked to the dining room and sat at the table. "Your grandfather died a Marine in 1943 when I was a little boy, only ten years old. You remember that summer we drove up to Arlington National Cemetery to see his grave? Now, I'm not saying anything against the U.S. Marine Corps. But I gave two years of my life to that outfit and I can tell you in all honesty it was a waste of my time and everybody else's time. I've never said this to you because I respect the men and women who serve this country, but those were the longest, loneliest years of my life. John Ed, you do not want to do this."

"I wasn't going to do it."

"Your sister said you were meeting with recruiters."

"I told her I was *thinking* about meeting with recruiters. On the news I saw what was going on in Iran, and I wanted to help out and be of some use to somebody for a change. I miss football so much. I miss it like you can't believe."

He nodded. "Me too, John Ed. It's a hard adjustment."

"I miss the things I didn't value or pay much attention to when I had them. I don't miss the games so much, the people in the stadium. I miss being a part of something. I only have myself to worry about now, and it's about worn me out. The weird thing is I've even started to miss the guys I didn't much care for when I was playing. And I miss August and the way the grass used to smell when we went out to start two-a-days."

He walked around the table and cupped the back of my neck with his hand.

"I guess I never saw my time running out. I thought I'd have it forever. And now if I could have anything back, it would be that—the feeling that came around every August when everything was new and anything could happen because the season was about to start."

I followed him out to his car. He paused and looked around, and it seemed he'd only now figured out that he wasn't in

Opelousas anymore. "It's going to be a nice day," he said and got behind the wheel.

"You drove all this way to give me a shirt and talk me out of joining the Marines. You know what, Daddy? You're getting soft."

He looked at me once more then put the car in gear. "Don't tell your mama," he said, then reached out the window and patted me on the arm.

AUGUST WAS THE ONLY TIME of year they gave you anything other than water and Gatorade at practice. Halfway into drills a break came, and the trainers handed you a double Popsicle and a frozen orange half, and you sat under a giant circus tent and tried to cool off. The tent was made of heavy green canvas, and it sucked up the heat, and it was damp and suffocating even in the morning shade with the industrial box fans blowing. Players competed for seats on the benches closest to the fans and the hot wind they made. One day one of them walked up next to a fan, dropped to a knee and brought his face up close to the blades. *"I ... hate ... this ... shit,"* he said, his voice breaking up and warbling. You knew he was talking about two-a-days.

I wondered why I had to come from Louisiana, when there were other nice parts of the country where my ancestors might've settled and where I might now be playing football. Minnesota, for instance. It got down to sixty degrees at night up there in the summer, and people wore sweaters and long pants, and when you drove down the street, you didn't see air-conditioning units sticking out of house windows and dripping water down into the weeds. It was hard to believe a place like that existed, sitting now in Baton Rouge with a Popsicle in my mouth.

"Sit down—you're blocking my air."

"*I ... hate ... this ... shit ...* "

"We're going to somebody's funeral, you don't sit your ugly ass down."

"*I ... hate ... this ...* "

"Sit down before I throw this orange at you."

"*I ... hate ...* "

He couldn't hear anything. And I was too tired to throw an orange anyway, so I sat shoulder to shoulder with the others on the long bench, and my muscles hadn't stopped twitching, and my sweat hadn't dried when the timekeeper blew an air horn and I was dropping the wrapper dripping syrup and the orange skin raggedy with pulp in one of a dozen open trashcans and slipping my hat back on and sprinting to the next drill, running over the slowpokes and the cripples to get there, knocking the managers to their knees and spilling their kits open. You had to show the coaches how bad you wanted it.

My freshman year, that first week, my heroic schoolboy past was laid to rest without ceremony, and I was born all over again. An inch above the top of my facemask, streaming across the helmet crown, was a strip of white tape with my name written in heavy black ink: BRADLEY. To the old coach who'd recruited me, and pretended only last year that the two of us were the best of buds, it was easier to reference a four-star general named Omar Bradley than a rook from the sticks oddly labeled with two first names; so I became Omar, as in, "You stepped with the wrong foot, Omar. The play goes to the right, you step right. Play goes left, step left. Okay," and now he blew his whistle. "Let's do it again for Omar."

They laughed afterward in the locker room—the veteran players whose names he'd had years to learn, the young ones who were no less invisible than I. "Why did he call you Omar?"

"I don't know. It isn't my name."

"You're not Omar?"

"No."

"Who are you?"

He had an audience now, everyone waiting.

"Look," I said, "it might've been the wrong name, but at least he called me *something*. I don't remember him calling you anything out there."

In the summer they had a breeze up in Minnesota. There were no mosquitoes, and people slept under quilts at night with the windows open and the softest breeze stirring the curtains. But you had to figure their football players weren't any different.

I LASTED LONGER in law school than I thought I would. I lasted until the last day students could resign and still recover a portion of their tuition. The morning I received the refund, I bought two shopping bags full of used paperbacks and invited a date to dinner—the first time I'd been to a restaurant in months. We went to the Fleur de Lis on Government Street and sat in the cool of the dining room eating a square pizza and listening to Frank Sinatra on the jukebox. I'd received a student loan to finance my first year, and I still had most of it in the bank. If I lived frugally, I figured I'd have enough money to survive for a year while I worked at my writing. I was sharing an apartment with four friends, and rent, at sixty-seven dollars a month, was my greatest expense.

We lived in the redbrick, World War II-era Villa Rose Apartments on Acadian Thruway, and our place—a three-bedroom, one-bathroom town house with golden oak floors and large extended families of silverfish and cockroaches—stood directly behind an

A&P grocery. One of the store's butchers was kind enough to offer me massive discounts on meat, so we barbecued, a few nights a week, slightly green pork chops, mainly, that came with labels showing that the dates of expiration had lapsed.

I wrote all day and deep into the night, my machine set up on the kitchen table. To save money, I typed my stories on the back of the résumés stored under my bed. My housemates were old friends from Opelousas High and a cousin from home, and they never complained about the incessant chatter from my electric Adler or my tendency to read fresh copy out loud while they were trying to listen to Johnny Cash and John Prine.

Feeling particularly self-destructive one night after a feast of generic beer and badly burned chicken parts, I vowed to write to the best newspapers and magazines in the country and appeal to them for a job. I would send out a letter a day, each an original piece of writing, packed with straightforward language and emotional honesty. The editors who received my letters probably wouldn't hire me, but at least they'd see I could turn a phrase. I'd tell them about the pretty girl I'd been dating who lived in the apartment next door, and how it felt to stand over a smoking barbecue pit in the rain. I'd describe autumn in Baton Rouge and the way my lungs burned when I ran the streets late at night after everyone had gone to bed. I'd pry their hearts open with beauty. I'd chop their heads off and stuff poetry down their necks. Better yet, I'd make them think of me when they sat in traffic at the end of the day.

I spent a long afternoon in the library gathering the addresses of newspapers in the cities where I could imagine myself living. I wanted to start all over again in a place where no one thought to ask me about LSU's most recent recruiting class or quarterback controversy. I wanted to go to a place where I didn't feel like crying every time I crossed a bridge and looked in the wrong direction.

The farther away, the better. I chose papers in Seattle and Portland and San Francisco and Los Angeles and San Diego and Minneapolis and Chicago and Boston and New York and Baltimore and Philadelphia and Washington, D.C., and Charleston and Charlotte and Atlanta and Jacksonville and Miami and Dallas. There were about fifty papers total, the largest being *The New York Times*, the smallest a daily in Fort Walton Beach, Florida. Fort Walton, located on the Florida panhandle, was where I'd vacationed with my family when I was a boy, and I always dreamed of returning to live in a white clapboard shack on the beach with a dog that played Frisbee and a girlfriend who wore bikinis at the dinner table. While I was in the library, I also gathered information about *The New Yorker, Esquire, Sports Illustrated, Playboy,* and *GQ*. Before I left for the day, I listed the names and addresses of some of the top movie studios in Hollywood, on the off chance that one of them was looking for a screenwriter. I'd never read a screenplay in my life, but I'd seen enough movies to know that there couldn't be much to writing one.

In the weeks before the replies began to pile up, I devoted myself to having a good time. I visited the planetarium, toured the Magnolia Mound plantation, and rode an elevator up twenty-seven floors to the observation deck at the top of the state capitol. I drove with Johnny Wartelle to visit the leprosarium in Carville, twenty miles downriver from Baton Rouge. My cousin and Villa Rose housemate, Johnny, drove an ancient Ford Falcon held together with kite string, Bondo, Super Glue and novenas to whichever saint was in charge of rust reduction. A tall chain-link fence surrounded the Louisiana Leper Home, as it was formerly called, but the front gates were open, and we drove right in as if we had pressing business.

The grounds, crowded with old buildings and so many oak trees they blotted out the sky, had a haunting beauty that dropped a heavy silence on Johnny and me. As we moved past a row of staff houses, I told Johnny that I wanted to memorize everything I saw this day because I planned to use it in a novel. Like all the other book ideas I'd pitched to my housemates, the one about lepers was sure to make me the voice of my generation. "Go slow, John," I told him. "I don't want to miss anything."

The rejection letters all seemed to have the same template. "We regret to inform you that there are no writing positions currently available. Best of luck in your future endeavors," etc. Only one, from an editor at the *Miami Herald,* had a personal message. At the bottom, he'd written in longhand, "Quite a background. Good luck to you, Mr. Bradley."

I decided to send him a thank-you letter, even as I wondered where our exchange would lead.

Just a note saying many heartfelt thanks for saying I had quite a background and wishing me luck. That was incredibly kind of you. If ever you come to Louisiana, or to Mississippi for that matter, which isn't far away, I want you to know you have a home here with me and my four housemates at the Villa Rose, and I'd be delighted to show you the sights, as there are many. The other day, for instance, I had the occasion to visit a leper colony with my cousin John Bradley Wartelle, and as we were inspecting the facility we encountered several unfortunate victims of this harrowing plague, also known as Hanson's Disease. One man was without ears and a nose and sadly many of his fingers were missing as well ...

I crushed the letter into a ball and tossed it in the trash. The *Herald* wouldn't hire me no matter how many lies I told about my visit to Carville. A lady gives you a smile as you're leaving the A&P with spoiled meat and dented cans of *petit pois* and you don't turn around and ask her to marry you, do you? I'd teach that poor editor never to say "Good luck" to another unemployed writer again.

I kept a list of the places I'd written to and scratched them off one by one. In six weeks I received thirty-five replies, and half a dozen of my own queries had been returned unopened. On the back of one were the words "Sorry, but Mr. Ross died in 1951."

My housemates moved on to jobs or more schooling, and I moved back to my parents' little brick rambler in Opelousas. Mom had offered to let me stay in their outdoor kitchen, a small outbuilding squeezed between the house and a hurricane fence overgrown with poison ivy. It had an old sofa that I could use as a bed and a small bathroom with a shower, toilet, and sink. My first day back, as I was unloading the Impala, one of the neighbors stood in the middle of his driveway and watched me with his hands on his hips. He was an older man, recently retired. My return seemed to violate some code concerning college-educated males. "You're back," he yelled.

"For now, anyway."

"Why aren't you playing pro ball?"

"I beg your pardon?"

He waved a dismissive hand then walked out to his mailbox.

It wasn't enough to make me reconsider the bank's offer to man the drive-thru window at its new Jim Bowie branch, but it did let me know that my days as a local celebrity were past. It also prompted me to drive out to the place where I'd had a job the previous summer. The Texas Eastern compressor station received few visitors, and any unfamiliar car immediately brought out the foreman, Roe Lewis. "Well, I'll be goddamned," he said, tossing a smoldering cigarette butt at my feet. "What are you doing here? I thought you went off to be a lawyer."

"I liked the law all right, but I couldn't take being in school another day."

"You quit?"

"I quit before the semester was even finished."

He put a fresh cigarette in his mouth and took his time lighting it. "Goes to show you're not as dumb as I thought."

I stepped back to escape his smoke, then closed the car door to keep my father from thinking that I'd taken up another bad habit. "You need anybody, Mr. Lewis?"

A thin man with a knotted bald head and a perpetual slouch, he removed his glasses and wiped them with a handkerchief decorated with his monogram. "Come on in the office and fill out some papers. I'll put you on the schedule for graveyard. You don't have a date tonight, do you, boy?"

THE STATION'S PURPOSE was to receive natural gas from a pipeline and pump it back out again, a chore accomplished by a dozen compressors that stood side by side in a metal building the size of a commercial air hangar. The compressors were as big as house trailers, and they made so much noise, running all at once, that most of the veteran workers suffered from hearing loss. As a result, they had little patience for cleanup crew members who tried to engage them in casual conversation. Only one of the men cared about football, and he was a fan of Louisiana Tech. Except for the threat of going deaf, I couldn't have found a better job while I shed the memory of football and considered what to do now that nearly fifty newspapers had turned me down.

Each day I wore a khaki shirt, a pair of gray electrician's pants, and steel-toe leather boots. Mr. Lewis had me push a mower, whack weeds, and wash his company pickup truck. He lived in one of the company houses, and some days he assigned me chores at his place. I washed his window screens, trimmed his hedges, and raked pine needles in his yard. When I worked at night, I arrived with a jug of Gatorade, a can of pork and beans, vegetable soup or beef chili and a few slices of bread wrapped in aluminum foil. If I placed the can on one of the compressors, my dinner was bubbling hot when I took my break. I always ate it straight from the can. The night shift started at 3 p.m. and ended at 11 p.m., but I was rarely assigned to work then. Mr. Lewis usually gave me graveyard—11 p.m. to 7 a.m.—and in those hours an operator and I made sure everything ran smoothly.

My job was to clean off the compressors when they leaked oil and to mop the red-painted floor in the morning before the day shift took over. I also had to assist if one of the compressors started running hot and the operator needed to shut it down and make a repair. The chores took only a couple of hours. The rest of the night I was free to sit on a bucket and read books or work on my writing. I scribbled longhand on résumé paper, filling the space with a tight scrawl. I wore sponge earplugs that failed to block out the roar of the compressors, although they did deepen my feeling of isolation and sharpen my ability to concentrate.

Most of the operators didn't care that I spent the better part of the shift writing, but a few made me stop by assigning odd jobs. Because of the noise, operators either mouthed instructions or wrote them out on slips of paper. "Rain coming," one said, moving his lips. "Go close the windows."

It took me an hour to complete the task. When I finished, he had another job for me. "Rain's left. Go open them back up."

Another operator yanked the pencil from my hand and wrote a question in the margin of his newspaper. "What was it like to play for LSU?"

I shrugged as if it were no big thing. He shook his head and said, mouthing the words, "Lots of girls?"

"Not so many," I answered.

He waited a minute, then wrote, "Don't lie!!!"

"We were too busy for girls."

This made him laugh. "I envy you."

In summer, the temperature inside the station rarely dropped below a hundred degrees. Some nights the combination of heat and sleep deprivation had me outside vomiting down into the darkness from an elevated gangplank. The worst nights were those when I had little sleep during the day and I struggled to keep awake while seated on the bucket. The operators considered it an unmanly display of weakness to nod off during the shift. The best nights were those when the compressors weren't giving trouble and I was able to write without interruption until the operator nudged me and signaled that it was time to get the push broom and clean up.

Mr. Lewis had me classified as a summer student worker, but he let me stay on past August, long after the station's other student workers had returned to school. I was earning a good wage—four dollars and fifteen cents an hour, eighty cents an hour above minimum wage—and it was more than enough to buy books and make payments on my law school loan. It also was enough to take a date out to dinner, if I felt so inclined.

Janet McGreal, a former college girlfriend, stopped by the house on Delmas Street one day on her way through town. Driving to Dallas from New Orleans, she pulled up in a blue and silver car with blue and silver pom-poms on the speaker panel behind the back seat. She was wearing tight blue shorts and a tight gray T-shirt with blue lettering that identified her as a Dallas Cowboys Cheerleader. The shirt was rolled up and knotted just below her breasts, revealing a tanned washboard stomach.

When I opened the door to let her in, I was still wearing soiled clothes and boots from work, and the lower half of my face was a grime of whiskers smudged with oil. I probably smelled like a goat. "John Ed?" Janet said with a laugh.

"I don't know all of a sudden."

It was truly painful to find myself in the presence of such a glamorous woman. If I was unable to speak, it wasn't because I lacked interest in Janet. She outclassed me now by more than either of us could begin to calculate. On the phone from the road she'd said she might stay the night, but she left after an hour.

I watched her drive off. The pom-poms in back looked like a pair of hairy lap dogs resting on the top of the seat.

"I'm a writer now," I shouted at her car.

MR. LEWIS LET ME GO a few days later. If I was still unemployed next summer, he said as he walked with me out to the lot, make sure to stop by and see if he had anything for me. "You're a good worker," he said. "We've had plenty of college boys out here trimming grass, but you're right up there with the best of them." He put a hand on my shoulder and looked me in the face. "You've got a real talent for the mower."

I could've reminded him that I was twenty-four years old and a college graduate, but I didn't want to insult him and lose the chance to land the gig next summer.

That night, I sat on a swing in the backyard and listened to the sounds coming from Donald Gardner Stadium, four blocks away. A breeze was blowing from the north, and I could smell the low odor of the cooking-oil plant on the other end of town. My old school was playing, and you could hear the crowd roar when something important happened, and then a band answered with a quick, brassy number. It had to be a big moment for the crowd to drown out the band—a kickoff return or a long pass for a touchdown. I wondered if I ever made a play big enough for the crowd to scream and the band to play at once.

Had it been a mistake to turn down Coach Stovall's offer? Maybe by now I'd be a full-fledged member of his staff, coach of the offensive line, on the fast track to landing a head coaching job one day. Or maybe I should've dedicated myself to trying to make it in the NFL. Less talented players were now enjoying rewarding careers as pros, making enough money to put them in sprawling suburban homes and nice cars. My only possessions were an old typewriter and a mountain of résumé paper with illegible scribbles. I'd composed more than eight hundred manuscript pages, every one of them a testament to my inability to produce anything but crap.

I left the swing and returned to the outdoor kitchen, pulling the door closed behind me. I wanted to shut the noise out, but the stadium racket penetrated the walls. Then I remembered the earplugs from work. I stuffed them in and lay back on the sofa with pillows over my head. The noise dissipated and I became aware of my own heart beating, *ba-dump ba-dump ba-dump*. And I couldn't decide which was worse, my heart or the stadium.

I removed the plugs and threw them across the room.

IT WAS FRIDAY, another one, and I was in a lousy mood. After being holed up for weeks, I let Timmy Miller talk me into leaving the kitchen and taking a drive. Timmy and I were still good friends, despite the fact that he'd gone and made a respectable life for himself. He worked as a pharmacist at his family's drugstore, drove a new car, and lived alone in his own apartment. He seemed to date a different girl every night, none older than nineteen. Like most of my friends, Timmy was already a success, and for about an hour now he'd been gabbing about what he planned to do when his investments paid off and he made his millions. He'd own a second home in Dallas, he said, and date tall, leggy Highland Park girls who came from good families. Until recently he'd never given much thought to gene pools, but then he'd started thinking about having children. "You ever think about girls and their gene pools?" he asked.

"Me?" I shook my head. "I don't even think about girls in swimming pools anymore."

We toured the old neighborhoods and the new ones, then slipped through the park past the baseball diamonds where we'd torn it up as kids. No one was around but a couple of old men swatting tennis balls under the lights. As we passed the funeral home, Timmy signaled for a left turn. We were going to Toby's Little Lodge, the last place I wanted to visit. I let out a groan. "Gotta hit the head," he said.

"Baloney," I told him. "I know why you're stopping."

Toby's was popular with locals who liked to drink and dance to Cajun music before sitting down to dinner and the best charbroiled steaks around. I hadn't visited the place in three years, not since the week after the Tangerine Bowl. "How long you gonna be?" I asked.

"Five minutes. Be right back, I promise."

Half an hour later, I was still waiting. I decided to kill him when he returned. I checked the glove box for something to hit him over the head with, but there was nothing but old road maps and gas station receipts.

I considered walking back to Delmas Street, a mile or so away. It seemed a better alternative to entering the restaurant and being seen.

136

I realized now that Timmy had set me up. He wasn't coming back, because he figured I'd eventually go in to get him, and when I did that I'd have no choice but to join him for a beer at the bar.

He was sitting on a stool with a woman on either side of him. I thought I knew everyone in town, but neither looked familiar. One was a blonde, the other a shade I couldn't rightly determine, honey perhaps. The nonblonde kept me standing there far longer than I'd planned, staring as I'd been taught not to do. "You ready, Timmy Miller?" I called out, without any conviction. My voice was feeble.

"Yeah, I'm ready."

But I was already moving in his direction, or, more accurately, her direction. Timmy and the blonde had vanished. I stood next to the woman and introduced myself.

"I think I saw you play football," she said. "Aren't you Coach Bradley's son?"

"You know my dad?"

She told me her name. I'd heard it before, most recently in a conversation with my mother who, for some reason, had felt compelled to share her ideas about the kind of woman I should marry. Rather than state directly that she wanted to see me with a good Catholic girl who'd never kissed a boy let alone played grownup with him, Mom entered her lecture through the back door, offering up an example of the type I might want to avoid. The most beautiful woman in town, she'd said, was Connie Dorsey, Louella and Bo Dorsey's daughter. But Connie, for all her charms, was considerably older than I was and the divorced mother of three. Mom didn't know Connie personally, but a young man of my potential, she said, needed someone who brought less history to a relationship.

It was sound advice, of course. My mother gave no other kind. But she seemed to forget that I aspired to write novels of the romantic sort and that I sought adventure with people whose experiences weren't limited to the ordinary. Gobblers, I called them, stealing a reference from an old Robert Service poem. Larry Henry had become my closest friend because he gobbled. When I found the woman who was right for me, she'd probably never have cheered in a football stadium or received a rhinestone tiara to end a beauty pageant, but you could bet she'd have gobbled life until it ran from her mouth in long, gooey streaks.

Timmy paid the tab, and the four of us left Toby's to rendezvous at other bars in town. At Bea's Lounge we stood talking on an empty dance floor as cowboy songs wailed from giant speakers and a disco ball shot sparkles from up near the ceiling. At the Tippin Inn I pumped coins into the jukebox and Connie chose old hits by Johnny Rivers and the Righteous Brothers. I watched her in the soft glow of the machine, trying to decide if she resembled more a young Catherine Deneuve or Ann-Margret before she went Vegas. We drank beer at a small table with a candle burning a warm scent of gardenia, while middle-aged couples in Western clothes danced on a parquet floor in the middle of the room.

I'd been shut off from people for so long it seemed I'd forgotten how to communicate. Connie appeared to be struggling with the same problem.

"I can't believe we never met," she said.

"Neither can I."

"In a town this small, I mean."

"You're right."

Somewhere along the way, Timmy must've given up and gone home. He was no longer in the bar, and neither was the other woman.

"How old are you?" Connie asked, shouting over the music.

"Twenty-four. What about you?"

"Thirty-one." She tapped the top of my hand. "Look, this isn't right, you know? I really don't want to do this."

"What are we doing?"

"I'm sorry, but I need to go."

I followed her outside into the parking lot, then down Edith Street toward Creswell Lane. "I'm not playing," she said. "Go. Leave me alone." We walked under streetlights swarming with bugs. I'd never picked up a girl before. Never dated a woman with kids. Never done anything that went against my parents' wishes. "John Ed, you should go," Connie said.

"What game was it?" I asked. "You said you saw me play."

"I couldn't tell you the name of the team or when it was," she said. "It was at Tiger Stadium. Somebody said Coach Bradley's son was down on the field playing for LSU. That's all I remember."

She lived only a block away. I trailed after her into a two-room apartment attached to a small, gray-painted rambler with a screened-in back porch. The place was no larger than the outdoor kitchen where I'd been living, but it had good furniture and a brass bed dressed with a fancy comforter and a collection of decorative pillows. On the wall there were framed pastel portraits of her children. The oldest was ten, a girl with blue eyes. A boy came next, then a second girl who must've still been in diapers when the painting was done. I'd visited the homes of women before, but never one with portraits of kids on the wall. "Where are they tonight?"

"In the house with my mother."

We weren't there long. As I stood studying the children's faces, Connie returned from the bedroom with her car keys and walked to the door. I followed her into the garage and a new Dodge convertible painted a glossy midnight blue, its seats finished with camel-colored leather. She still hadn't invited me to join her, and I sensed that she didn't welcome my company, but tonight I was willing to chance most anything. We ended up at the Oaks Motel, a 1950s motor court with a funky bar where certain men played

Bourré at a table in back. I'd never dared to enter until now. Sometime in the past there must've been oaks shading the grounds, but the only tree in sight glowed in spooky neon on a sign in front. I glanced at the office and a vacancy card standing in the window. The door to the bar was propped open with a stool, and Connie was inside before I could check to see if I had any cash left in my wallet.

We sat in smoke and too little light and appraised everyone in the room but each other. I made a game of peeling labels from our beer bottles. As soon as you remove one without tearing the paper, I told myself, you have permission to speak to her.

"I can't believe we never met," I said some fifteen minutes into the game. I immediately chastised myself for repeating her line from a couple of hours earlier.

"What's that?" She leaned forward with a hand at her ear.

"Nothing. Never mind."

Later, in her garage apartment, it came to me that I should tell her everything. "Connie, I need to show you something."

She was on the other side of the room. I could smell the smoke on my clothes. Music from the Oaks still rang in my ears.

"I don't think you know me well enough yet to show me anything."

"I need to show you my chest." I began to unbutton my shirt. My hand was trembling.

"What happened?" she said.

"Football," I whispered then let out a breath.

She walked up to me and inspected the scar, her eyes washing over with tears as she brought her face close.

"It's like this is all I have left," I said. "LSU took everything else. Or else I left it there."

She shushed me and put a finger to my lips, the painted nail touching the tip of my nose. "I think you're beautiful," she said.

"Don't lie to me."

"You're beautiful," she said again. She leaned forward, holding her long hair, and kissed the scar with such tenderness that for once I believed it might go away forever.

Chapter Five

A LETTER FROM THE POST

I FOUND a letter from *The Washington Post* forwarded to Delmas Street from my former Villa Rose address. It was in a pile of mail on the counter in my mother's kitchen. Weeks had passed since my last rejection, and I didn't need another. I went back to the outdoor kitchen, lay on the sofa, and peeled the envelope open with a finger. I'd sent my query to Ben Bradlee, the paper's executive editor, but the letter in my hands was from an assistant managing editor, whatever that was.

He regretted to inform me that there were no writing positions currently available at the paper. "Really?" I said out loud. "Well, I'm shocked." However, he continued, he enjoyed my letter and had passed it on to the editor of the sports section, George Solomon, who now wanted me to write to him directly. I ran outside and shouted loud enough to chase the birds from the trees.

Not counting the time Roe Lewis said I had a talent for the

mower, it was the most encouragement I'd received in the three years since I'd left football.

The *Post* was the last place I expected to hear from. I'd never actually read the paper, but I had seen the film *All the President's Men*. The paper's staff still included many of the journalists who exposed the Watergate scandal—Ben Bradlee among them. Jason Robards had played him in the movie.

So what did I do now? I wondered. What did I write to this Solomon fellow? Hell, I'd already given Bradlee my best stuff.

My typewriter sat on a small table next to the window that looked out on the oak tree. I rolled some paper in and started pecking the keys. I introduced myself to George Solomon and told him I was unemployed and looking for work. Hopeful that my background in football might interest him, I told him about Coach Mac and my LSU teammates. I covered three pages with single-spaced copy that ran from one edge to the other. I typed deep into the night, slept for a few hours, and then finished the letter in the morning. There was so much copy filling the third page I barely had room to sign it.

I kissed the envelope before I walked to the front of the house and posted the letter on the mailbox with a clothes clip.

Like most players I knew, I never entered a game believing we were going to lose. It didn't matter who we were facing, didn't matter if the man I was lining up against was an All-American twice my size, we were going to win, and I was going to beat him. For some reason, the same bullheaded confidence carried over to my work. I might've grown up in a town whose most famous sons were a frontiersman and a cook, but I never doubted that the writer's life could be mine. They could send me their rejection letters until the daytime ended and the nighttime began, it was going to happen for me.

Alone with Connie in her garage apartment, I fought off the fear of being turned down again. I quoted from imaginary reviews of books I hadn't written yet, and I took her on imaginary shopping sprees and spent the millions I'd made from my best sellers. Did she want to dump her little Dodge and get a Mercedes-Benz? Let me take care of that. "Who's the finest unpublished twenty-four-year-old writer in America?" I asked.

"You are," she answered.

"And who's the greatest author alive nobody ever heard of?"

"You."

"You're two-for-two. Now here's a tough one: Who's going to write so many beautiful books he'll make them forget he ever played football?"

"You will."

"And who's going to go off and make everybody proud again?"

"You."

It took Solomon more than a week to reply. He'd attended the University of Florida, he said, and he closely followed SEC football. Would I be interested in rewriting my letter to him in essay form? If the paper chose to publish it, he would pay me a hundred dollars. If not, there was no kill fee, but at least I'd know the satisfaction of having given it a shot.

I didn't have a copy of the letter I'd sent to Solomon, so I had to write the story all over again. Before I'd talked to one man, now I was communicating with millions of readers, and it seemed they'd all crowded into the room with me and were standing behind my back as I sat at the typewriter scanning my brain for words. Four days went by, and I couldn't come up with a single sentence. Bent forward, I sat on the bench swing outside and stared at the ground between my feet.

My father's fancy Florsheims crunched the pecan leaves. Fresh from work, he'd loosened his tie and unbuttoned his shirt collar.

"Aren't you supposed to be in there writing?" he asked.

"I don't think I can do it."

"You can't do it?"

"I don't think I can."

He sat next to me, and the chains holding the swing gave a rusty squeak taking the extra weight. "You don't want to quit, do you?"

"Yes, I do. I definitely do want to quit."

He nodded as if he understood, as if he himself wanted to quit every day. "Am I going to have to tell everybody you turned down a chance to write for *The Washington Post?*"

"I didn't say I was going to quit. I said I *wanted* to quit. We've had this conversation before, remember?"

We swung back and forth, neither of us saying anything. Finally, he put his hand on my thigh and gave it a squeeze. "Go back and try again. Give it two hours. Two hours isn't very long, is it?" He looked at his watch. "I'll come check on you again at five o'clock sharp."

I returned to the kitchen and put my head down. Using a trick I'd learned from a writing instructor, I got everyone out of the room by pretending to write a letter. It was to one person only. "Dear Pip," I began, calling my father by his nickname. I told him about my old teammates and what it was like to play in Tiger Stadium on a Saturday night. One sentence followed another; the pages piled up. Someone was knocking at the door. "How's it coming?"

"You told me two hours."

He tapped the face of his watch. "It has been two hours."

Solomon's office called about a week later. There was no phone in the outdoor kitchen, so my mother had to walk outside and shout for me to come. The caller identified herself as Jill Grisco, an assistant in the paper's sports department. She asked me for my Social Security number. This was how I learned that the paper planned to run my story. She wouldn't have needed the number if they didn't intend to pay me.

More than the prospect of seeing my byline in one of the country's best newspapers, I was excited about the money. I was broke again, having used up the last of my earnings from Texas Eastern. Rather than celebrate with more books and typewriter ribbons, I decided to buy Connie something—a big bunch of flowers or maybe that little see-through number I'd seen the last time I visited the mall.

WE USUALLY MET AT NIGHT after my parents had gone to bed. I sat outside on the stone bench under the oak tree until the light in their bedroom window went dark, then I started the mile-long walk to the little garage apartment where a lamp burned in the window and Connie waited on a corduroy love seat by the door. The walk took me past the clutter of darkened tennis courts and baseball diamonds at South City Park and down by the football field at Donald Gardner Stadium. I liked to pause at the fence surrounding the stadium and gaze out at the field. The painted yard lines glowed in a white grid and the scoreboard was a large black rectangle in the far trees. When the moon was bright, the clouds seemed to swim past in a rush. I liked how the tall light standards looked against the silver bellies of the clouds. To train in the summers of my high school and college years, I'd run the steps from bottom to top, most days in the hot sun while wearing ankle and wrist weights. Now the steps seemed to float up to the press box, and I fought off an impulse to scale the fence and run two at a time. I wished I could feel again the way I'd felt when I was a player. It seemed a long time ago, although it had been only a few years. My time in the game was moving away from me, like the clouds in the sky.

By the time I reached Connie's door, I was shivering from the cold. She held my hands between hers and rubbed and patted them to warm me. When she kissed me, I closed my eyes and drank in the heat.

I'd missed out on a lot when I was playing football, and I tried now to catch up. There were nights when I walked through Connie's door and headed straight for her bed without even saying hello. I dropped my clothes one after another on my way and I didn't pick them up until later when I made my way back to her door. Other nights we sat up for hours talking about our favorite writers and the movies we'd seen. I brought her books from my collection and read to her while she spun records on her turntable. We laughed a lot, and there was never enough time to say to each other all the things that needed saying.

I left before dawn, staggering out on legs with little left. I was in a hurry to return home before my father walked out for the morning paper, so I ran most of the way, dogs barking as I jogged past houses that had not yet come awake, my football knees and ankles creaking in the cold. That I was twenty-four years old and felt compelled to hide my girlfriend from my parents surely was evidence that I needed a place of my own. It also indicated a maturity level closer to boyhood than manhood, but I was determined to change that as soon as I found regular work. If *The Washington Post* turned out to be a dead end, I planned to call Coach Stovall to see if he still had a graduate assistantship for me. If he didn't, I planned to track down Coach Mac and ask him to help me find a job in football.

Lots of people had to work at jobs they didn't like. I didn't know why I should be any different. I would've coached the junior varsity team at OHS for the rest of my life if it meant I got to go home to Connie at the end of the day.

When I asked her about her failed marriage and ex-husband, she refused to provide even the smallest piece of information. I asked her about a man I heard she'd dated. She kept silent on this subject as well. It seemed she wanted me to believe she didn't have a past, and when I finally recognized that this was indeed her position, I was free to forget mine, too.

I decided that no one had ever loved a woman as much as I loved Connie. I'd read books and seen movies about men and women in love, their passion for each other described in poetic language, soaring music, and dramatic visuals, but none came close to what we had together. I was romantic enough to believe that we'd be with each other forever. Silver-bellied clouds would continue to rush by in the sky above the football field, and the day would come when we ended up side by side at Bellevue Memorial on the edge of town, sharing a single plaque with a brass vase between our names and a single line of poetry that told the whole story. Even after we were gone, we'd exist in the hours late at night when everyone else in the town was asleep, the stadium dark in the park that stood between her house and mine.

Some nights we went for drives in her car. She liked to keep the top down, even when it was cold outside. In a futile effort to keep warm, I burrowed my hands deep into my coat pockets and lowered the bill of my cap. I leaned forward against the hot-air vent. Football is over, I thought to myself. Football is definitely over.

She showed me rent houses in neighborhoods where she'd lived when she was a kid, every one of the houses derelict and peeling paint. At one place, the lawn was decorated with a large cement-cast statue of the Virgin Mary embracing Jesus after they'd taken him off the cross. As we toured downtown and the courthouse square, she talked about shopping as a girl in the buildings that now stood empty, their windows covered with sheets of plywood and FOR RENT signs. We ended up at Donald Gardner Stadium, parked by a side entrance that for some reason was unlocked. I removed the chain, pushed the gate open, and held a solitary finger high as I ran out on the field, a champion at loving Connie if at nothing else. I gently tackled her in the end zone and we fell in the grass and tumbled toward the goalpost.

This field was hallowed ground. I could picture my father stalking the sideline and my brothers at play. And yet I never felt better there than I did with Connie. It was like being in a church with no one to tell you how to think or how to feel, the moment when God at last comes to you in the quiet of the empty pews and the colored light falling from stained-glass windows.

Connie was lying in the middle of the end zone. I crawled to her and put my arms around her. She lifted her face to mine. I pulled her farm coat open and slipped my hands under her sweater. She winced, feeling the cold on her breasts. I pulled her bra up, letting her breasts come loose, and placed my face against her side, listening for her heart. "Who do you love?" I asked. "Tell me, Connie. Tell me who you love."

"You. I love you. I love you."

FOR MY NEXT ASSIGNMENT, Solomon sent me to Tuscaloosa, Alabama, to interview Bear Bryant. I met the old coach in his office, and we talked for about an hour as a television set played vintage cartoons, the volume turned down low. Bryant's voice was deep and dark and beautiful, but he was a less-than-confessional interview. He seemed to have little interest in discussing his past or his future, and the subject of football didn't interest him much either. If he remembered our meeting at the Birmingham Touchdown Club banquet he didn't mention it. He ignored many of my questions and instead asked me about my family in Louisiana. He wanted to know if I had brothers and sisters and how old they were. Then he quizzed me about Coach Mac, one of his favorite former players and a tough adversary. "Charles is a helluva man," he said.

"Yes, sir, I never knew a better one."

"Always respect your father, son."

"I do, Coach. Thank you." He returned his attention to the TV. "Coach Bryant, I was wondering if you had any plans to retire after the season. There's been a lot of speculation about the possibility of that happening."

"Your mother, too," he said after long consideration. His eyes were still on the cartoon. "We only get one of those, don't we, son?"

"That's true, Coach."

I'd rented a room in a family motel somewhere near campus. That night I wrote the story out longhand as kids next door turned beds into trampolines and flung their bodies against the wall. I kneeled beside the bed and used the mattress as a desk. The door and window to my room were open, and I let the electric heater blow at full speed. The noise died down at around midnight, and I walked to a nearby gas station for supper: a jumbo cup of coffee and a bag of red-hot pork rinds.

Toward daybreak I finished writing and fell asleep on top of the bedspread, marked-up drafts of the story scattered all around me. I knew I should get up and close the curtains and chain the door, but my head wouldn't let me. I was having another LSU dream.

We were playing Alabama at Birmingham's Legion Field, and somehow I'd misplaced my helmet. I rarely took my helmet off during games, even when the defense was on the field, but today I'd put it down somewhere and couldn't find it. I checked the entire length of the bench. No helmet. I checked behind the ice chests and the Gatorade and water Igloos, and I checked under the ball bags and the Army duffels holding spare pads. I checked behind the box fans churning at either end of the bench. I opened first aid kits and looked in them, even though they were too small. "Where is it?" I said. I could feel myself beginning to panic. "Anybody see my helmet?"

My teammates shook their heads no. "Is that my helmet?" I pointed to the one Marty Dufrene was holding under his arm. But it wasn't mine, and the expression on his face let me know he resented being singled out. We didn't all wear helmets from the same manufacturer, but most of them, mine included, were supplied by a company called Kelley. I walked from one teammate to another checking for Kelley headgear. None was right.

What if a fan stole it? I wondered. What if he jumped from his seat down to the sideline when I had my head turned and made off with it? I checked the faces of the crowd closest to the bench. If one of them was the thief, he would've been watching me with a guilty look on his face. But no one was watching me. They were focused on the game.

Suddenly the stadium erupted. The defense had forced a turnover; the ball was ours. Charles McDuff and Big Ed Stanton pushed past me, buckling their chinstraps as they ran out on the field. Tom Tully and John Watson jogged to where the referee had placed the ball. The line was now complete, except for me, and it was my job to call the huddle and make sure everyone was present and accounted for. God, where's my helmet? I prayed. Lead me to my helmet, God. I was approaching hysteria as I ran down the sideline, bumping into players, knocking things over. "Lock and load,

John Ed," shouted Dave McCarty, our line coach. I knew he'd put Marty in if I didn't come up with the helmet fast. And if Marty played well, I could lose the starting job. I'd spend the rest of my senior year on the sideline, shamed and disgraced. "Get in the game, son," McCarty yelled.

"Coach, I can't find my helmet."

"*You can't find your ...* "

I tried to pull the helmet off the head of a reserve player. He pushed me away with a violence I never would've expected from a teammate. I tried for another helmet and its owner wouldn't let me have it either. He punched me so hard in the face that I was momentarily stunned and fell to the ground. I tumbled over on my back. In the sky above, an eternity of clouds moved past at such a pace that it was impossible to single one out. I reached a hand up, hoping someone would help me. No one did.

I finally rose to my feet on my own and started for the field with no helmet on. I pressed past teammates and assistant coaches who attempted to stop me. "Not like that," Coach Mac said, arms thrust out to block me. I slipped by him with a shifty move that made him stumble. The cap fell off his head.

The crowd spotted me and began to laugh. Then I was at the door to my hotel room. I pulled it open and stepped outside wearing only boxers and a T-shirt. The parking lot was empty. I glanced at a maid several doors down counting little bars of soap. "I thought I lost my helmet," I said.

She didn't answer.

I should keep my dreams to myself, I realized, if only to avoid burdening people with them. How do you begin to explain the fear of losing a helmet to someone who never wore one?

I sucked in a breath and went back inside.

SOLOMON SOUNDED DIFFERENT from all the other times he'd called with assignments. He was whispering the way Coach Mac used to do when he had a matter of epic importance to discuss. "We want to send you back to Alabama to cover the LSU game," he said.

I didn't reply.

"It's coming up this weekend."

"Can I think about it?"

"What's there to think about? It's the biggest college game in the country this week. We want you to cover it."

I told him I'd have to get back to him with an answer.

For two days I lay on the sofa in the outdoor kitchen studying cloud formations in the water-stained Celotex and wondering why I ever quit law school. He wasn't going to make me go to the game, and I didn't care if it meant I'd never write for *The Post* again. I could call Uncle Harold for work. There wasn't a thing wrong with blowing insulation for a living. I wasn't going anywhere near a football stadium where LSU was playing for as long as I lived.

On Wednesday my mother shuffled outside in her slippers and yelled for me to come get the phone. I could see her through the window, and I knew that look on her face. She was excited because she'd talked long-distance to someone in Washington, D.C. And not just anyone. I yelled back that I was busy.

"But it's Mr. Solomon," she said.

"Take a message."

"You come talk to him, John Ed."

And so I did. Before I could find words to politely decline the assignment, Solomon started talking as if I were already on board. Jill had made all the arrangements, he said. All I had to do was report to Legion Field an hour or so before kickoff, pick up my credentials at the Will Call window, and take the elevator to the press box. He wanted me to interview players and coaches after the game and file the story by 7 p.m.

I listened in horror, wondering how to make him stop. Somebody needed to tell the man that I wasn't the kind of writer who wrote game stories, especially ones about LSU. He wished me luck and put the phone down. I stumbled back to the outdoor kitchen in a black fog.

I lacked the funds to rent a car, so I called Greyhound about a ticket. The round-trip fare was more than I could afford. After I rented a room for two nights in the cheapest motel in all of Alabama, I'd be lucky to break even. And if I ate anything other than crackers and Vienna sausages, I was sure to land in the red. It never occurred to me to ask Solomon to cover my expenses. That would've been rude. More, it would've obligated me to actually attend the game and write something.

My sisters were former sorority girls with wide connections. Donna knew an LSU grad who was planning to drive home to Birmingham for the weekend. I gave the young woman a call and explained my predicament. She assured me that she was only too happy to have me join her. I asked her to recommend an inexpensive hotel. She said she was pretty sure her parents could put me up.

On Saturday I accepted one more invitation and rode to the stadium with the girl's parents. I sat in the back seat with a borrowed typewriter on my lap, my arms folded on top of the carrying case. I wore a white shirt, khaki pants, a red club tie, and a blue blazer. Though I looked professional enough, I'd forgotten to bring typing paper, a pen, or a notebook. I figured I could borrow them when I reached the press box. There would be plenty of reporters who'd covered the team when I was a player, quite a few of whom I'd once regarded as friends. If they couldn't help, I could always steal a pencil and use the back of the stat sheets. I was good at recycling paper.

As I stepped off the elevator, a huddle of reporters paused in mid-conversation to stare at me with pinched and curious expressions. One of them, a columnist from the *Morning Advocate*, said he'd read some of my stories in *The Post*. "How on earth did you land that gig?" he asked.

"I wrote Ben Bradlee a letter."

"You wrote him a letter?"

"No kidding. I wrote him a letter."

My seat was in the first row, close to the 40-yard line. To my left sat a senior writer for *Sports Illustrated*. To my right, a staff writer for *The New York Times*. The *Times* reporter was already typing away on a new computer, even though kickoff was still half an hour away. The *Sports Illustrated* writer was filling a legal tablet with notes. It shamed me to put the powder-blue Smith Corona on the table. What was the *Washington Post* stringer doing with that shitty little typewriter? To the pros on either side of me, watching me remove the cover must've been like watching a tuxedoed waiter remove the silver dome from a serving tray to reveal a half-eaten corn dog.

Someone was tapping my shoulder. It was Roger Brandt, editor of the sports section for the Opelousas *Daily World*. Roger had written stories about my father when he was coaching and not a few about me when it was my turn in the game. "Is that really you, John Ed?" he said. "I overheard some reporters in the men's room saying you were here covering the game for *The Washington Post*. I couldn't believe it."

I leaned in close and whispered in his ear, "Can I borrow some paper from you, Roger? Would you mind?"

"Of course. I'll give you however much you need."

"What about a pen or a pencil? Something to write with?"

He began to laugh then stopped himself. "You're not kidding, are you?"

I shook my head.

"Anything else?"

I leaned in closer. "You wouldn't have a spare notebook, would you?"

My head started reeling the moment LSU came running out on the field, led by captains James Britt and Alan Risher, both of them old friends. The players moved in a beautiful corn-yellow parade, the roar of the crowd muted in the press box. I saw Ramsey Dardar, Mike Turner, Leonard Marshall, and Malcolm Scott. Next came Coach Stovall—*Cherry Snowball!*—destined to take this team to the Orange Bowl. I recalled the day in his office when he put his arm around me and said, "Never forget us." Clearly I hadn't. But had they forgotten me?

Unable to watch more than the first few minutes, I retired to the men's room and locked myself in a stall. People knocked on the door. "I'm in here," I snapped. By the time I returned to my seat, the half was almost over. I pretended to take notes but in fact I was somewhere else. In Connie's bed telling her what a great writer I was going to be. Out driving the back roads in her convertible, wind blowing her long pretty hair. In the old church cemetery at Grand Coteau where we went to hide from the world, the huge oaks black against the sky as the two of us walked among the tombs.

With five minutes left on the game clock, reporters started moving to the elevator. I joined a group and traveled down. We stood on the sideline in a loose arrangement behind the photographers, as newspaper credentials hanging from our belts flapped in the breeze like children waving goodbye. Was it true? Had I really been a player once? It all seemed a ridiculous lie, to look at the LSU squad now. I fit in with them about as well as I fit in with the reporters.

I looked across the field and spotted Bear Bryant, and even more clearly than our recent interview I remembered the night we'd had cocktails with Mac in that hotel bar. Bear seemed infinitely older today. As a senior against Alabama, I'd broken a finger in the cold and the rain of a 3-0 loss that was probably my worst game of the year. But LSU was the winner today, 20-10, in what would turn out to be Bryant's last game against the Tigers. One month after retiring at season's end, he would succumb to a heart attack.

The players ran to the locker rooms, and the reporters followed. LSU's victory made me feel even more confused about where I belonged. With a different result, the team and I would've had something in common.

As I stepped into the LSU locker room, somebody shouted my name, and then one of the players grabbed me from behind and lifted me off my feet. Was it Ramsey? Lenny Marshall? There was so much chaos that I never did identify him, but his sweaty underclothes dampened my jacket and shirt, and left them clinging to my back. I walked around and embraced the players I knew. Everyone wanted to know where I'd vanished to. What I'd done with my life. "I'm a newspaperman now," I said. "Seriously."

They hadn't forgotten me, after all. I could've thanked each of them for that. Could've kissed them too. It came to me that I really wasn't much different from those former players who kept going back to the games and reminding everybody how great they once were. In the end, I'd just wanted my teammates to remember me.

I never did get around to interviewing anyone. And, at 7 p.m., I still hadn't written the first line of my story. "Dear Pip," I typed, over and over. But I couldn't continue.

The reporters on either side of me had left for the airport. The press box was almost empty. Roger moved down to where I was sitting and glanced at the blank page in the Smith Corona. I lowered my head and rested my forehead on the typewriter's cool metal frame.

"Just say you wrote it," he said. "Go ahead, John Ed. I won't tell anyone."

He was holding several sheets of paper out to me. For a moment I didn't understand. He was offering me the story he'd written for his own paper.

"I can't, Roger. You know that."

"Use the body of the story. We can rewrite the lede. No one will know."

"It isn't right." I stood and walked over to him. "Thank you, Roger. That's awfully nice of you, and I appreciate it more than I can tell you. Look, will you do me a favor? Don't ever write anything in the *Daily World* about this. I'd rather not let anybody know what happened today, my dad especially."

"John Ed, I'm sure he'd understand."

"I'm sure he would too. But I'd rather he didn't know."

He swallowed hard then gave a nod. "Sure. I won't say anything. I promise."

I called the office and asked to speak to George Solomon. He wasn't working tonight. A man named Leonard Shapiro, one of the section's best writers, came on the line. "I don't have it," I told him. I cleared my throat. "I'm sorry, Mr. Shapiro, but I wasn't able to write the story. I tried to, but I just couldn't do it."

He didn't say anything for awhile. I figured he was ramping up to let me have it. I deserved whatever he had to tell me, and I knew my days with *The Post* were done. Give it to me, I was thinking. Get it the hell over with. But he surprised me as much as I'd ever been surprised. "Don't worry about it, kid," he said. "It happens to the best of us."

I wasn't sure I'd heard him right.

"It's okay," Shapiro repeated. "Go home and get some rest. We'll call you in a few days with your next assignment."

THEY MIGHT'VE WAITED until the end of two-a-days. They might've given the dorm monitors time to finish curfew check. It wasn't yet midnight, and I could hear them out in the hall. My neck and chest were on fire, and I wanted to go to bed and dream about life after football. I wanted to see myself leafing through rare books at the stall of a bouquiniste in Paris or walking a Florida beach with a healthy, tanned girl who had hair like Farrah Fawcett's. These dreams helped you survive August and camp, and they let you know your purpose as a human being wasn't limited to how best to protect the quarterback.

Big Ed was asleep. I still hadn't made up my mind what to do, but I knew the right thing was to stay put. I'd never violated curfew before, and I recalled what had happened to those of my team-mates who had. In prison movies, inmates dig tunnels that lead to the other side of a wall topped with barbed wire. If they reach the other side, they have to avoid the sweep of lights from guard tow-ers and the drooling bloodhounds that track their scent. Most of them get caught, and then they end up in isolation or being whipped. Mac was no more lenient in his treatment of curfew offenders, so I knew better than to answer the door. But in some prison movies, I recalled, inmates lived to regale others with their courageous act in a moment of risk when to say no would've doomed them to a cell forever.

The bank of fluorescent lights overhead gave them a sickly cast. "You comin'?" It was David Woodley, looking even more disheveled than usual.

I shook my head. "No, Bones. Not tonight."

"Yes, you are too coming," said Charles McDuff from behind him.

They glanced down the hall, one looking left, the other right, to make sure they hadn't drawn any attention, while I looked back in the room at Big Ed. His Bible lay on the bed next to his pillow, and he slept without moving or making a sound. I wondered if he was faking it. If so, it was a smart strategy. He wouldn't have to rat on us when Mac quizzed him about what he knew.

"What if we get caught?" I said.

"Then Mac loses three of his starters. Put some shoes on, Omar. You're coming with us."

The beer, Old Milwaukee in a can, was the cheapest they could find, and they'd iced it down in a cooler that was roped to the wall of Charles's little green pickup truck. The cab was too small for the three of us, so I volunteered to ride in back, with the beer. I kept my head low until we were a safe distance from the dorm.

The prison break had been David's idea, and I'd been hearing about it for days. He and I were going to celebrate our last camp by visiting the Ponderosa after curfew and drinking cocktails under the stars. Charles would join us, of course, since he and David were roommates and best friends. So what if we didn't get any sleep and had to be up the next morning at 6? We were seniors, and we had to do something special to mark the end. This was going to be one great night. When we were lying on our deathbeds, looking back, we'd count it among the best we ever had.

The truck slowed crossing the railroad tracks that ran along the perimeter of the practice fields. We pulled up to a gate, and Charles cut off the headlights. I got out and held the gate open. Charles parked on the grass, and David and I carried the cooler and placed it on the 50-yard line. I passed around icy cold cans, and we lay back and gazed at the night sky, and for a long time none of us spoke or seemed to breathe for the beauty of what burned way off in the darkness. The longer we were quiet, the harder the light seemed.

Now that we'd done it, there wasn't much to say, so we drank the beers one after another until the last can was gone. David turned the cooler over and left a mound of ice to melt in the sod. I started to gather up the empties and put them in the cooler, but he stopped me. "Leave them where we dropped them, Bradley Boy."

The cans were still there, scattered in the grass, when we arrived later that morning in team buses and filed through the pedestrian gate. The sun beat down on them and kicked up a wet reflection. "Some fraternity boys sure had themselves quite a time out here last night," Coach Mac said as he got in his golf cart. "Look, fellas. Look at what those fraternity boys did to the Ponderosa. Look at what they think of you."

We lined up to stretch then dropped to the ground to work our hamstrings, and I looked at David a few bodies away. As seniors it was our job to loosen up the squad before drills started, and we faced the younger guys now and pretended to be worthy of the assignment. David looked fine, as if he'd had a good night's rest, but Charles and I were green around the edges and a weird sort of pale everywhere else. I prayed that I wouldn't throw up when McCarty and Klaczak had us running ropes, and then I shouted for the guys to get back on their feet for windmill stretches, right hand to left toe, left hand to right toe.

Three and a half years from that day, David told reporters in Florida that I was a liar for betraying him in a story I wrote for *The Washington Post*. At age twenty-four, he was playing for the Miami Dolphins in the 1983 Super Bowl, then the youngest quarterback ever to lead a team to the championship game. I'd filled my story with personal anecdotes and casual observations about a player whom most reporters had considered enigmatic if not altogether impossible to know. I thought it was a flattering, insightful portrait. David disagreed.

Among other things, he objected to my description of the night we broke curfew. He denied it ever happened. I was confused as to why he would take offense at such an innocuous tale. He never called or wrote me, and I didn't contact him to find out what I'd done wrong. Then years later, in 1992, I learned that he was suffering from alcoholism and needed a liver transplant. I reached him by phone in Shreveport. "Look, man, I'm sorry I ever wrote that stupid, piece-of-shit story," I said.

I asked him to let me make it up to him. I'd write something else about him, this time for *Sports Illustrated*. The story would bring attention to his situation and help him out. If there was anything he didn't want me to include, all he had to do was tell me. "Leave me alone, Bradley Boy," he said, then quietly laughed and hung up the phone.

Maybe I did betray him, in the way all writers betray the people they write about. He was a private man who wanted to be left alone, and I'd flung his door open and stepped inside. I often wondered if he remembered what it was like to stretch out in the grass with Charles and me, only weeks away from the first game. We believed we were better than the prognosticators thought. We had to get by Colorado, USC, Alabama, Georgia, Florida, and Florida State, not to mention five other teams, but we could go undefeated. Why not? Why couldn't we shock the world? Less talented teams had done it. And so we offered up toasts to the future, and we drank the beer, and we knew that no matter what happened, we'd never let each other down.

Without that night my life might've turned out different. To begin, the story I wrote about the Dolphins' mysterious young quarterback would've been a lot less compelling, and George Solomon and *The Post* might not have run it. I might not have received another freelance assignment. And without that assignment, maybe I never would've been able to prove that I was good enough to work there as a full-time writer. Maybe I never would've written my books. Maybe I'd be making my living today selling garage-sale finds on eBay.

It was May of 2003. The TV set was muted when David's face came up on the screen, a photo from his days with the Dolphins. He looked like I remembered him, but a photo can deceive as easily as memory can. I sat up and stared at the image, the years of his birth and death printed beneath it.

"Good God, Bones," I said to the empty room.

The deal is, you can't make someone forgive you unless he wants to. David was dead at age forty-four of kidney and liver failure.

THE JOB OFFER came about six months after my first story was published. Solomon said he wanted to bring me in as an intern, but Ben Bradlee had overruled him. He'd told Solomon to go ahead and put me on staff. They asked me to start on Monday, April 4, and offered to pay me around eighteen thousand dollars a year, a figure I found hard to believe. I thanked Solomon for his generosity and put the phone down, and then I punched the sky in celebration. Later I would learn that my salary was the lowest in Solomon's department and the least amount the paper could pay a full-time staff writer under the terms of its union contract. But for the moment I was counting cash and dreaming about how to spend it. If I worked hard and impressed my bosses, in a year or two I might earn enough to qualify for a mortgage, and then I could send for Connie and her kids.

"Let's talk about our house," Connie said one night. And I described it for her room by room. I walked her into a light-filled kitchen with red cypress cabinets and glistening floors, and then I took her upstairs to a bedroom filled with windows and views of a flower garden. There was wood flooring dressed with a single antique rug, real oil paintings on the walls, and a four-poster bed so tall it almost touched the ceiling. I finished by walking her out to the screened-in back porch, where we had coffee in the morning and read the paper in the evening.

I told her about the children we were going to have together: the girl who'd look just like her mother, the boy who'd grow up and play football for LSU, if he wanted to. I always made sure to add the caveat "if he wants to."

I went to see her about an hour before I left for Washington. I should've told her that I was so sad I felt like I was about to die. I should've fallen to my knees and pleaded with her to come with me. Instead, I led her outside and had her stand in front of a used Toyota Corolla, until this morning the property of my sister Gina's husband. I opened the hood and showed Connie the engine. She cried with her face in her hands while I pointed out how good it looked for a car with nearly eighty thousand miles.

"I don't know why you have to get so emotional," I said.

"You really don't understand anything, do you?"

I lowered the hood and she slipped a hand inside my shirt, placed it over the scar on my chest, and came up on her toes to kiss me.

When I drove off a minute later, belching smoke, she had to think I was the most insensitive sonofabitch that ever lived.

I'D BORROWED my uncle's farm truck, and my brothers helped me load my things into the bed—books mostly, boxes and boxes of books. There wasn't enough room to fit both the mattress and the box spring. Rather than abandon any of my paperbacks, I left the box spring behind. Daddy drove the pickup. I followed in the Corolla.

As we were crossing the river into Baton Rouge, I looked to my right toward Tiger Stadium, prepared to confront the old ghost one last time. But rain was coming down so hard I couldn't see past the guardrails. For years, I'd avoided looking in that direction, and now that I was willing to have an honest moment, I couldn't see a thing. Had I been in a better mood, I might've registered the irony. All I could think about was Connie.

We were two days on the road, fighting rain all the way to northern Virginia. We pulled into Washington at dusk and found a hotel downtown on 14th Street, only a block away from *The Post*. The blue plastic tarp that covered the back of the truck had been ripped to shreds. The mattress was soaking wet, so too were the books. We parked in an underground garage, and I asked the hotel manager for a guarantee that my things would still be there in the morning. "This is a city, sir. You know … a metropolitan area?"

"So if I come down here in the morning and find everything gone, the hotel isn't liable. Is that what you're telling me?"

He looked in the back of the truck, reached down, and picked up a soggy copy of *One Flew Over the Cuckoo's Nest*. "Sir, trust me, no one's going to steal your things."

I had only the weekend to find an apartment. It would be two weeks before I received a paycheck, and I had ten bucks in my wallet. I still hadn't figured out how to ask my father for a loan.

My brother Brent stood at a window in our room, staring down several floors to the street. "What are those ladies doing?" he asked.

I walked up behind him and had a look. The street was thick with hookers.

"Get away from there," my father said.

I put my hands on Brent's shoulders and guided him to the side then claimed his position at the window.

We were within walking distance of the White House, but apparently this was the city's red-light district.

"You too, boy," Daddy said.

He was lying on his side in bed, playing solitaire. I'd never disobeyed him before, and it wasn't time to start now. Forget how old I was or why we were there today. I did as I was told.

The next day, we looked at half a dozen places. The only apartment complex that had something available immediately was in Rosslyn, a congested, high-rise suburb directly across Key Bridge and the Potomac River from Georgetown. I liked other apartments better, but none would let me move in until the deposit check had cleared and my references were contacted. "This isn't some motel on the side of the road," one apartment manager told me when I asked if I could move in that day. The place I chose was an efficiency located on the flight path to National Airport. Air traffic shook the building every few minutes, the planes flying so close to the ground it seemed you could reach up and grab them. Guests entering and leaving did so with fingers in their ears. I waited until moments before I signed the lease to ask my father for help. "Can you loan me the deposit and first month? I promise I'm good for it."

"Don't worry about that. Send it when you get on your feet. I want you to work hard and make a new life for yourself. This is your chance."

"I don't know anybody here."

"You know Mr. Solomon, and you've met Mr. Bradlee. You'll make friends."

"Everybody at the paper writes on computers," I said. "I noticed that when we visited the newsroom."

"You can learn how to use a computer."

"I don't see why I can't use a typewriter and turn my stories in and let somebody else put them in the computer."

"Can't be much to writing on a computer, John Ed."

"I don't know." I looked at him. "I think I want to go back with you."

My brothers were standing nearby with their hands in their pockets. I was the first of the family to move away from home, and I knew they expected a lot from me. "Aren't you going to tell them good-bye?" my father asked.

I hugged them both, then stood back and watched them pile into the truck. Tonight they'd sleep in Tennessee, and tomorrow, late, they'd drive into Opelousas, relieved to have found their way home again.

What I really wanted to tell my father was that I was afraid I wasn't good enough, but you didn't win ball games with that attitude, and you didn't say such things to a coach. "Remember to call your mama when you get a chance." He stepped up closer and kissed the side of my face, brushing my cheek with his whiskers.

He got in the truck and drove away.

MY UNIT was on a lower floor in one of those big-city brick piles of indeterminate architectural design. When you stepped off the elevator and walked down the hall, the smells and sounds took you around the globe, past doors behind which people spoke in Spanish, German, and Chinese, others where they cooked Indian and Lebanese food, and still others where they played punk rock, R&B, and what sounded to my ear like Irish folk songs. There was so much aural and olfactory stimulation that I was exhausted before I could put the key in my door.

From my window I saw a parking lot crowded with cars and past it an interstate that serviced the Virginia suburbs and the countryside beyond. The exit and entrance ramps were constructed on a low grade, about the same angle as the ramps in Tiger Stadium that we used to run in the off-season. I put my chair in a corner and placed my gooseneck reading lamp next to it. I carried the Adler over to the saloon table and centered it on the golden boards. The mattress went on the floor in the middle of the room. I stacked the books along a wall. I owned two dinner plates, one bowl, three coffee cups, three forks, one spoon, and seven butter knives. I couldn't say why I was so rich in knives. In the kitchenette I put the china in the cupboard and the silverware in a drawer, and I listened to them rattle when planes flew overhead.

It took less than an hour to pull the place together. I wanted to go out for something to eat, but I wasn't certain that I could find my way back. I had what remained of a sandwich Brent couldn't finish and a long sip of water from the tap. It was dusk and the lights had come on, along the interstate dropping yellow-green pools on the ramps, and in my mind, now, I was at Tiger Stadium again, running the exterior stairwells that climbed to the stadium's west-side upper deck, which was under construction. We ran them one man at a time, our feet hitting the steps and sounding like firecrackers echoing in the empty space. The stairwells had been built first, before the massive elevated structure for the seating, and they took us up several hundred feet to nowhere. I could see down into the stadium from the top of the wells, to the river looking fat and brown snaking under the bridge on its way to the capitol, and the air suddenly seemed less dense than before. I contemplated the beauty of the field at the center of the bowl, the white goalposts, the grass so green it seemed hyperreal. A whistle blew and we came down again one man at a time, moving faster than we had on the way up. At the foot of the stadium we spread out randomly, our hands on our knees, sucking air. Then the strength coach told us it was time to run to the levee, and so as a group we ran past Alex Box Stadium, where the baseball team played, over the railroad tracks, and past the Ponderosa and the veterinary school, and then across River Road to the tall grass at the bottom of the levee. We divided into groups and started climbing the levee one group at a time—skill people first, linemen next, finally the kickers and punters. As we ran to the top and down again, tall weeds grabbed at our shoes and gnats and mosquitoes lifted in clouds. A ship moved past on the river with men on deck standing along the rails watching us and smoking cigarettes you could smell on the breeze.

We were almost done when a freshman defensive lineman collapsed on the way up and somebody said, "Come on, let's carry him." And together we lifted him up and ferried him back to the stadium, four and five men at a time. I couldn't believe how heavy he was, all two hundred and sixty pounds of blue-chip muscle and bone, how sick he looked, and how he said nothing even though his eyes were open.

Running past the vet school and the Ponderosa, over the tracks, and down by the baseball field. Running with that boy in our arms all the way back to the stadium.

I NEEDED TO PUT IN some work before I could arrange for Connie to visit. I'd maxed out my credit card, and her airfare was more than I'd be able to handle for awhile. I wrote her a letter every few days and told her my plans for when we were together again. The paper had a WATS line that was supposed to be for business only, but I used it at least once a day to call her and avoid having to make expensive long-distance calls from my apartment. Solomon and the rest of the sports staff returned from lunch at downtown restaurants like Duke Zeibert's and Mel Krupin's, and there I was on the phone with some chips and a half-eaten sandwich on a paper plate next to my keyboard. I was pretending to interview someone for a story. I added to the picture by scribbling in a notebook—quotes from Connie describing how much she missed me.

She finally came to see me. From National Airport we took a cab to my apartment, the view from the window providing one famous sight after another as we toured the tree-lined parkway past the Capitol and the national monuments in the distance. I draped my left arm around her shoulders, and with my right hand I cupped her inner thigh. Nearly two months had passed since I'd seen her, and she was even better to look at than the pictures in my head. I kissed her, pointed to something she needed to see, and then kissed her again.

I paid the driver and carried her luggage to my room. I hadn't taken more than a single day off since I started the job, and now I'd arranged with Solomon for a three-day weekend. I removed the cassette tape from my answering machine and took the phone off the hook in case a story broke and he called with the assignment.

We left the apartment the next morning and hopped the Metro to the Mall. We came up from underground into sunlight, and I led her by the hand to the National Portrait Gallery. She followed me down a corridor to a black-and-white photograph of the writer James Agee. Walker Evans had taken the picture in 1937 when the two men were working on the magazine assignment that would evolve into the book *Let Us Now Praise Famous Men*. In the photo, Agee's eyes were so clear it seemed his irises had been bleached. His hair was thick and unkempt; stubble covered his face.

"That's him?" Connie asked.

"That's him."

She too had read Agee's books and she closely identified with *A Death in the Family*, the autobiographical story of a boy in Knoxville, Tennessee, whose father was killed in a car accident. One of my instructors at LSU, Warren Eyster, had known Agee when both men were young writers in New York, and Eyster had made Agee required reading in his classes. Since moving to Washington, I'd taken half a dozen trips to the museum to see the portrait, once skipping out of the office in the middle of the afternoon to spend nearly five full minutes in front of the picture before heading back. All I needed was to look into Agee's eyes and my doubts about my own writing vanished. He could've passed for one of my brothers, and yet his picture hung in a museum.

I still questioned if I was just a former college ball player masquerading as a newspaper reporter, but no one had to know that as long as my stories kept being published and my colleagues at work didn't ask how I was doing and expect an honest answer.

I'd never been happier. Connie and I were finally alone together, free to come and go in public as we pleased. We were tourists in a new city, visiting the museums and monuments and crowding as much as we could into the brief time we had together. At night we watched old movies at the Biograph in Georgetown and the Circle Theatre on Pennsylvania Avenue, often staying for a second feature that kept us there past midnight. For dinner we sat in a booth in a candlelit French bistro on M Street and had omelets, *pommes frites*, and cheesecake. Still unwilling to turn in for the night, we took the Corolla for drives around the White House, Connie leaning out the window as she searched in vain for a glimpse of President Reagan in an upstairs window.

It was a long way from those nights in her convertible. A long way from LSU. "I'll never go back," I told her. "Never. Not in a million years."

"You'll go back. That's your home."

"It *was* my home. We're starting over. You're going to love it here, Connie. Wait until you and the kids come up. Nobody cares who we are. They don't know anything about us."

"It's not always bad when people care."

"Maybe not," I said, "but it's bad when they care too much. Trust me on that."

Solomon sent me on the road for a couple of days, and Connie delayed her flight after her mother agreed to watch the kids. I came back to Washington lugging a travel bag in one hand and a portable computer in the other and found that she'd kept busy while I was away. There was a tiny dressing room next to the bathroom in my studio, and the door to this room was now covered with a montage of photographs from my years at LSU. Most of the images showed Missy Crews and me at sorority and football events. Connie had taped a word balloon next to each one. Several of the balloons included words I thought we'd held sacred until now—words I'd spoken to her in clumsy attempts to express how much I loved her.

"It isn't funny," I said.

"It is funny."

"You went through my things, my private papers and things from school. Those are my pictures, Connie."

"Don't be mean. Why do you always have to ruin it by being mean?"

"I'd never do something like this to you. It wouldn't occur to me to do something like this to you."

"It was a joke." And now she was shouting, "What has happened to you? Can't you see it was a joke?"

I was tired from the road and suddenly the apartment felt even smaller than usual. It would've been nice to have my old helmet to throw through the window, but I'd left it back home in a closet in the outdoor kitchen. I probably could've reached the interstate, smashed a windshield, and taken out a passenger or two. I settled for a hot shower and a change of clothes. When I left the dressing room, I found her sitting on the mattress, her legs crossed beneath her, head hanging down. "I really meant it to be funny," she said and began to cry. "I don't know why you'd want to keep those old pictures anyway. All that ended a long time ago."

"I know it ended."

"Your cheerleader ended, football ended."

"I know. I know it ended."

I kissed the side of her face, but she didn't respond. I held her in my arms and pulled her close, but she didn't move. Why did I have to say anything? Why couldn't I have laughed it off? Maybe Connie was right: The pictures were from long ago, and I didn't need them anymore, especially the ones of Missy.

If you can walk away from football, I thought, you surely should be able to walk away from the memory of a girl who went off and married somebody else after school.

I spent the next few days hunkered down at work. I left the apartment early each morning and returned after dark, too exhausted to do much of anything. We fried chicken in the kitchenette and called out for pizza, but there were no more movies, fancy meals in Georgetown, or drives around the White House. "Had I really been in love with Missy, I'd have married her when I had the chance," I told Connie.

"Are we still on football?" she asked, mistakenly believing we'd been discussing something else.

SOLOMON SENT ME everywhere there was to go—to New York, Las Vegas, and Miami Beach to interview fighters and their trainers, to Daytona, Indianapolis, and Darlington to write about auto racing, to the Florida Keys and the Chesapeake Bay to fish, to Annapolis to find out what it was like to be a midshipman and an athlete, to the penthouse suite of a Georgetown hotel to question a lesbian tennis star about her love life. He had me write about basketball and hockey, sports about which I knew next to nothing. I interviewed heroes of the Olympics and the World Series, professional softball players, jockeys and the widows of jockeys, young NFL superstars with so much money they lived in suburban castles and owned fleets of sports cars and SUVs, grizzled old coaches who reminded me of Coach Mac and gave long, warm handshakes when the interviews were done.

I spent a week in Reno writing stories about a lightweight title fight between Livingstone Bramble and Ray "Boom Boom" Mancini. Mancini spilled so much blood in the ring that I was sprayed at ringside, my shirt speckled crimson. After Bramble won the decision, I threw the shirt away. Next the paper sent me to Lake Tahoe to write a story about snow skiing for the Travel section. From there I drove by Jeep to the Nevada desert to interview members of the Washoe Tribe and write about their struggles to overcome poverty and isolation in the shadow of one of this country's richest playgrounds.

The pace was brutal, taking me away from Washington for weeks at a time, but the paper kept publishing my stories and paying my bills, so I had no complaints. Connie came back up for another visit, and we traveled to Boston and New Haven for the 100th anniversary of the Harvard-Yale game, or, as fans called it, The Game. I stayed up all night writing a long feature, and in the morning I looked over to find that she'd been watching me work, a pillow pulled up close to her body as a surrogate partner. "You've been thinking about it again," she said. "I can always tell."

"Thinking about what?"

"You're still not over it, are you?"

I shrugged, pretending not to understand.

I rarely had a weekend off. Every month or so, Solomon called me into his office to offer advice on how to make my writing better. Leonard Shapiro did the same, patiently deconstructing my stories that needed improvement, encouraging me to work harder at being a good reporter. I had a lot to learn, if I hoped to keep pace with my colleagues, some of the best journalists in the country. At times, I was so awed by their talent that I wondered what I was doing on staff with them. In addition to me, Solomon recently had hired David Remnick, Gary Pomerantz, and Michael Wilbon. John Feinstein joined the department from Metro. Tony Kornheiser and William Gildea moved over from the Style section. Shirley Povich, Dave Kindred, Denis Collins, and Ken Denlinger wrote columns. Paul Attner covered the NFL, David DuPree the NBA beat. Mark Asher was the staff investigator, and Jane Leavy floated from sport to sport contributing long takeouts of such elegance they made me feel like a hack. Soon Solomon would bring in Christine Brennan, Sally Jenkins, Richard Justice, and Dave Sell. Norman Chad wrote the sports TV column. And there were others, many others, whose stories routinely put mine to shame.

The best twenty-four-year-old writer in America? I was with the paper for less than half an hour when I realized that I wasn't the best one in our little corner of the newsroom.

Each morning I took the Metro to the McPherson Square station and walked in half light to the office on 15th Street, arriving hours before the other writers. I was trying too hard perhaps, reaching too high, wishing for more than my talent could deliver. I wore rumpled khakis and a white button-down shirt with one of the wide-body, polyester neckties I'd taken from my father's closet when I left home. I carried a hand-me-down briefcase holding bottled water, peanut-butter crackers, and a banana. In a back pocket I'd stuffed a paperback copy of Hemingway's *In Our Time*, there for me to glance at if I got stuck and the words wouldn't come.

I hoped to get some writing done before the phones started ringing or Solomon sent me out to sub for a beat writer who'd called in sick. I liked thinking about the other reporters at home asleep or just now having breakfast, their long commutes to the city still ahead of them. It recalled the days when I borrowed Coach Guidry's key to the OHS weight room and I worked out on weekend nights when other kids were out partying or sitting at home in front of the TV. I'd often thought of those kids while I trained in front of the mirrors, and I believed I was doing more than building my body. I was gaining an edge. If I put in the hours and the effort before the game began, the fourth quarter would be mine. All I had to do was work harder than everybody else.

I was determined to take nothing for granted. If I wanted the respect of my colleagues, I had to get better. If I wanted to get better, I had to work harder. I might've been a staff writer for *The Washington Post*, but I was still a lineman on the team.

My desk was out in the open. It wasn't in a cubicle with dividers, and it wasn't in one of the offices occupied by the paper's columnists and senior editors. People exiting the service elevator on the L Street side of the building walked past me as soon as they cleared Book World and turned a corner, and in the morning when the workday was beginning, many of them didn't hesitate to shout out greetings or ask me something about the latest sports news, even as I sat there trying to write. "Hear what Riggins said to Sandra Day O'Connor?" "You really think Hagler has a shot?" "Where'd

George send you this week? *Tibet?*"

I'd arrived at the office early, beating both a rainstorm and the staffers who reported en masse at 10 o'clock sharp. I was at my desk, staring at a computer screen with a file opened to a blank page and a green cursor beating like a heart in the upper left corner. Jill Grisco, the office assistant, was doing paperwork at her desk.

For the past few hours, I'd been laboring over yet another story that was resisting my every effort to infuse it with beauty. Stories often did that, especially when the subject matter was an upcoming boxing card featuring fighters nobody had ever heard of, or amateur stock car racing in the Maryland and Virginia exurbs, or the future of the United States Football League and its local franchise, the Federals, otherwise known among my co-workers as the Gerbils. These were the assignments Solomon insisted on throwing at me, and every day I faced the same impossible task, to make something worth reading out of material that, by its very nature, wasn't even remotely interesting.

I opened the Hemingway paperback and flipped to a story about a boy named Krebs who came home from war and didn't know where he belonged anymore. He didn't fit in with his family, and even his hometown seemed a strange place. He couldn't imagine a future for himself. Sometimes the simple beauty of Hemingway's language broke the logjam and I was able to type again, but even the maestro was of no use to me today. It was suddenly 10 o'clock and people were starting to pour in. I wished I could write a sentence, just one. Was that too much to ask, God? A sentence?

The phone was ringing. I felt like answering it and giving the caller an earful, but that was Jill's job. Most calls at this hour were from readers with complaints about factual errors, misspellings, grammatical mistakes, or some leftist writer's alleged editorializing in what should've been an objective news story. Every *Post* reporter, in fact, was a leftist at this hour of the day. I listened as Jill took the call. She stood, looked in my direction, and held a finger up for line one.

"Who is it? Did you get a name?"

"John Ed, it's important," she said.

"But who?"

"Says he's your coach."

"My coach?" I swiveled in my chair.

A button was flashing at the bottom of the phone. I reached out to press it then stopped myself and whirled back around. "Tell him I'll call back."

To my dismay, Jill was no longer in hearing range and there was no one nearby to handle the call. I had no choice but to speak to him. And I'd need to quickly come up with a reply to his inevitable question: "Where on earth have you gone, son?"

The elevator doors opened, and a large group came striding out. Somebody stopped to ask me what I was working on. I stood and spoke to him, giving more to the conversation than he either expected or wanted. When I sat down again, I read over my story and made changes. I reconstructed the lede, adding words then quickly deleting them. I read the text out loud to hear how it sounded. It sounded terrible. So I cut the opening paragraph and tried again. I composed a new one, crowded with arcane words that required me to consult a dictionary. Oh my, the phone. I looked at it now. Lines two and three were lighted. Line one had gone dark.

If it really was so important, he could call back.

"John Ed, line four."

Line *four*? How could this be? Only ten minutes had passed. The intern who'd taken the call was standing at his desk, the receiver held against his chest, waiting. I glanced at the phone next to my keyboard and the flashing button for line four. "Take a message," I said.

"It's important. You'll want to get it."

I grabbed my umbrella and headed for the service elevator. "Take a message," I said again, as I stepped inside and waited for the doors to close. "Tell him I'll call back." We were going down now, and the only person who heard me was the bewildered courier standing in the corner.

It was raining as I left the building. I popped the umbrella open and took a right down 15th Street toward the Mall, water soaking my shoes and pants and blowing up in my face. The wind tunneled down the street, and the panels of the umbrella flapped and sucked inward, exposing me to still more rain. By the time I reached the National Portrait Gallery, every part of me was wet. In the bathroom, I tried to dry myself with brown paper towels, but they broke apart when I rubbed them against my clothes. I didn't dare look at myself in the mirror. I already knew all I needed to know about that man. He was the coward who was afraid to talk to his old coach.

I was shaking from nerves and the cold as I left the bathroom and walked to the photograph of James Agee. My shoes left prints on the floor, and my hair was black and plastered against my skull. How do the things and the people we love most become the things and the people we run from? I'd been here only a week ago, when Connie and I were fighting, but Coach Mac had always been good to me, and what would it have hurt to speak to him again now?

I looked in Agee's eyes and they looked back at me. He was a slight man, too small for football. I sat on a bench nearby until the legs of my pants had dried. I squeezed my socks to drive the last of the water from them. As a rule I didn't speak to inanimate objects, but there was a moment when I almost told Agee that it was a shame he never wrote about football. I could've used his help in understanding why I couldn't let go of it even though I'd already let go of it.

By the time I went back outside, the rain was over and the air was quiet and still. I took long strides and stopped only once, to stuff my umbrella in a trashcan. The newsroom was filled with people, there was a great bustle of activity, and Solomon gave me a wave from his office as I made my way to the department's mail cubby. There was a single piece of paper, and it was signed at the bottom with the intern's initials. "Joyce says your ticket is ready in Travel."

So it had been Joyce—Joyce who arranged our travel plans when Solomon sent us out on the road.

Coach Mac hadn't been on line four, after all.

THE ONLY NEWS STORY I wrote for the *Post* about LSU was a long takeout describing the life and times of Billy Cannon, the school's lone Heisman Trophy winner, who pleaded guilty in 1983 to federal counterfeiting charges and served nearly three years in prison. I'd never met Cannon, although I did see him once in the training room before a home game. Kickoff was still an hour away, and I was standing on a padded gurney as team trainers wrapped my shredded right hamstring with tape and Ace bandages. I was debating whether to ask them to shoot it up with cortisone when a large, dark-haired man appeared in the room. I assumed he was the father of a teammate, but one of the trainers, his eyes open wide, said in an excited whisper, "God Almighty, it's Billy Cannon."

To build a picture of the man, I interviewed school officials and a few of his friends, but I carefully avoided calling Mac and my former coaches. Mac had been the defensive line coach when Cannon played, and several of our assistants had been teammates of his.

Solomon seemed pleased with the story and ran it with photos across the fold, but I'd done the paper a disservice by not arranging interviews with the people who'd once been closest to Cannon. Until recently some of them had been friends of mine, as well, and they could've offered me better anecdotes to help illustrate the kind of person he was. How could anyone with such obvious gifts be reduced to printing funny money? I never adequately answered the question, because I was too afraid to make the right calls.

The morning the story appeared, I accepted a heady share of praise from my colleagues, and I alone seemed to recognize what a failure the piece was. Given another chance to write it, however, I probably couldn't have done any better. I'd almost have preferred to resign my job than speak to my old coaches again. I'd moved on, and not even my obligation to my profession was going to have me reverse course now.

Besides, I couldn't imagine those interviews—about Cannon or anyone else. They would take my questions and then what? If at the end they asked what had happened to me, I'd have to tell them that it was like loving a woman who didn't want you any-more. Better to steer clear of her if you hoped to survive having lost her. Better to pretend you never had her than to own up to still wanting her.

Perhaps to avoid an appearance of bias, Solomon didn't send me to Baton Rouge to write about the current LSU program. But he did send me to other college towns and to NFL cities for stories about football, and several times I ran into former teammates or opponents of mine. One morning, at the Miami Dolphins' training complex, I heard someone shouting at me from a walkway that connected one building to another. I turned around and spotted A.J. Duhe standing about twenty feet away. Duhe, a former All-SEC defensive tackle at LSU, had been a senior my freshman year, and in his first season with the Dolphins he was named the NFL Defensive Rookie of the Year. Today he was wearing a soft cast on his leg. "Weren't we in school together?" he called out. Before I could answer, he said, "John Ed Bradley, right?"

I walked over to talk to him.

"What are you doing here?" he asked. "You come to work out for the coaches or something?"

I took a step back and spread my arms out to let him have a look. I didn't resemble an NFL lineman so much as a scarecrow that had lost its filling.

I probably interviewed a score of pro players I'd faced in college, but I never brought up the fact that we'd met before. Most of the interviews were conducted after practice or games and were only a few minutes long, hardly enough time to make personal connections. The players wanted to get out of their uniforms and into the showers, and I wanted to get quotes for stories that too often were already pushed up hard against a deadline. It was rare when I told a player my name or provided any personal information; I usually identified the paper I worked for then started asking questions. Once, however, I interviewed a defensive lineman I'd played against who seemed to remember me. He interrupted the interview with "You look familiar."

"Do I?"

He made a slow circle in front of my face. "Something about your eyes."

I shrugged and returned to my questions, never letting on that we'd had quite a battle back in school.

I handled coaches the same way, not wishing to impose my little memory of college ball on them. After a Rams game in Los Angeles, I interviewed the team's coach, John Robinson, for a feature about the quarterback. Five years before, Robinson had coached USC in that nailbiter in Tiger Stadium. As I asked him questions for my story, I wondered what he remembered about the

183

night in Baton Rouge when his Trojans entered the field so certain of their greatness and left a few hours later looking for the fastest way to the airport. As I was wrapping up, I paused a moment before wishing Robinson well. "Anything else?" he asked.

I shook my head and tucked my notebook away.

Years later I interviewed then-Redskins Coach Norv Turner, one of Robinson's USC assistants. I also interviewed Tennessee Titans Coach Jeff Fisher, a defensive back at USC in 1979. In both instances, I sidestepped our shared histories. Some coaches liked to think they had nothing in common with reporters. If these men held that view, far be it for me to try to change their opinion.

But of course, you didn't have to tell some of them. One afternoon I was interviewing Georgia's Vince Dooley when he paused in mid-conversation and asked me about LSU. "What was Cholly Mac like to play for?" he said suddenly, ignoring the question I'd asked him.

I needed a few seconds to get my bearings. "Oh, I loved him," I said finally, "and I loved playing for him. Next to my father, he's the finest man I ever knew. He's had a bigger impact on my life than anyone. I'll forever be indebted to him."

This was my stock answer. And though I'd leaned too heavily on cliché, every word of it was true. I was sure I'd have been even more forthcoming with someone other than a coach. "Oh, I loved him," I'd have said. "But there were days when I came close to hating him too. Like the times he embarrassed me in film sessions, playing my mistakes over and over for all my teammates to see. And that Friday afternoon he called me out for wearing a T-shirt, painter's pants, and sandals. This is true. We were getting ready to go to a movie, and I'd disobeyed his dress code. And, well ... he really let me have it for that. He asked me if my mother and father taught me to dress that way or if I'd learned it on my own. I never forgot that. And I never forgave him, either, even though I was the one who should've asked *him* for forgiveness, wearing what I did when everyone else had on dress slacks and nice shirts. My point being ... yes, I loved Coach Mac. I loved him very much."

"When you talk to him again," Dooley said, "please be sure to tell him I asked about him."

"I sure will. I'm sure he'll appreciate that."

Coach Mac tried to reach me at the office one more time. He called my parents' home in Opelousas and spoke to my father. "Can you ask John Ed to give me a call?" he said. I was away on assignment when Daddy left the message on my answering machine. By the time I returned to Washington almost a week later, I was sure the reason Mac had called was old news, hardly worth his time or mine. Besides, I didn't want to bother him.

I TOOK A WEEK off from work and returned to Opelousas. On my first day home, my father challenged me to a round of golf at the Indian Hills Country Club. I accepted on the condition that he and I play the course alone. I hoped to talk to him about Connie and my intention to marry her at last.

I'd known her for more than four years, and although I'd gone as long as seven months at a stretch without seeing her, whenever we did get together I understood with certainty that I'd never be truly happy unless I closed the distance between us. After countless arguments, breakups, and vows never to see each other again, we always managed to find our way back together.

Even though I was twenty-eight years old, Connie and I continued to see each other in secret, not wishing to upset my parents. It was absurd that at my age I was still hiding her from them, but I'd long ago stopped blaming myself for the subterfuge. Mom and Dad, I learned, had endured their own struggle to reconcile the end of my LSU story. I was seventeen when I left home to join Coach Mac and the team, and my parents continued to mistake me for that boy, the one whose room across the hall still had trophies lining the shelves, purple-and-gold pennants hanging from the walls, and baskets filled with letters from recruiters telling him how great he was going to be.

At Christmas I'd tried to talk to my mother about Connie. She'd collapsed in a fit of tears, and my father had carried her in his arms to bed. As she lay there crying, Daddy had walked up to me and stared in my eyes until I turned away. He then asked me to leave the house, his voice breaking as he pointed to the door.

I was finally ready to set a wedding date, and I wanted my father to support my decision even if he didn't like it. I had no doubt that my announcement would upset him, and as we played the course I tried in vain to speak the words I'd rehearsed so many times in my head. In the end I couldn't do it—I couldn't speak her name in front of him, let alone tell him how much I loved her. When I was sixty and my father was eighty-six years old, I'd still need him to be proud of me.

As we moved slowly from hole to hole in his cart, I realized I'd never really talked to him at length about anything except football. Our inability to communicate was as much my fault as his. There were things I either never learned how to do or never had been taught how to do, and talking to my father about love was one of them.

Seeing him in the sun that day, I couldn't get over the peppery gray that highlighted what only a few years ago had been a bristly blond mustache. He was fifty-four now. "You're getting old, Pip," I said as he prepared to clobber a ball with an expensive graphite club.

We had reached the ninth hole, and I'd quit worrying about how to bring up Connie. Instead, I was trying to enjoy what remained of our time on the course. I hoped to wreck his concentration so he'd muff the shot.

"You've gone gray," I told him. "You're skinny, and the muscles in your arms have shrunk down to nothing. What's happened to your arms, Pip?"

"I can still drive the ball farther than you."

"Those days are numbered. Enjoy them while they last."

He looked up from the tee and his eyes blazed, and he smiled the most extraordinary smile, as if he held some secret over me. He swiveled his hips the way he'd seen the pros do on television, and he reset his spiked shoes.

"Don't blow it," I told him. "We've already lost six balls."

"Yeah, but you've lost five of 'em."

"Please don't make it seven."

He pulled the club back, ready to swing, and it came to me that I needed to say something. "I love you, Pip. Pip, you know I love you, don't you?"

But my father was quiet, fixed in concentration, watching the ball sail off to the right, deep into the tall pine trees.

WHENEVER THE PAPER sent me out on the road, I brought a hard copy of my novel along with me. I worked on the manuscript in airports, hotel rooms, car rental agencies, press boxes, all-night diners, and any other place where I found myself with a little extra time.

The book was about a former LSU football player, the unfortunately named John Girlie, whose girlfriend, an older woman, didn't meet his mother's approval. John lived for the hours late at night when he stole away from his mother's house and met with his mysterious lover. John's father was nowhere in the picture. He'd abandoned the family years before.

After years of work, the manuscript pages were dog-eared and ringed with coffee stains, and some were so crowded with editing marks that they looked like drip paintings. I enjoyed working on stories for the paper, but I liked time on the book more. Connie came back to me in a character named Emma Groves, and I revisited the cold winter nights in Opelousas—called Old Field in the story—when I walked through the park to meet her and stopped to look at the football field. I borrowed from memory to build the love scenes between John and Emma, and I lifted dialogue spoken by Connie and me. The book let me escape to that time before our problems became so profound that I quit trying to repair them.

As I reached the end of the novel, I struggled to come up with a way to pull it all together. In one draft, John and Emma left Old Field and drove north, determined to find a new life in a place where they didn't have to hide. In another, the one I decided to stick with, John left town alone in search of a new identity and soon learned from a news report that Emma had killed herself.

Neither of the endings was rooted in the truth, but I preferred the second version because it tapped the deep well of guilt I felt for not delivering on the promises I'd made to Connie. I never did move her and her children up to Washington. I never built her a house filled with light and decorated with oil paintings; we didn't get married and have kids together. After I couldn't tell my father that I wanted to marry her, Connie and I quickly devolved from the world's greatest lovers to phone friends. I had both the job at the paper and a novel to finish. I promised to see her when I could. Connie had no illusions about what that meant.

I called the book *Famous Days and Tupelo Nights*, a title that was as clumsy as it was long, and one destined to be shortened. The tupelo gum tree grew in the bottomlands surrounding Opelousas, and it made an appearance in the cemeteries of Old Field, where John and Emma, having so few other options, retreated at night to be alone.

After my literary agent sold the book to a New York publisher, I handed in my letter of resignation to the *Post*. The advance was less than a third of what I earned in a year at the paper, but I'd saved some money, and if finances got tight I could always write magazine articles. To celebrate the deal, the paper threw a lunch in my honor in a room off the publisher's suite. Katharine Graham wasn't around, and neither was Ben Bradlee, but the party did draw plenty of the talent that made the paper what it was each day.

One after another, colleagues gave toasts and testimonials, and I sat there and let them have their fun with me. We had cake and champagne, and toward the end of the party I thanked everyone then invited them to come visit me in Louisiana if ever they found themselves down South with nothing to do.

I left the office later that day feeling the way I had when I walked off the field at Tiger Stadium after my last game. "Don't take it with you," Coach Mac had told us. "Leave it out there. Leave it all out on the field."

A few weeks later I called my father and told him I planned to mail him a copy of the novel as soon as I could have one made. The prospect of my father sitting down with my tawdry little tale was a source of tremendous dread. Ex-football coaches didn't go for flowery love talk. They could do without hearing about sex, either. And apparently they weren't good on the phone. "That's nice," my dad said. "Here, want to talk to your mother?"

That night the phone in my apartment rang at around 3 a.m. I was living in Georgetown, a place with twelve-foot ceilings and an antique chandelier in the bathroom. It wasn't the house I'd fantasized about years before, but I never knew a better bachelor pad. It couldn't have been an editor calling with an assignment. I no longer worked for the paper. I found the phone after a couple of stabs, nearly knocking a lamp off the bedside table.

It was my brother Bobby, calling from a hospital waiting room. I could hear people crying in the background even before he said anything.

THEY TOOK ME to see him one last time. He was wearing a suit and tie and one of my football watches, the white face with the Sun Bowl emblem peeking out from under the cuff of his dress shirt. I placed my hand over the watch and felt it ticking. My mother walked up and stood next to me. "So his heart stops but the watch doesn't," I said.

"I'll make sure to remove it later."

"No, leave it on him. I'd just stick it in a closet, anyway."

"But you'll want it one day."

I shook my head. "I don't think so, Mama."

Hundreds of people turned out, many of them his players from long ago. They were all middle-aged men now, and they stood by the flower arrangements and cried like babies. Some came over to talk about the days when they played at OHS. They called him Coach, a name that still sounded right even though he hadn't worn that hat in almost twenty years.

He'd been out playing golf at Indian Hills, this time with my brothers and a family friend, when he seemed to pull a muscle in his back as he chipped out of the sand trap on the fourteenth hole. They'd cut the game short and gone home, and he'd had lunch outside on the patio. His skin was dull and gray, and he wouldn't stop sweating. "Don't you think it's your heart?" Mom had said to him. "No, I don't think so," he'd answered, although the expression on his face told a different story.

She'd persuaded him to let her drive him to the hospital, and moments after they arrived at the emergency room he told her he was sorry. They'd planned a family barbecue to celebrate Memorial Day weekend, and it didn't look like he'd be able to help her with dinner. "Johnny, don't worry about that," Mom had said, then a nurse had led her to the waiting room.

It wasn't long after, half an hour perhaps, when the doctor arrived to tell her he'd suffered a heart attack. In the hours that followed, more than a hundred people from the town showed up. At around 2 a.m., when half a dozen family members remained, my mother suddenly sat up in her chair. "Daddy's gone," she said.

My sister Gina had been lying on the floor, trying to sleep. She sat up, too. "Why do you say that, Mama?"

"I just have a feeling he's gone."

Minutes later a doctor walked into the room and told her he was dead.

We drove him out to the cemetery at Bellevue in a long procession and placed him at the foot of his mother's grave. My paternal grandmother's name was Louisiana Guilbeau Bradley. She wasn't Missouri or California or Wisconsin Bradley. She was *Louisiana* Bradley. I didn't want to leave him out there, but the gravediggers were waiting not far away in the shade of a cedar tree. I looked at them standing by their backhoe and smoking cigarettes in the heat, and my head was screaming curse words, letting God have it as surely He deserved it. Finally, my brothers cuffed me under the arms and led me away.

I stayed that week in the house on Delmas Street. This one night I was lying in bed in the small room I once shared with my brothers. The hours moved by, my mother's clocks chiming every fifteen minutes, a big one in the kitchen ringing bells that left a hum in the hall long after they'd stopped. Near dawn, I got out of bed and put on some gym shorts, a T-shirt, and running shoes. I started toward the park, taking it slow at first because I hadn't bothered to stretch. I couldn't outrun the images that kept flooding my head, but I figured I could replace one kind of hurt with another.

The stadium was dark, all the gates closed and locked with chains. Three parallel strands of barbed wire ran along the top of the fence, but they didn't keep me from scaling it. I climbed a ramp up to the seats and ran the stairs to the top. There was still enough starlight to see by. My legs seemed driven by memory, recalling the distance from one step to the next. The stadium was divided into three sections. I ran down the stairs of the first section, sprinted to the center section stairs, and climbed them to the press box, and then I descended again and raced to the third section. It was how I used to run the stadium in those long-ago summers before two-a-days, gobbling up one section at a time. It was harder now than it had been then. My legs began to cramp, and my knees and ankles hurt. I quit after covering only a couple of sections.

In Washington I had a rowing machine in my bedroom, but I used it more as a clothes hanger. I walked up the center section to the uppermost bleacher and stretched out on my back on the aluminum bench. The old press box, no bigger than a house trailer, filled the space above me, blocking the stars from view. I was hot and sweating, but I somehow managed to sleep. When I woke, about an hour later, there was sunlight on the grass, and cars were beginning to move past the trees on Union Street.

I took it all in then started home again.

Chapter Six

SEE MARTY

THE OUTDOOR KITCHEN seemed smaller than before. The air smelled of dust and mold; dead insects lay on the windowsills. It took hours to clean the place and coax the sunshine back in. I replaced the sofa and chairs with new living room furniture and a cherry bedroom suite. I cleared my work clothes from the closet and hung the suits and sport jackets I'd worn at the paper, most of them of no use to me anymore. I carried the Adler typewriter out to the shed and laid it on the floor next to a plastic milk crate holding my dad's golf balls, and in its place, I put a new computer straight out of the box.

In the mornings, I drove out to Bellevue. It was a pretty thing to see the light coming up behind the trees and drying off the dew and gossamer. I sat on my father's grave and picked weeds and chewed the ends, some days talking out loud to him, other times listening to the trucks rattling down Highway 182 and the birds in the nearby bean fields. August came, and with it the start of two-a-days, and nothing I'd ever known was harder than accepting that he wouldn't be there for football season.

Brent, now sixteen, was a star receiver at Opelousas Catholic, and I regarded it as yet another pathetic failure on God's part that my father wasn't around to see him play. On weeknights, when my mother sat in a chair in the living room with the lights off, I knew better than to disturb her. Those days were long. But always we knew that Friday was coming and soon we'd be at the game, sitting on bleacher seats in the old stadium where Daddy still seemed more alive than anyplace else.

Mom and I applauded every time Brent touched the ball or made a big hit, and when the game was over, we waited for him outside the stadium dressing room to tell him how well he'd played. I felt it was my duty to do this. I couldn't figure out how he did it, but the boy went the entire season without once pulling me aside to tell me I had a long way to go if I meant to walk in our father's shoes.

Tupelo Nights had already come and gone from the stores, and my publisher informed me that it was cheaper to sell the unsold copies by the pound or convert them to pulp than to continue warehousing them. The book had made me neither rich nor famous. "One day they'll find it again and it'll get the attention it deserves," Connie said.

"Right," I said and laughed.

I hid my remaining copies in the back of a closet—in much the same way that I'd squirreled away football memorabilia years before. This seemed a better alternative than to have to look at them on a shelf and acknowledge that the book had once meant everything. In her bedroom, Connie displayed a framed copy of the author photo that appeared on the book's dust jacket. Every night, I tipped it over and left it lying facedown. By the time I returned the next day, she'd put it upright again.

Connie was a good nurse. When the dark days began to pile up one after the other, I could always count on her to help me get through them.

Somewhere along the way she had stopped asking me when I planned to marry her, and her desire to spend time with me now seemed driven less by a lover's passion than by a caregiver's pity. We tried to pretend that my father's ghost didn't sit with us every time I went to her house to visit. He hadn't wanted me to marry her when he was alive. Was there any way I was going to disappoint him now that he was dead? But she sidled up to me once. I knew what was coming before she said it. "What about later in the summer, before the kids go back to school?"

"Let me think about it," I answered.

In the afternoon, the high point of my day, I threw a football out in the yard with her twelve-year-old son, Brandt. Every now and then I checked my punt snap, firing the ball back between my legs the way I'd done it in the old days. Brandt ran fly patterns, and I tried to hit him in stride. The ball wobbled like a duck, missed the mark, and bounded away in the weeds. We played until it got dark, and I returned to the outdoor kitchen and lay in bed composing letters in my head to Ben Bradlee. Like the first one I sent, they were filled with stories about how I'd gone about the business of wasting my life. At the end of each, I politely asked him to consider hiring me back.

Connie wanted me to call the LSU football office for tickets. She thought it would be fun for Brandt and the girls to attend a game in Tiger Stadium. "The games are all sellouts," I said, hoping she'd believe me. "There are no tickets to be had."

"There would be for you, John Ed."

"Connie, I don't have any pull over there anymore."

"You don't need pull. Just call and tell them who you are. You gave a lot to that school. The least they could do is find you some tickets."

"Nobody there remembers me. And I won't put myself through that, calling there and having them tell me no."

That night I caught her staring at me. "You know what your problem is? You're too proud."

"Yes, I am. I am too proud."

She never asked me to take them to a game again.

On Saturday nights, I did my best to sit with Brandt and watch the LSU games that were televised. When they were on the radio only, I tried to listen. Either way, I never lasted long. The sound of the band in the minutes before kickoff was enough to send me outside. I stood in the middle of the yard looking up at the stars—the same stars that shone now over the field at Tiger Stadium and had lit up the sky when I was a player. The ones from all those years ago when my father had barbecued with his radio blaring. I could hide from the radio and the TV, but I knew I'd never be able to live another autumn Saturday night without missing him.

I finally went back inside and sat alone in Connie's living room with a book. By 8:30, I knew, it was halftime, and the players had returned to the locker room. Divided into groups by position, they studied still photos of their opponents' formations and tried to figure out what adjustments to make. I could conjure up these meetings, hear the questions from the players and the answers from the coaches, their voices hoarse from trying to be heard above the crowd. *"Hey, Coach, how am I supposed to get the backside backer if the nose guard is shading my shoulder and throwing interference at me as soon as I snap the ball?"*

"Do the guard and I call off the double-team when mike steps up and fills the hole like that?"

"Since I can't feel anything in my right shoulder, Coach, you think we could get John to scoot up a little and take the punt snap at twelve yards rather than fifteen? I can barely get the damn thing back to him."

By 9:30 the players were on the field, holding up four fingers to indicate that the final quarter belonged to them. By 10:30 they were peeling off jerseys and pads, removing ankle wraps, and either celebrating or talking about the week to come. *"We're not Ole Miss, I tell you that. They don't come to Tiger Stadium and score four touchdowns by halftime. And nobody keeps this offense out of the end zone. Hell, no, they don't."*

By the time I left Connie for the night, the players had returned to the dorm and settled into their rooms for curfew check. Some had ice packs fitted with wraps over injuries, others hobbled on crutches. When you walked the hall to the bathroom, you heard moans coming up in a chorus, a sound you knew you'd never forget. I wondered if this year's squad had a guy like Big Ed Stanton, who prayed on his knees on the side of his bed, thanking God in a whisper for helping him win another one. I wondered too if there was anybody like John Adams, whose legs cramped so bad he had to beat them against his bed frame to get the muscles to loosen up. *Ba-boom, ba-boom, ba-boom, ba-boom, ba-boom, ba-boom ...*

"Damn, John, what the damn hell are you doing to your damn self?"

Ba-boom, ba-boom, ba-boom, ba-boom ...

WE WERE TOUGH PEOPLE, those of us on the offensive line. A guy might have skinny arms and a flat ass, and his three-point stance might make him look like he was digging for a contact lens in the grass, but at the snap of the ball, he was the bitter end of dreams for anyone who tried to get past him and touch our quarterback. Likewise, I saw fat boys with stretch marks and acres of jiggling flesh dominate linebackers that Arnold Schwarzenegger himself might've chiseled out of stone.

We reported to class in the morning with leaky sores on our knuckles and forearms and wounds on our necks that looked like hickeys left as souvenirs by sexually rapacious girlfriends. Some of us had hematomas on our triceps that stayed purple from August through January. The bruising came from helmet blows delivered by fellow linemen who crashed against us while executing double-team blocks. Many of us limped. And many of us shaved our heads as proof that we really didn't give a crap. We didn't give a crap about *anything*, including the fact that we were so ugly we scared people and gave them strokes and heart attacks.

Most of us were too large for classroom desks that were roomy for other students. Some of us had to duck and turn sideways when we entered narrow doorways with low overheads. Strangers approached us on the street and stood staring. "How tall are you?" they asked. "How much do you weigh? Think you could lift a cow over your head?"

Most of us were exceptionally quiet men who didn't want to expend unnecessary energy by speaking. People who talked too much—receivers and cornerbacks—deserved our suspicion. We were not frivolous. We hoarded each word as if it were the difference between winning and losing. We knew our value, even when others did not.

Nobody worked harder than the offensive line, and nobody with any sense ever questioned this point.

On our team, number 50 belonged to Jay Whitley, pride of Baton Rouge's Lee High. Fifty-one was Lou deLaunay, 52 Kevin Lair and later Leigh Shepard, 53 Steve Estes and Jim Holsombake, 54 Rocky Guillot. Fifty-five was linebacker S.J. Saia, and then, at the start of my sophomore year, the number went to Marty Dufrene, who probably was the toughest offensive lineman ever to come out of Lafourche Parish, a place known for good football.

"Where you come from, Dufrene, talking with an accent like *dat*?"

"Down de bayou, *cher*. Where else you think I'm from?"

My number, 56, came next. Look in any souvenir program from 1979, and there, side-by-side, were Marty and me, two peas in a pod.

How did I first learn about his accident? Did it turn up in a news story about efforts to raise money to help pay his medical bills? Did I receive another tearful call from one of my siblings?

I went into my office and closed the door. I called information for his number, and then I did an amazing thing: I dialed it. Marty's wife, Lynne, answered, and I went through the awkward business of introducing myself, my voice betraying a slight wobble as I told her my name. "Lynne, do you remember me from back in school?" I said.

"Yes, I remember you," she said. "You want to talk to Marty? Hold on, John Ed. It's going to take a few minutes because I have to put him on the speakerphone."

When he finally came on, he sounded as if he were trapped at the bottom of a well.

"Marty, is it true you got hurt?"

"Yeah. Yeah, it is true."

"You're paralyzed, man?"

"Yeah—" He raised his voice to make sure I could hear him. "I broke my neck. Can you believe that shit?"

It had happened a few years earlier, in June of 1986, when he was a student at a chiropractic college in Texas. He and Lynne were at a school party, and he was standing on the steps leading down to a wading pool. One of his schoolmates grabbed him and held him in a headlock. The guy was horsing around, and there was no way he could handle Marty alone. So a second student slammed against Marty, driving him toward the water. The pool was only about two and a half feet deep. Marty smashed hard against the liquid surface, and then he struck bottom, shattering a vertebra.

As he gave the details, I kept seeing the boy I knew at LSU, the one who had pushed me so hard that at times I cursed him to hell and back. I didn't tell him that I'd avoided my teammates with the kind of dedication a recovering alcoholic devoted to avoiding the bottle. He would've laughed at that, considering what he'd been through. Instead I said, "Marty, I'd like to come see you. Can I do that?"

"Yeah, sure, it would be great to see you again."

"I'll do it. I promise. Just give me some time."

"Sure, whatever you need, John Ed. I'd like to catch up."

"Marty, I'm sorry I didn't call earlier. I only got the news a few minutes ago."

"Don't worry about that. It's fine, man. We're teammates, right?"

But I didn't visit Marty or follow up with another call. I didn't even bother to write to him with an excuse or an explanation. I thought about him all the time, though, and I imagined what he must have been thinking: Why'd that sonofabitch call me? Why'd he tell me he was coming if he had no intention of doing it?

My own questions weren't much different: What made me think I had the right to bother him? Did being his teammate entitle me to ask him to revisit the worst day he'd ever lived?

But the big question, the one I asked myself more than any other, was this: What was my obligation to my teammates, the people I'd played football with all those years ago? I never did come up with an answer.

See Marty, I wrote on the memo pad I kept on my desk. The next day I put a square around the words. The day after that, I added a circle. By the end of the week, I'd drawn a star around the encircled square and obliterated the words with squiggles.

The odd-looking doodle kept growing until it took up every bit of the paper. To anyone else, it might've served as evidence that I had too much time on my hands. I saw something else—the message under the ink.

I ripped the paper off the pad and threw it away.

See Marty, I began again, and then added a square around the words first thing the next morning when I sat down to start my day.

THEY PUT SOMETHING in Dennis Quaid's hair to lighten it, and although the new color translated well on screen, in person it was an unusual combination of metallic greens and yellows, rather like the leaves of a banana plant after the first cold snap in winter. When it wasn't swept straight back, imitating a 1950s pompadour, it was loosely parted down the middle, bangs hanging and partially obscuring Quaid's eyes. His new film, *Everybody's All-American*, was being released nationwide this week, and Quaid was living in a suite in the Peabody Hotel in Memphis while he worked on his next project, *Great Balls of Fire!*, a biopic about vintage rocker Jerry Lee Lewis.

The actor and I had a lot in common, the editor at *Esquire* magazine said when he called to offer me the assignment. *Everybody's All-American* had been shot in Baton Rouge with Tiger Stadium as a key location. And Quaid, a Houston native, apparently loved the state of Louisiana as much as I did, in part because he'd scored his biggest hit to date playing the role of a New Orleans cop in *The Big Easy*. Also like me, he had enjoyed a close relationship with his father, who died of a heart attack in 1987, the same year that my own dad died. Quaid liked to have a good time, and he'd so immersed himself in the role of Jerry Lee Lewis that, like The Killer himself, he seemed to be rushing headlong into trouble. "See if you two can go out together and knock back a few," my editor had said. "We're going to run it on the cover, so make it good."

Quaid was smaller than any football player I'd ever known, but he was as easy to be around as the best of my old teammates. We talked for hours in the living room of his suite and in his mobile home near the set. One afternoon in the trailer, he popped a bag of popcorn in the microwave, then emptied the contents on a table-top. Holding his head a few inches from the pile, he shoveled the popcorn into his mouth using both hands, pushing in as much as he could accommodate. I moved my tape recorder out of the way. I didn't want to hear the noise again when I transcribed the inter-view. He wiped the table down with a paper towel, then lowered himself to the floor and knocked out a set of crunches. Finished with the exercise, he drank from a large bottle of water, wheezing through his nose for air.

One moment he came across as candid, sincere, and down-to-earth. The next he was wild and unpredictable, acting out with a barely restrained lunacy. He liked telling stories about his father and his older brother, Randy, a fine actor himself. He told me about Meg Ryan, whom he would one day marry, although he was reluctant to provide many details. He answered all of my questions without complaining, and yet the one thing I couldn't bring myself to ask him, the one thing I most wanted to know, was how it had felt to be in Tiger Stadium filming the game scenes for *Everybody's All-American*.

Memphis was cold and breezy the night I joined Quaid for a rehearsal with veteran musicians at Sun Studio, where Lewis had recorded many of his hits. They played for hours before Quaid called for a break. He walked outside behind the building with a portable TV and spent several minutes searching for the local station that aired *Siskel & Ebert*, the syndicated movie review show featur-ing Chicago critics Gene Siskel and Roger Ebert. If the critics stuck to schedule, tonight's reviews would include *Everybody's All-American*.

Quaid was fidgety when the program began. Though the screen was only about five inches wide and the reception lousy, it was still painful to watch as the critics, even snider than usual, gave the film two thumbs-down. Quaid's performance, which had received effusive praise from other important reviewers, was hardly mentioned.

Quaid put the TV down and returned to the piano. He started banging out a tune but then suddenly broke off. "You work on a film as hard as we worked on that one," he said, "and you're as proud of it as I am, and everybody has great things to say about it, and then these two guys in a couple of minutes tell you it isn't any good and you're not any good."

I was tempted to tell him about one particularly bad review of *Tupelo Nights*, received from a literary critic whose opinion strongly influenced those who bought and read books, but I knew better than to trip in that hole. I'd only get upset again, and the night would turn into a pitch-and-catch about the cruelty of certain people, and we'd have to quit early and return to our hotel rooms to work out in private the reasons why we were so misunderstood.

Quaid eyed the bottle of Jack Daniel's that one of the musicians had placed on top of the piano. "Hey, Killer," somebody said, "can I pour you a drink?"

"Yeah, what the hell. Pour me a drink."

The next day, Quaid and I drove south to the rural estate in Mississippi where Jerry Lee Lewis lived. We passed through enormous iron gates shaped like a grand piano and stopped at the end of a drive next to a rambling brick house. On the far side of the lake in front of us, three large dogs chased after a goose and a mallard duck. Lewis's wife, Kerrie, stood at the water's edge, shouting *"Kill-her, Kill-her, Kill-her.* Stop that and come back here, *Kill-her."*

The back door opened, and Jerry Lee Lewis stuck his head out. "What'd I do now?" he said, looking befuddled.

The three dogs came bounding toward us. "Which one is Killer?" I said.

"All three of them," Kerrie answered. She pointed each one out. "That one there is Killer, this one here's Killer, and he's Killer too."

"Well, that sure makes it easy, doesn't it?" Quaid said, flashing the large, white-toothed smile that had become his signature.

We went inside the house to a small den. The room held a collection of decorative ceramic decanters, and I spotted a couple made in the likeness of Elvis Presley, Lewis's onetime rival. Another looked like an LSU tiger holding a football. As I stood before the shelves, I asked Lewis if he recalled performing for the LSU team in December of 1978 at an event sponsored by the Liberty Bowl. My teammates and I, along with members of the Missouri team, had caught the show at the popular local restaurant where we'd stopped for breakfast one morning after practice. Although it was the most electrifying musical performance I'd ever seen, Lewis had begun cursing and screaming when we shouted for him to play "Great Balls of Fire." "You don't just play 'Great Balls of Fire,'" he'd said. "Singing a song like 'Great Balls of Fire' is like making love to a woman. Let me ask you boys something: Any of you ever make love to a woman? I didn't think so. You ever made love to a woman, you'd know what I'm talking about."

"What year did you say that was?" Lewis asked.

I told him.

"No," he said, "I can't say I do remember. But there was a stretch there when I did things that people still ask me about and I have little or no memory of them at all."

Lewis sat quietly and pondered a past that others owned with more authority than he did. I wondered if this might be a way for me to retire large chunks of my own memory: get so wasted day after day that the mind forgot to remember. But what did the mind

206

do with all those days that had been lived before the bingeing began? Did it purge them, too? Or did they become the only memory and grow all the larger? If that was the result, I supposed it made more sense not to drink at all.

Lewis asked Quaid how filming was coming along, and Quaid encouraged him to stop by the set for a visit. Except for their hairdos, the two bore little resemblance to each other, but it was still curious to sit with them in the same room, the man and the man who would play him. If Lewis seemed distant, it probably had something to do with his much-publicized battle with the IRS over unpaid taxes. I'd read in one news report that Lewis had installed a security door at the entrance to his bedroom to keep the authorities out. I considered asking him for a look at the famous door, but I didn't want to come across as insensitive. He'd been so gracious.

We walked back outside. The dogs were sleeping in the shade of a tree. "We used to have a dozen other ducks and geese," Lewis said, "but the boys got hungry one day and had them for supper."

I looked around for the goose and the duck we'd seen earlier, but they were nowhere to be found. There wasn't even a ripple on the lake.

On Friday I traveled with Quaid and his assistant to a suburban shopping mall and the multiplex cinema that was screening *Everybody's All-American*. We waited in an office until moments before the movie began, then a manager led us into the dark and crowded theater, his flashlight moving a dim circle over spongy red carpet. Our chairs were next to an aisle in the center section, roped off with yellow crime-scene tape. Quaid sat up tall and squeezed his lips together, the fingers of his right hand nervously tugging at his chin.

Everybody's All-American, based on a novel by Frank Deford, told the story of a football star named Gavin Grey who struggled to find a meaningful life after his playing days ended. In the book,

Grey was a Tar Heel from North Carolina, but the film's producers shot the film in Louisiana, in large part because of LSU's legendary program and the epic beauty of Tiger Stadium. I had little in common with Grey the superstar. In his time he was the best, most celebrated player in the land, more akin to Billy Cannon. And yet I understood Grey's confusion and frustration as he attempted to carve out a new identity in a world without football. On-screen, Quaid wore a purple-and-gold jacket similar to the one I had at home. A big, yellow L decorated with gold bars signified the number of years he'd lettered. As the story unfolded, he was so convincing that I got lost in the narrative and forgot that he was seated next to me. And suddenly I was back in Baton Rouge, on the field under the stars. It was Saturday night.

The crowd noises awakened an old feeling in me, and soon I was slumped in my chair, pinned down by nostalgia. Once again, I began to plot my exit. But how could I get up and walk out without offending Quaid? On the screen, Grey and his teammates were battling to come from behind in the Sugar Bowl. I bought into the illusion. Somehow Quaid was now the one who'd played for LSU. I felt a deep, jealous burn, seeing him race down the sideline to the end zone and the last-minute, come-from-behind victory. A camera panned the stadium, resplendent as always in purple and gold. Cheers came up like an ocean roar.

I had decided to tell Quaid that I wasn't feeling well and needed to go to the men's room when Quaid himself rose to his feet and started up the aisle toward the lobby. I watched him disappear, and then I turned back to the screen. When will you let it go? I thought to myself. Is your assignment to have a panic attack and embarrass yourself in front of the movie star or to write a story about him? I closed my eyes, and the stadium scenes gave way to Grey's domestic troubles with his wife, former beauty queen and sorority belle Babs Rogers, played by Jessica Lange. Even with the period makeup and hairdo, Lange was too old to play Babs. Her interaction with Quaid was the movie's biggest weakness, and their unconvincing duet helped me get my mind off the football scenes and regain my equilibrium.

Moments before the movie ended, Quaid returned to his seat. He wasn't as jittery as before. Smiling the way he always did, he said, "Go Tigers," then slumped down deep in his chair.

In the Lincoln Town Car on the way to Sun Studio for another rehearsal, I watched the city recede from the rear window, and I wondered what my teammates would make of the film. Would Quaid's performance move them as it had me? Would they recognize themselves in Gavin Grey?

We ended up at Rum Boogie Cafe on Beale Street later that night. Quaid climbed on the bandstand and started playing an old Jerry Lee Lewis song on the piano. I sought out the company of one of the film's co-stars. She told me she had someone at home, and of course, I had Connie waiting, but the booze and the music soon had the two of us clinging to each other on the dance floor. Quaid, lacquered in sweat, hair flying, seemed to be channeling The Killer with exceptional ease. He performed until the house lights came up and management kicked the doors open.

The actress and I staggered back to the hotel and stood holding each other in the hallway outside her room. I wanted to tell her how lost I'd felt watching *Everybody's All-American*, how a small, greedy part of me had been ready to discredit Quaid even as I'd applauded him and thanked him for letting me share in his triumph. But it was 3 a.m. and she was leading me toward her bed, dropping articles of clothing a piece at a time the way I once had with Connie. The actress was lying naked on the sheets. "We can't, you know?" I told her between kisses. "We might want to, but we can't."

"No one has to know."

"But we would know."

The next time I saw her was at a theater back home. Connie and I had gone for a Friday matinee of *Great Balls of Fire!* "She's really a whole lot prettier in person," I said, whispering because the room was full.

EVEN THOUGH I'D MOVED from the outdoor kitchen years before, the Post Office still delivered some of my mail to Delmas Street. Mama put it in the basket on her kitchen counter, the same one that had held fan letters and news clippings when I was in school. As soon as the basket filled up, she called and told me to come by and get them.

I should've sat her down and tried to explain myself. I should've told her how unnerved I got every time I received a padded bag holding a vintage souvenir program or a trading card for me to sign. The notes about reunions and tailgate parties upset me too, and I should've tried to tell her why. I still loved it too much, and I was sick of the burden of loving it too much, and I should've been able to say that. "Mom," I should've said, "it stopped being about LSU football a long time ago and started being about who I can't ever be again no matter what I do or how hard I try."

Instead I told her, "It'll be fine. Trust me. Put it in the trash."

We were on the phone together. "But it might be important," she said.

"Does it look important? Hold it by a corner, and swing it up to the ceiling light. If you see something that looks like a check, then don't throw it away. Everything else can go."

The athletic department wrote twice and invited me back. In both instances, I was slow to respond. And so the phone rang, and that was how I found myself speaking in an enthusiastic tone with a person of note, who was explaining how nice it would be for everybody to see me again. The person of note was such a charming fellow, so friendly and persuasive, that if he'd asked me to hitchhike to Krotz Springs and take a leap from the Atchafalaya River Bridge, I'm sure I'd have strongly considered doing it.

"You're right," I said. "It really wouldn't hurt, would it?"

They wanted me to walk out on the field before kickoff and accept an honorary captain's award. I showed up wearing a gold sport coat and khaki pants, spooked beyond telling to be in the stadium again. Fifteen years had passed since the 1979 USC game, which now seemed to have achieved legendary status among the fans, and I had come to celebrate with them.

All I had to do was stand at the hash mark and receive a plaque. But a delay left me alone on the sideline, waiting to be introduced. I knew better than to look away from the field. There were eighty thousand people filling the seats, most of them anxious to see the Tigers win, not a one of them caring about what I cared about, and that was to make sure to lift my feet high and avoid the divots.

The fans had to be tired of this stunt. Every home game, the school trotted out another one—the old, the crippled, the fat, and the bald. I was this week's reminder to enjoy your youth while you had it, proof that college football stars were no more immune to the cruelties of time than anybody else. Eat your veggies, boys and girls. And don't forget to floss!

To get past the nervousness, I found myself doing something I'd done when I was a player. Using my right index finger, I wrote lines from poems I'd memorized on my thigh. James Whitehead, Richard Hugo, Philip Levine, Miller Williams—these were the voices that had spoken to me back then. The effect of writing on my leg had never failed as a miracle cure for pain. It soothed me, taking my mind away from the neck burn or chest wound leaking blood, giving me beauty in that moment when I thought I couldn't endure. Tonight the words and the act of writing them provided the same relief.

As I walked to the hash mark, the announcer listed some of the awards I'd won as a player. Then he named my books. By this time I'd published four novels, and he announced the first, third, and fourth titles, before finishing with the second one: *The Best There Ever Was.* Only about eighteen people in the whole world had read it, but somehow the announcer made it sound as if I were the best there ever was. His voice rose louder and louder, and the crowd chased after him with roars. When he finished, people jumped to their feet and beat their hands together, really letting me hear it for being so great. I knew that most of them were scratching their heads before they could even sit back down, everyone saying to everybody else, "Who was that again?"

"That there was the best there ever was."

"Yeah, but who was he?"

And everybody at the same time giving a shrug. "I don't know. I don't remember who he was. But he was the best, I'll tell you that much."

When they trotted me out again, several years later, it was raining, and like a fool I showed up without an umbrella or a poncho. I must've wanted everybody to see my outfit—a navy jacket that looked purple in a certain light and khaki slacks with gold thread in the weave. I must've thought that by wearing the LSU team colors, I was showing my loyalty. As long as I was wearing those clothes, no one had to know that I'd set foot in the stadium only twice since my eligibility had run out two decades before.

It was late in the year, and the game had failed to sell out. This time the announcer didn't bother to name my books, so no one was tricked into standing and making noise. I was no longer *the best there ever was ... !* I was just some schmo who looked like he was scribbling on his leg with his finger as they ushered him out before kickoff.

I accepted the plaque and raised an arm above my head in salute, and all the while I was somewhere else. There was applause, but so little, it sounded like a trout stream on Sunday night after all the fishermen went home. I left the field and entered a stadium corridor to get out of the rain.

I didn't want to seem ungrateful, but my hair was soaking wet and my clothes were clinging to my body. On top of that, it was starting to get cold, and my nipples were showing through my shirt. At halftime, when everyone was visiting the bathroom or going for food, I excused myself and started down the ramps. I walked straight out past the main gate and marched half a mile to my truck, some of the way in mud, the rain still falling. My good shoes were ruined. I kept my head down, trying to shield my face. When I got home I'd have to remove the cash from my wallet and lay it out on the kitchen table to dry. I'd have to pay the cleaners to see if they could do something to save my jacket. I'd found it at the Dillard's remainder store, and it must've been pretty cheap, because it was already bleeding a purplish cloud into my shirt.

"It never rains in Tiger Stadium." That was what people used to say when I was a kid. And I'd always believed them, imagining a large, oval patch of sky above the field that stayed clear all year long. I saw sunshine there even when it was wet and dark and brooding everywhere else. "It never rains in Tiger Stadium," they'd said. It was too bad I had to grow up and become a man to finally learn better.

I reached the truck and got inside and warmed the engine, letting the wipers thwack across the windshield. They were probably looking for me by now, wondering where I'd slipped off to. Or maybe they'd caught my exit and stood watching, struggling to understand why anyone would want to head for the parking lot with the outcome of the game still undecided. "What is wrong with that fellow?" I could hear them saying. "Why can't he get over himself?" And turning back to the field, they watched as the team came streaming out under the goalpost for the second half, and my retreat was forgotten, and their questions were never answered or visited again, even as they echoed in my head the rest of the night.

What is wrong with you? Why can't you get over yourself?

"It never rains in Tiger Stadium," they'd said. But tonight it seemed all I'd ever known there was the rain.

I put the truck in drive and started for the interstate.

I HATED MONDAYS. I hated the monotony of stretching and warmups, the drudgery of running the ropes and driving the eight- and single-man sleds, the frustration of facing scout-squad guys who were so eager to impress the coaches that they were doing bull rushes and swim moves even before I could get the ball to the quarterback and come up out of my stance. "It's Monday," you could tell them. "We're supposed to be half speed." And the next play they were doing it again. I hated how sometimes when I snapped the ball, it banged against my nuts and I felt an immediate urge to puke even though there was someone to block and no time to puke. Monday wasn't the only day I banged my nuts, but for some reason it hurt more then.

I hated how the thigh pads sucked and pulled at your hair and pinched your skin. I hated the restrictive hip girdle, with pads for the right and left flanks and a third pad that fitted over the crack of your ass and protected your tailbone. Truth is, my ass didn't need protecting; it was so corked with muscle that a master sushi chef couldn't have carved his initials in either buttock with a Ginsu knife.

On Mondays we ran conditioning drills after practice—another reason to hate the day. We drilled for ninety minutes, then lined up on the goal line and ran sprints in position groups. Most Mondays, we ran ten consecutive fifty-yard dashes with barely a break. Other Mondays we ran progressions. We began with a ten-yard sprint, then added ten yards to each successive sprint until we finished by running a hundred yards in the tall, soft grass. My sophomore year, the coaches introduced us to gassers. We ran ten yards, touched a foot on the line, broke back hard to the goal line, touched a foot on that line, then raced as hard as we could to the twenty-yard-line. At this point, every man started to feel a sharp pain in his ribs, and his lungs burned, and maybe his hamstrings were starting to cramp, but the drill didn't end there. We planted a foot on the 20 and cut back again for the goal line, then kept advancing by a distance of ten yards until we reached the 50. As soon as we hit that mark, we sprinted all the way back to the goal line, where it had all started. That was a gasser.

I used to wonder, even as I ran them: What kind of evil, twisted mind invents such a thing?

When we were done, I ripped my helmet off and flung it to the ground. I fell to a knee under the goalpost, making sure to keep a distance from the other players to prevent them from stealing my air. I screamed if anyone touched me. At this moment I was in such physical distress, I couldn't bear the weight of another man's finger, let alone his whole hand. Always, I endured the period by telling myself that it would make me stronger come Saturday night—my legs more resilient, my lungs more robust. I wondered if my opponent was running gassers. I wondered if he was sprinting back and forth in twenty pounds of equipment on days when the local TV weathermen were warning people that the best way to avoid death by heatstroke was to stay inside.

The coaches called it conditioning. But wasn't conditioning what you used after you rinsed the shampoo out?

On Mondays, I even hated my knee pads. I could complain to the equipment manager that they were as big and soft as goose-down pillows and did nothing to protect me from tearing an ACL, but NCAA rules said you had to wear them, so I wore them. On Mondays I had nearly as much contempt for my shoes. I hated the black leather cleats dressed with white stripes and strings so long I had to lace them a couple of times around the meat of my foot before tying them off. I hated how blisters formed on the edges of each ankle wrap and hurt so bad that they made me want to find a hacksaw and chop the bottom half of my leg off. I hated how the cleats, screwed into the bottoms of the shoes, felt as if they were poking up through my soles, drilling holes into my flesh, and, in some spots, tapping bone.

Mondays were for masochists. On Monday there was always a fraternity boy driving his new convertible on River Road with the top down and music blaring—Boz Scaggs, Barry White, the Bee Gees, ELO. On the milky-white leather seat next to him sat a sorority girl with golden hair flowing in the sun. Never a brunette or a redhead. How her little tube top didn't rip in two was one of life's great mysteries. When you spotted them from out on the Ponderosa, your misery meter started to chirp. They were out enjoying a romantic car ride while you were condemned to a life of suffering and sacrifice.

"Get away from me, helmet. I'm in no mood for you, helmet."

Of course, I couldn't actually talk at this moment. My mouth was too dry, too busy sucking the heat to get any words out.

"Forgive me, helmet. I'm having a bad day, helmet. Remember, it is Monday, helmet. You know me and Mondays, helmet."

I hated Tuesdays every bit as much. On Tuesday we were tired and sore from Monday, and the uniform hurt when you put it on. On Tuesday you wished somebody would escort you out into the high weeds on the other side of the levee and shoot you dead and let the river wash you out to sea. We ended Tuesday with twenty minutes of team offense and another hard round of conditioning, the coaches having to scream louder now to get us to run.

"Will the damn thing never come?" I yelled one day, loud enough for everyone to hear.

"What thing?" Coach Mac asked.

"Saturday. I want it to be Saturday."

"Only trying to make you better, Omar."

He sat in the shade of his golf cart, watching from the middle of the field, so we had to run around him and waste more energy.

"Only doing this because we love you. Don't think about yourself. Think about the people of the great state of Louisiana. They're counting on you. Every last one of them is counting on you."

The governor was counting on me. The rednecks in the northern part of the state were counting on me. The Cajuns in the south were counting on me. The black people and the Creoles were counting on me. The Asians and the Hispanics were counting on me. The Catholics and the Baptists and the Jews and the Jehovah's Witnesses and the Hare Krishnas—even the nondenominationalists were counting on me. Under the stars in Tiger Stadium on Saturday night, we were all the same.

"Can't let the people down, buddy. *Can ... not ... let ... them ... down ...*"

Wednesdays were okay. On Wednesday the coaches let up a little. Thursdays we went out in shorts, shoulder pads, and helmets, and the lighter load made everyone feel better. Our legs felt new, and when the days began to cool, we felt downright frisky. On Thursday there was no conditioning, not a single gasser to run until next Monday, four days away, and this made me inestimably happy and pleased with the world. I reunited with my helmet, my pads, and my blisters. I forgave them for what they'd done to me, and they forgave me for hating them.

At the end of practice on Thursday, Mac called us around him and instructed us to take a knee. "They put their jockey shorts on the same way we do, fellas," he said. "One leg at a time, fellas. One leg at a time."

We nodded to show we were listening. Sweat ran down our faces, drained down our necks, and tickled our rib cages, settling in our ass cracks and our cleats. In the cold, steam rose from our bodies like smoke from a barbecue pit. When we were heavily favored, Mac's tone was cautionary: "Don't take them lightly. Don't let them slip up behind you and take what you've worked so hard for. Nothing sneaky, fellas."

We roared, lifted our helmets high, and punched holes in the sky. As soon as the noise stopped, Mac extracted a folded sheet of paper from his shorts and read the list of films playing at the local cinemas. This too was tradition. On Fridays we always went as a team to a movie. "Okay, who wants the Burt Reynolds?" His lips moved as he counted the show of hands. "And now, who wants the Clint Eastwood? And the Charles Bronson? Anybody want the Charles Bronson?"

James Bond movies were the most popular; they outscored even shark and bikini flicks. Movies with fast cars were big too. Only once did we watch the same movie two weeks in a row. That was

Walking Tall, where a good man facing long odds beat his opponents senseless with a stick. This was how we saw ourselves—as underdogs—even when we were ranked in the Top 20 and beating hell out of teams week after week.

We did not attend romantic comedies or love stories, and we always avoided any movie that critics had touted as worthy of Oscar consideration. "This fellow says this is one of the greatest movies ever made," Mac said.

He held out the newspaper ad for everyone to see.

"Got anything better, Coach?"

We traveled to the movie in a pair of Continental Trailways buses. Team captains passed around shoeboxes filled with fudge made by an elderly Baton Rouge woman, a friend of the football program. According to legend, she had been supplying candy to the team since Coach Mac replaced Paul Dietzel as coach, and either tradition or superstition had kept her as part of the team's Friday routine ever since. "Everybody has a role to play," Mac reminded us. "The big and the small, those who get the attention and those who don't. What is your role?" He pointed to a player, selected at random. "What about yours? And yours? And *yours?* Will you be the difference come Saturday night? Or will it be you? Or you? Or *you* ... ?"

We never doubted what the fudge lady's role was.

Fifty varsity players filed into the theater and plopped into seats in a roped-off section. Fellow moviegoers cheered when we entered the room, all dressed in slacks and identical white polo shirts with tiger emblems. At times they stood and applauded, whistled and shouted for victory. We never got tired of it. We never stopped believing that they were right to love us. When we were on the road, the movie crowds didn't boo us, but they did make their allegiances known, yelling out, "Roll Tide" and "Go Dawgs" and

"Gator Bait." No one seemed to mind. It was Friday before the game, and the cracks of our teeth were black with fudge, and the show was about to start.

My senior year, we went to a movie about Adolph Hitler, hardly the kind of film we typically attended. Players voted to see it after one of our trainers, Dell Flair, campaigned for us to go. Dell was Broussard Hall's resident intellectual. I never knew if he was having a joke at our expense, but so many players fell asleep that patrons in the theater complained to the manager about the snoring. And then suddenly Mac's hand was on my shoulder, nudging me awake. I blinked to consciousness, and there he stood, his big moon face looming inches away. "Are you sure you're ready to show the world what you're made of, buddy?"

I loved Fridays. But I loved Saturdays even more.

WE WERE FIGHTING AGAIN, arguing about why I'd never married her. I'd wasted the best years of her life, she said, and she'd had enough and she wanted me to leave her alone. I was a commitmentphobe, she said, and still afraid to disappoint my father, the coach, even though he'd been dead for years. This is it, she said. It was over between us and she never wanted to see me again. If I came anywhere near her house, *if I so much as drove down her street,* I'd give her no choice but to call the cops. She'd do it, too. Did I know what a peace bond was?

"Come around here, and there's going to be a big story in tomorrow's *Daily World,*" she said. "It won't be on the sports page, either."

"Nobody remembers me," I told her.

"*Please.* Are you on that again?"

"They hardly knew me when I was playing. They won't know me

now." And yet, even as I said that, I could see the headline in tomorrow's paper: EX-LSU FOOTBALLER JAILED AFTER DOMESTIC DISPUTE.

No mention of the books I'd written, no reference to my time as a staff writer for *The Washington Post*, nothing about the stories I'd published in *Esquire, GQ,* and *Sports Illustrated.* Before I drove to her house and a deputy hauled me in, I wondered, maybe I should call editors at the paper and remind them that I really did do something with my life after football.

AUTHOR BRADLEY, FORMER TIGER STANDOUT, HELD IN PARISH PEN.

"If people in this town knew who you really are," Connie said, "they'd be shocked. The big football hero. You're such an unbelievable fraud, with all your lies and empty promises. You make me sick."

It wasn't anything she hadn't told me before, and she was right to feel that way. I had lied and broken promises. But after hearing it all morning long, I'd finally had enough. I yanked the line from the jack, and then in a fluid, practiced motion, I tossed the phone out a window.

"Scared of commitment, am I?"

Lucky for me, the window was open, unlike other times when we'd fought. I listened as the phone tumbled through a pink azalea and struck the ground, making the bell hum.

"Let me tell you something," I shouted out the window, aiming my words at the phone. "My whole, entire life has been about commitment. Do you hear me? I played football for Cholly Mac at LSU. How many people do you know who can say that? Do you know *any?*"

I paced the room, trying to decide whether to drive out to her house and confront her and risk being arrested. Pausing by the window, I shouted his name again, *"Cholly Mac,"* in case the phone under the bush had missed it the first time.

If the arresting officer needed proof of my character, I could always let him rummage around in my bedroom closet. He could have a look at my trophies and the scrapbook filled with newspaper stories, each a testament to my ability to commit. THE HEART AND SOUL OF LSU, a headline in the *Lake Charles American Press* once said about me.

The neighbors across the street, Mr. and Mrs. Richard, enjoyed sitting by the curb in lawn chairs and waiting for cars to pass. They waved whether they knew the people or not. "Everything okay?" Mr. Richard asked when I stormed outside.

I was carrying a trash can. "Everything's fine."

I crouched down to pick up the busted telephone, keeping my back to him so he couldn't see my face.

"You sure everything's okay?"

"I'm sure, Mr. Richard. Thank you for asking."

I went back inside, and they remained in their chairs on the lawn for another two hours, even as the shadows grew longer and the temperature began to drop. Every fifteen minutes or so, I got up off the sofa and checked on them from the kitchen window. I wondered if they planned to spend the night out there. When they weren't watching the street, they watched my house, waiting, I was sure, for another telephone to fly out the window.

The day had turned gray and threatening; a damp breeze swayed the treetops. I slipped on a jacket and drove to Connie's, passing my old high school on the way. They wouldn't remember me there, either, I knew. Too many teams had come and gone since my senior year at OHS, and it was hard to remember last year's players, much less those from a generation ago. There would always be more blue-chippers who bent over footballs and punt-snapped spirals toward the basketball goal at the other end of the gym.

Connie lived in a nice neighborhood. Wood smoke poured from the chimneys, and the smell mixed with the smell of gumbo simmering on kitchen stoves. It wasn't the sort of place where you expected bad things to happen, especially at this time of day. I parked halfway down the driveway, walked to the side door, and punched the bell. I could hear it chime inside the house, and a moment later I heard footsteps and muffled laughter. I put my face against the glass in the door and glimpsed Connie's children retreating up the stairs, then Connie came sliding in her socks on the polished wood floor. I'd never seen her move so fast. She lost her balance and fell clutching the banister, only to hop to her feet in the next instant and start back up.

This was just like her, pretending I'd come to harm her family. My God, I thought. She was willing to hurt herself to prove it.

"Connie, let me in," I called out, pulling against the knob.

Had any of my teammates been issued peace bonds after fighting with their wives or girlfriends? I'd never seen any news reports about such a thing. Most had gone on to lead exemplary lives, according to the stories I'd read. They had families and successful careers. I could name a few who became doctors and several more who were lawyers. Some were millionaires. But I could name others who courted and found trouble, their famous days at LSU granting them not a whit of protection against the problems that awaited them. They'd seemed no less upstanding than those who went to church on Sunday. Each of them was "good people," as Coach Mac had liked to say.

They put Ramsey Dardar in the state pen after he pled guilty to burglarizing homes in Baton Rouge, apparently to finance a drug addiction. Ramsey a crackhead? I refused to believe it. A freshman defensive lineman my senior year, Ramsey had been one of the best-liked guys on the team. I could still see his beautiful smile past his face mask in the moment before I snapped the ball and felt the impact of his headgear, his hands clutching my jersey as he tried to rush past me. Ramsey was from Acadiana, Cajun country, where I was from, and at practice we'd compliment each other in French, often after trading blows: "*C'est bon, mon ami. C'est tres bon.*"

If I survived this day without going to jail, I vowed to see Ramsey again.

"What did I do to you?" I yelled at the house. "What did I ever do to you?"

Years after this day, in the fall of 2005, Lyman White would be sent to a federal prison for Medicaid fraud. I'd played against him in high school, back when he was a star at Franklin High, and I never knew a finer guy or a better teammate. Lyman made the big hits that stopped drives inches from the goal line. He blocked passes meant for open receivers. And he always looked good getting off the bus, his smile in place, his big right hand extended to whoever was there to greet him.

"Go home," I heard somebody shout from inside the house.

"Tell me what I did first."

"Go home," came the voice again. It was Connie's son, Brandt.

How could he take her side, I wondered, after all the times we threw passes out in the yard?

"Tell your mother to let me in, Brandt."

Now there was laughter. This was all a big joke to them. "No."

"Tell her."

"She doesn't want to see you. Go home, John Ed."

The same year the feds nailed Lyman, they arrested George Atiyeh for operating an unlicensed bookmaking business and, later, in a separate case, convicted him of bankruptcy fraud, a crime motivated by the need to feed his family, or so George told the court. A nose guard, George was also a heavyweight wrestling champion, and he and I often faced off against each other in practice. I once sucker punched him for laughing after he beat me in a three-on-three drill, instigating a brawl between the offense and the defense that turned so ugly, the coaches could only stand back and let us go at each other until we ran out of gas. After order was restored, Coach Mac grabbed me by the shoulder pads and led me to one side of the field, his face red and running sweat. I thought he was going to give my head a slap or make me run extra conditioning. Instead he said, "Buddy, thank you. The boys have been sleepwalking all day long."

I glanced toward the street now, half expecting to find a police car. "You don't know me," I shouted at the house. "You never knew me."

More laughter—squeals of it—then a long silence.

"You didn't know me, Connie. Not then, you didn't. You wouldn't be doing this to me now if you knew me then."

Strange how you went from showing her the scar on your chest to scaring her so bad she locked the doors and hid her children upstairs. How you went from Tiger Stadium to the town where you grew up and a life where you had to convince yourself every day that you hadn't outgrown your usefulness.

I stepped back and walked to the truck. As I reached to open the door, something moved beyond my vision. I wheeled around and looked toward the house. She was at a window on the second floor—Connie's youngest child—gazing down at me. She let out a laugh, then ran off screaming.

In real life, there was no extra conditioning to run as punishment for behaving badly. In real life, you got in your truck and drove home and tried to understand how you'd slipped so far away from being the person who once had them pleading for his autograph. Like football and everything else that mattered too much, this relationship showed signs of having reached an unsatisfactory conclusion.

There was no more beer in the fridge, and Mr. and Mrs. Richard were hours away from resuming their curbside vigil. Inside my head, the same invented dialogue played over and over. I was talking to my old coach, the one I hadn't seen since my last day on the team, the one I'd refused to see. "I guess I got lost along the way, Coach."

"What happened to you, son?"

"I think I finally realized I was like Charles McDuff, capable of dying."

"It ends for everybody, John Ed."

"Yes, but I thought I was different."

BY NOW it was too late to explain. Cancer had left him bedridden at his home in Baton Rouge; the prognosis wasn't good. It was December of 2001, a balmy morning too warm for a coat and too cool for shirtsleeves. I needed to make a dozen trips around the neighborhood before I could find what it took to park and leave the truck.

Susan Raborn had called the night before and urged me to see him again. A friend from my LSU days, back when she was the most golden of the golden girls and the object of universal admiration among my teammates, Susan still lived in Baton Rouge. And she had stayed in touch with Coach Mac's daughter, Dee. "It's only a matter of time," Susan had told me on the phone. "Dee says it probably won't be a week."

"Well, I appreciate the information. I'll try to get there as soon as I can."

"John Ed, Coach Mac won't be here much longer. You need to go now."

"But I can't, Susan."

"Then you'll never see him again." She waited a moment. "This can't be what you want, can it?"

My hand was shaking as I lifted a finger to ring the bell. I stopped myself and glanced back at the truck, wondering if anyone in the house had seen me. I could walk back to the street and leave without being noticed, send a note explaining the mechanical trouble I'd had on the way. But no, I turned back to the door in time to see it swing open. Coach Mac's wife, Dorothy Faye, was standing inside.

Susan must've called to tell her I was coming. Otherwise, I was certain, she would've been more alarmed by the sight of a grown man weeping at her front door. "Why, John Ed Bradley," she said. "Come in. Come in, John Ed."

She put her arms around me and kissed the side of my face, then she used her fingertips to wipe my tears away. She was treating me better than I deserved, smiling and saying all the right things. I could only imagine the hell she'd been through. She looked sleepy, but she was still beautiful, still the best-looking coach's wife I'd ever known. Coach Mac had once lectured me on the importance of finding a good woman, using his own luck in marrying Dorothy Faye as an example of how the right choice can improve the standing of a man and make a life given to football tolerable. When we flew out of Baton Rouge for away games, I always looked for her on the team plane, knowing she'd add some class to the trip and boost our chances. After weeks in the locker room, there was nothing quite as wonderful as the smell of her perfume as she walked the aisle, tapping each of us on the shoulder. And letting me sit with her husband today was her kindest act yet. He didn't have much time left—three days, as it would turn out.

"We're so glad you've come," she said.

"Thank you."

Dee stepped up from behind her mother and gave me a hug. "Good to see you again, John Ed."

I nodded but found it too hard to say anything.

Dorothy Faye led me down a hall to his bedroom, and I could see him before I walked in the door, lying on a hospital gurney, white sheets and a spread covering his body from the chest down. His head was bald, the hair lost to chemotherapy. He looked much older than seventy-eight. And he was smaller than I remembered, his bones poking up against loose-hanging skin, an odd, yellow-gray color. I paused at the door. It had been twenty-two years, but that was Coach Mac, all right. I knew it for certain when he called out my name. "Is that you, John Ed?" he said, then patted a spot by his side on the mattress. "Come on over here and talk to me, buddy."

Dorothy Faye found a chair for me, and I pulled it up close to the bed. Coach Mac reached for my hand and held it in his own, and then he let his head fall to the side so he could see me better. "Your old position coach was here yesterday," he said.

"Coach McCarty?"

"He sat right there." He nodded in the general direction, and we both looked at the empty space, as if waiting for McCarty to appear there again.

"And you're a writer now," he said.

"Yes, sir, I'm a writer."

"Well, I'm proud of you, John Ed."

He ticked off the names of the other assistants who'd visited in recent days, and then he listed the players from my era who had stopped by. I asked him what had become of some of them, and in every case he had an answer. "I was so sorry to hear what happened to Marty," he said. "When you see him, you make sure to tell him I asked about him. Will you do that for me?"

I considered telling him that I hadn't seen Marty in years, but I didn't want him to know that about me. "I'll be sure to tell him," I said.

He gave my hand a squeeze and asked me if I remembered the night USC came to Tiger Stadium and how the fans stood on their feet for four straight quarters and watched as we showed the Trojans what LSU football was all about. "I remember it all the time," I answered. "I don't always want to, because we lost, Coach, but I remember it."

"I remember it too," he said in a wistful way. He reached a hand up and raked it in front of his face. "They called face-masking against Benjy," he whispered.

"Sir?"

"That penalty. The one at the end."

"Yes, sir. They sure did call it. And it cost us the game. The officials stole it from us."

He swallowed, and I waited for him to castigate me for criticizing the refs. But he didn't correct me. In fact, he didn't say anything for a long while. And it seemed I could see moments from the game play out behind his eyes: the yellow flag going up, the fifteen yards marched off, the touchdown with less than a minute to play that gave the wrong team the win.

"Coach, Benjy Thibodeaux didn't face-mask anybody," I said. I could feel the pace of my heart quicken as I began to argue against a referee's call that would never change. "He didn't, did he, Coach? I still can't believe they did that to us."

Coach Mac eased his grip on my hand and closed his eyes. Only about twenty minutes had gone by, but I understood it was time for me to leave.

I stood and moved toward the door, determined not to look back, not to cry again. His voice stopped me. "Hey, buddy?" He waited until I faced him. "Always remember I'm with you. I'm with all you boys."

He lifted a hand off the bed and held it high, just as he'd done that night in Orlando when Big Ed and I carried him from the field on our shoulders and he waved to the crowd for the last time.

"I know you are, Coach. I know you're with us."

"And buddy?" A lopsided smile found his face. "Next time, don't wait so long before you come see your old coach again."

I CALLED MARTY not long after. Once again, his wife asked me to wait while she put him on the speakerphone. He answered after a few minutes, and I asked him if there was a good day for me to come by. "Today is good," he said.

"I can't today."

"Tomorrow's good too."

I didn't say anything, and he seemed to understand that I was having a hard time. "You tell me when you want to come, John Ed. I'll be here for you."

WE LEAVE THE HOUSE, and I follow a few steps behind him as he motors his wheelchair to the end of a long drive and faces the barn. He and Lynne own thirty-eight acres, plenty of room for the five horses standing along the fence watching us. "Mark my words," Marty says, "I'm going to be riding before the end of the year."

I look down at him. One of his hands is resting on the control that operates the chair. "You're telling me you're going to ride a horse, Marty?"

"I'm having a saddle made with the back beefed up for support so I can strap myself in. Of course, I'm going to have to use a lift to put me in the saddle, but I'm going to do it. See that big, gray mare? I think she'll let me ride her."

We've been together only a few hours, but already the force of his personality has eased my fears about seeing him again, and it's helped me see past the chair. After the accident, Marty's muscles atrophied, his midsection grew large and outsize, his face swollen. But when I look in his eyes, I see the same guy I knew back in school. This might be weird to say, all things considered, but Marty hasn't changed much. "One thing about him," his wife, Lynne, says, "he might've broken his neck, he might be paralyzed and in that chair, but he is still a football player."

The house is on the outskirts of Larose—a large Acadian standing only a few hundred feet from Bayou Lafourche on Highway 1, with a FOR SALE sign out front. Marty works for the Lafourche Parish Sheriff's Department as a major in its civil department, a desk job that keeps him in an office most of the day. He and Lynne have one child, seventeen-year-old Amy, a high school senior. Marty and Lynne are selling because Amy is going off to college, and the house, with five thousand square feet, is more than Lynne can handle by herself.

In addition to managing the household, she mows and trims the lawn and tends to Marty's needs, which includes getting him ready for work each morning. She removes his external catheter and inserts a new one. She gives him a sponge bath, shaves his face, and washes his hair. She makes breakfast for him. She loads him into a van and drives him to the sheriff's office, almost an hour away.

Later in the day, she returns to bring him back to Larose. Then she cooks dinner. Once or twice a week she helps him shower, a chore that often requires up to three hours.

Marty has no feeling in his hands and fingers and only limited use of his arms, but he can feed himself with a fork attached to a brace on his wrist. He uses the same brace, or strap, as he calls it, to brush his teeth and type at his computer. He has a voice-activated software program at work for dictation, but his hunt-and-peck typing method, at twenty-five words a minute, outpaces it. He once owned a twelve-thousand-dollar chair that lifted up and tilted forward, allowing him to stand, but it stopped working, and he can't afford the repairs. The chair he uses now is much less sophisticated—it cost about five thousand dollars—and he drives it with an athlete's dexterity, maneuvering through tight spots and around corners without slowing down. "You're a maniac in that thing," I tell him.

"I'm a maniac out of it too," he replies.

We move over to the shade of the carport, the horses still watching us from the fence. I reach to touch the top of his shoulder, one of the few places where he still has feeling, but I stop and withdraw my hand. It's an awkward gesture; I'm sure he noticed it. "Marty, you must've resented the hell out of me," I say.

He looks up, his eyes moving from left to right and back again.

"I mean, you really must've hated me."

And now I see surprise on his face. His body bucks forward and back in the chair, in a way that suggests he's trying to escape it, and I know it isn't necessary for me to explain what prompted the statement. "No, never," he says. He gives his head a shake. "I'm not that type of guy, John Ed. I saw you as my competition, but I always have a lot of respect for my competition. You were standing in my way, standing in the way of where I wanted to be. But even then I knew my role and accepted it. I was going to push you as hard as I could. That was my duty to you and to the team. I looked up to you as a teacher, just as you looked up to Jay Whitley as a teacher when he was playing ahead of you." He pauses to catch his breath. "We were teammates. That was the most important thing."

I still feel as though I owe him something—an explanation more than an apology. But he pivots the chair hard and drives it back toward the house.

We sit down to a big lasagna dinner that puts every meal Li'l Bit ever served us to shame. After coffee and blueberry cheesecake, we move into the den, and Marty and I sit close together and talk in conspiratorial whispers, dusk coming fast and darkening the windows. Marty shares details about the accident with a strange mix of awe and bravado, almost as if he's describing someone else's experience. "When we hit the water, we separated," he says. "I thought everything was fine, like I'd done a bad dive that turned into a belly flop or something. I opened my eyes, and I could see my arms spread out, and I could see my feet touching the bottom. And you know, my brain's saying, 'Stand up, Marty. Move your arms.' But I couldn't feel anything. 'Turn your head and get a breath of air.' I couldn't do it. So my brain is giving me directions and I can see everything, but my limbs won't move. And it's, like, instant panic and then instant calm. I don't know how else to explain it. It was like everything just became so peaceful because I knew I was going to die. 'This is it, this is how it's going to happen.' But just in that moment I could hear again, and it was like I was deep inside a tunnel. People were yelling, 'Marty, get up. Marty, get up.' But their voices were very faint and distant, and then suddenly the guy who had fallen into the pool with me turned my face out of the water. All I said was, 'I'm not kidding.' And when I said that, I heard a bunch of splashes, and one of my classmates grabbed my neck and immediately put it in traction, and they carried me out of the pool.

"One of my classmates came and knelt over me. 'Wayne,' I said, 'are my toes moving?' He said, 'No, Marty.' I said, 'Pinch 'em. Are you pinchin' 'em?' He said, 'Yeah.' I said, 'God, I don't feel it.' He worked his way up my body, pinching as he went, and every place was dead. Finally he got to my upper torso, and I could just barely feel the tops of my shoulders. No movement, no feeling. So I'm paralyzed, totally paralyzed from the shoulders down."

He'd shattered the fifth cervical vertebra, and one large bone fragment, shaped like a teardrop, had compressed his spinal cord "like a noodle," Marty says. He was twenty-seven years old, and he and Lynne had been married five years. Amy was only fourteen months old, too young to form any memory of her father beyond a bed or a chair. Marty spent six months in the hospital. "My classmates would come every other day and read my notes to me," he says. "When I thought I was prepared, my professors would come in and give me an oral quiz. So I continued to go to class and take exams, and I was making good grades, because I had nothing else to do but lie there. We did this for the rest of the trimester, and the whole time I expected to get out and continue my education."

Marty had been the school's student body president. But he abandoned his studies and later enrolled at Nicholls State University in Thibodaux, earning a degree in secondary education. He was teaching GED-preparation classes to problem students when he met a candidate for Lafourche Parish sheriff at a banquet. Craig Webre was a dark horse running on a reform platform, and he asked Marty to support his campaign. After he was elected, Webre offered Marty a job. "I told him right then, 'I don't care if you're the sheriff, and I don't care if you're my boss, I will not lie for you, I will not cheat for you, and I will not go to jail for you.' I said, 'If you do something incorrect and I have knowledge of it, I'll turn you in.' Webre said, 'I respect that, Marty, and I wouldn't expect anything different from you.' And so we hit it off right away. We had the same goals and direction."

Marty could be full of bluster when he was a player, and he's showing it now as he talks about his work. "There are people, every now and then, they'll come up to me and say, 'Man, you've got a lot of courage.' I take that in stride, but I always tell them, 'Look, it's not courage. It's *survival.*' You know me, John Ed. I would be the same person, doing the same things, if I weren't in this chair."

Not until we talk about LSU does Marty become more candid about his losses. After I left the team, Marty never started a game at center. In the spring of his junior year, he reinjured a shoulder and had to have pins surgically inserted to repair it. By the time he was strong enough to play again, at the start of the 1980 season, he was at the bottom of the depth chart. First a guard was moved to center, and then a talented freshman beat them both out for the job. Marty was furious. Playing on special teams and occasionally in mop-up situations, he felt cheated. In the third game, he injured a knee and decided to give up football at year's end. "It was a very difficult, painful time," he says. To keep his scholarship, he worked for the team as a student trainer. Lynne helped him transition to life without football, but who goes from being the heir apparent to the starting center position at LSU to a guy who wraps ankles and tends to sprained fingers? Marty finally quit the program and left the school and Baton Rouge. Years would pass before he got over it.

"I always assumed the job would be yours," I tell him. "I didn't know you never started. I'm sorry, man. It doesn't seem fair."

Marty's eyes fill with tears. "It's all right," he says.

"No, it isn't all right."

"It's all right," he says.

He takes a deep breath and lifts his head. The tears are still coming down, but he has a smile on his face. "Nothing I've ever experienced compares to that first time I ran out with the team as a freshman—out into Tiger Stadium. God, I was fifteen feet off the ground and covered with *frissons*. You know what *frissons* are, John Ed? They're goose bumps. It's the French word for goose bumps. It was the highest high you could have, and no drugs could match it—the way it felt to run out there with the crowd standing and yelling for you. I wish every kid could experience that."

"If every kid could," I say, "then it wouldn't be what it is. It's because so few get there that it has such power."

He sits staring, and I can tell it's his turn to ask me a question. "You became a ghost," he says.

"What's that?"

"You vanished. We never saw you again."

"Well, I got a job up in Washington. I lived away for a long time."

He nods, but I can tell he knows there's more to it than that.

Marty bought season tickets and attended LSU's home games until 1994. He also kept in touch with some of our teammates. One day, Charles McDuff and his wife, Janet, surprised him with a visit. They were headed south on a fishing trip, and they wanted to see how he was doing. Spencer Smith called him and insisted he attend the grand opening of a motel he'd bought in Grand Isle. Spencer, a former Parade High School All-American who played offensive guard, was more notorious for his off-the-field exploits. After nights on the town, he liked to forearm streetlights, hitting them so hard, the bulbs broke high up on the poles. One night before the Sun Bowl at a bar in El Paso, an All-American tackle for Stanford tried to intimidate us by tearing a phone book in half with his bare hands. Spencer's answer was to take a large bite out of a whiskey glass.

Marty and Lynne drove to Grand Isle for Spencer's motel event and ran into still more players. When Jerry Murphree, a splitback on the team, learned that Marty worked for the sheriff's department, he asked him for a favor. He and his wife were separated, Jerry explained, and he wanted to do something special for his son. "Do you have a badge I can have? My little boy keeps telling me he wants a badge, a real one."

And in 1987, less than a year after the accident, Marty was lying on a hospital bed in the living room of his parents' home when the phone rang. "You'll never believe who it is," his father said. He brought the phone over and held it to Marty's ear. "Buddy, how you doin'?" a voice said. Marty recognized it immediately, even though he hadn't talked to Coach Mac in years. "Buddy," Mac went on, "I'm sorry about your accident. But knowing what you're made of, you're going to fight hard and overcome it. Everybody's counting on you, Marty. You can do it."

"He gave me a little pep talk," Marty says, "just like he used to do when we were playing. At the time I was nothing but a body in a bed; his timing couldn't have been better. Because, you see, I still had little movement or feeling in my arms. I couldn't even lift my head up. Coach Mac reached me when I needed him most."

I tell him about my recent visit to the McClendon home in Baton Rouge, how Mac had wanted me to let Marty know that he'd asked about him. Marty is quiet in his chair. "I've got something to confess to you," he says, "something I'm sure you better than anyone will understand. Whenever I'm feeling sorry for myself, whenever life is more than I can bear at the moment, I always do the same thing. I put the Tiger fight song on the stereo, and all the memories come back, and somehow it makes everything okay. 'All right,' I say to myself. 'I can do it. *I can do it*. Let's go.'"

It's late now, and I know I should leave. Marty seems oblivious to the time. I make a move for the door, and he tells me to sit back down. "Where do you think you're going? You don't have anywhere to go." A lamp drops a pool of light between us, but otherwise the room is dark. Lynne has spent the last few hours cleaning the house, breaking only to check on Marty, and it's time for her to get him ready for bed. She comes in, stands next to his chair, and gives him a smile when he looks up at her. Exhaustion shows in the dark circles under her eyes. She reaches her hand out and strokes the back of his head, whispering softly to him. His eyes flutter closed, and she bends down and kisses the top of his head. She's the one people in a stadium should stand and cheer for, I think to myself.

Marty wheels his chair as far as the door. "John Ed, don't be a ghost," he says.

As I back my truck down the drive, he's still sitting there, back-lit by the lamp in the room, his arm raised as high as he can hold it in goodbye.

Chapter Seven

| ADDICTION

THE CLOSET is on your left at the end of the hall. It's where I keep my old football things, along with broken vacuum cleaners, never-used Christmas ornaments, spare air-conditioning filters for units in apartments I rented years ago, and clothes from my days at the *Post* that don't fit me anymore. A large framed photograph, taken in Baton Rouge on the night of November 10, 1979, hangs on one of the side walls. Granted, a closet is an odd place to hang a picture. It is odder, still, if you consider the subject.

To see the thing, you need to slide the clothes out of the way. Be brave. This requires not just strength but determination. The closet is so dark it's impossible to make much sense of the grainy, black-and-white image. A string hangs down from a light in the ceiling, but the bulb is burned out. I haven't bothered to replace it. The photo is the reason.

I should've wrapped it in brown paper and stored it in the attic years ago, or given it to a nephew, or driven it out to the landfill and tossed it high on a mound of hurricane debris. It's not something I need to see anymore. Seeing it makes me think too much, and everybody knows what I'm like when I do that. But early one December morning, when I should be sleeping, I decide to have a look. The lighted display on my cable TV box says 4:14. I get up and put on some clothes.

I retrieve a flashlight from the kitchen, then start removing things from the closet, stacking clothes and assorted objects on the bed in the spare bedroom. I turn the flashlight on and bring the beam around. The picture is hanging crooked, and the glass covering the photo is covered in dust. I use a sleeve from one of my old suits to clean it off. I own other photos of myself in my playing days, but only this one shows me in action with my teammates on the offensive line.

We're protecting David Woodley from Alabama's defense. At the center of the photo, I've uncoiled into the trunk of a nose guard who's come up off his feet and lifted his hands to try to block David's pass. I've speared him with my helmet and thrust forward with everything I've got, but the man is so big, you have to wonder if he even feels the hit. To be honest, the photo makes me look good, when in fact I had a terrible go of it that night. On my left, guard Tom Tully has broken from the pocket in search of somebody to block, and on my right, John Watson clearly has his assignment in hand. With his left arm fully extended, he's punching his man in the chest, pushing him back. On the far right of the picture, Big Ed Stanton stands tall between the quarterback and a defensive end, and fullback Danny Soileau is hovering over a fallen Alabama player.

Only one of us has lost his feet: left tackle Charles McDuff. He's sprawled on the turf. For twenty years, I thought the photo showed

Charles being beaten. I thought the player he was assigned to block had slipped past him just as David was preparing to throw. I thought I was looking at a sack in progress, a mugging about to happen. And I thought it was unfair that the camera had captured Charles at that moment. We all got beat at one time or another. God knows I did. And I believed Charles deserved better. So I hung the picture in the closet, behind a lifetime of garbage, where only I could find it.

Did David say something to Charles when we huddled for the next play? I used to wonder. Did Charles apologize and explain how he'd lost his footing on the soggy ground? Or did Charles tell David to shut up and let him do his job?

But I had it wrong: Charles did not miss that block after all. The Alabama player that Danny Soileau is standing over is down on the ground because Charles put him there. Until this moment, I'd never studied the image close enough to see that.

I train the flashlight on Charles's prone figure. I wish I could go back to that night and help him to his feet. I wish I could offer him a hand. "Hey, Charlie," and pull him up off the ground.

But it's too late for that. It's nearly 5 a.m., and I'm sitting on the floor of a closet, and I will never speak to Charles McDuff again.

LATER THAT MORNING, I drive to Baton Rouge and park in front of a large brick house in the Bocage subdivision. The neighborhood is filled with sprawling ramblers, West Indies-style reproductions, and ersatz plantation homes with copper lanterns on each side of the front door and fat, vanilla-white columns standing in rows along bricked galleries. Up and down the street, discarded Christmas trees lay curbside for trash pickup, some of them still decorated with sparkles that hang from the branches and give a shine when the wind kicks up.

My head throbbing from too little sleep, stomach churning from the coffee I drank at a gas station on the way, I get out of the truck and start up the sidewalk. I'm trying to figure out how to begin and rehearsing a few things to say when the front door opens and Charles's brother, Michael, comes walking out to greet me.

Four years younger than Charles, Michael used to spend a lot of time hanging out in Charles's dorm room, so much so that he became everybody's little brother. I haven't seen him since he was seventeen. His hair is powdered gray now, and he's retired his shabby gym clothes for the kind of casual attire worn by successful, white-collar professionals. In a phone conversation he told me how he made his living, but all that registered was that it had to do with money.

Michael ushers me into the living room, where three young men are sitting. They stand when I enter, and Michael tells me their names, starting with Charles Jr., the oldest. I move from one to the next shaking hands. None is as big as his father, but I see Charles in each of them. Charles Jr., twenty-three this day, has his dad's feathery blond hair, John Edward, twenty-two, his open, expressive face, and Chris, twenty, his laidback demeanor. Charles Jr. is attending Brooklyn Law School in New York. His younger brothers are studying at a community college in Baton Rouge. Only after I sit do Charles's sons return to their own seats.

"You boys are much more polite than your father was," I say, laughing uneasily. They can't seem to decide how to reply. "You turned out to be gentlemen. Now, what would he think of that, I wonder."

"Maybe that their mother raised them well," says Michael, adding a laugh of his own. Then, without urging, he tells the story.

On a hot summer day nearly ten years earlier, Charles was towing his boat from New Orleans to the family condo in Orange Beach, Alabama, when a flat tire forced him to the side of the road. By the time he changed it and reached the marina where he'd docked the boat, some two hours later, he was in obvious physical distress. A woman who worked at the marina offered to call him an ambulance, but Charles declined, saying he was running late and needed to join his family, who'd arrived the day before. When he arrived at the condo, the boys were at the beach playing in the surf. Normally he would've gone down to speak to them, but today he remained inside. Charles told Janet, his wife, that he thought he might be suffering from heat exhaustion and he wanted to take a cold shower. He finished in the bathroom and went to bed, still sweating and struggling to catch his breath.

"He told her he was going to rest, and that's when it hit him," Michael says. "It was instant. Charles was very overweight—he weighed about three hundred and forty pounds. After football he stopped taking care of himself, and he'd been on high blood pressure medicine, taking it on and off. There was never an autopsy done. The medical examiner's report said it was a pulmonary embolism, but it could've been a heart attack."

While Charles's body was being transported to the hospital, the three boys left the beach and went swimming in the complex pool. Charles Jr. remembers hearing a siren, but it never occurred to him that it might have something to do his father. The boys toweled off and returned to an empty condo. They walked from room to room, calling for their parents. Charles Jr. wondered out loud if they'd gone for a walk on the beach. Two hours later, Janet returned and told them their father was dead.

"I remember thinking my dad wouldn't want me to set a bad example for my brothers," Charles Jr. says, "so after awhile I stopped crying. If I didn't cry, maybe my brothers wouldn't cry."

Michael received the news via telephone and immediately left Baton Rouge for the condo. The boys were waiting for him when he arrived, their bags packed. "They were in shock," he says. "They were trying to understand it. They kept telling me it was all right because he'd gone to a better place, which is what their mother must've told them. It broke my heart, you know? Those three boys trying to be little men, trying to be brave the way their father would've wanted."

On the drive back to Louisiana, Michael recalled his own childhood trauma: the father who died when he was thirteen. "My dad died of a heart attack," he tells me. "That's why I was with you guys at the stadium all the time. Charles took me under his wing; he wanted to keep me close. I was actually closer to Charles and his teammates than I was to kids my own age. I'm getting to hang out with LSU football players—you can't believe what that was like for me, even under the circumstances."

After weight room workouts, Charles had Michael sit behind the wheel of an old family car and steer the thing while Charles pushed it from behind. They went up and down the street, stopping only after Charles's legs had started to shake so much he could no longer stand. Charles had seemed invincible to Michael. And he wasn't afraid to have fun. Once at a Hawaiian party at a Tigerland bar, somebody complained that Charles was underdressed. Charles stood in the middle of the room and looked around—everybody else was wearing leis. So he went to the men's room, ripped the seat from a toilet, and wore it around his neck the rest of the night.

At the end of each season, the team's upperclassmen sponsored a party called the Perry Bowl, named in honor of a former player who'd organized the inaugural event. It featured tequila, draft beer, and a handful of LSU's more devoted female fans. The idea was to get so drunk you forgot your mother's maiden name, your favorite pet's name, and your own name. I attended only once, when I was a freshman. I swore off going to another when I woke up in a puddle of something on a pool table, a girl I didn't know lying next to me. Michael invited a date to the 1980 Perry Bowl. Minutes after arriving, he watched in horror as a two-hundred-and-eighty-pound defensive lineman pinned the young woman against a wall. "Charles," Michael said, "you've got to do something." Charles casually tapped the lineman on the shoulder and whispered in his ear. Michael's girlfriend was set free.

None of us enjoyed much anonymity in Baton Rouge, but Charles got more attention than most because of his size. When people saw him, they instantly identified him as an LSU football player. At least one person, however, apparently wondered if he was something else. In the summer during his college years, Charles worked for a labor union with a powerful local chapter and a reputation for getting what it wanted. One of its leaders liked to have Charles accompany him to meetings. Charles's job was to stand off to the side with his arms crossed. "At one of these meetings the other guy got upset, seeing Charles there," says Michael, recalling the story as Charles had told it to him. "The man turned to Charles's boss and said, 'Look, don't be bringing your goons around here again.' The boss said, 'Hey, don't be calling my goon a goon.' But Charles was there to intimidate, and there were never any confrontations."

Charles had less success scaring people on the football field. Although he started several games in 1979, he eventually lost the job to a freshman. Disappointed with the limited playing time, he became one of the team rebels. He hung out in bars and drank a lot, often with David Woodley by his side. Charles had one more season of eligibility after David and I left the team, but that spring he injured an ankle and never fully recovered.

He and Janet were married in May, and although she helped settle him down, coaches still regarded him as a malcontent. They put him on the freshman team, which usually played on Thursday afternoons before a few hundred fans at Bernie Moore Stadium, the track field in the shadow of Tiger Stadium. Charles was humiliated. After two games he told Michael he'd had enough. "What's the point?" he said as he was undressing at his locker. Charles quit later that afternoon.

"He had a lot of pride, and it was difficult for him," says Michael. "So much of his identity was tied to being an LSU football player. And the way it ended really shook him up. Like most guys who've played at that level, it was hard for him to adjust to a life without the game. For years he worked as a dispatcher for a trucking company, and then he got on with a shipping company. Charles provided for his family, but he never got much satisfaction from his work. I think he always regretted how football ended for him, but he finally reached a point where he could look back and be philosophical about it. 'You know,' he said to me once, 'that was the best time of my life, those years with Coach Mac. I was in great physical condition, I felt like nobody could beat me, and I was part of something really wonderful. No matter what comes, I'll always have LSU.'"

Charles took his sons to games at Tiger Stadium and introduced them to his former teammates at pregame tailgate parties. "Huge men," recalls John Edward. "It would take two hours for us to get to our seats; Dad had to stop and talk to everybody." At home, Charles told the boys stories about the players they'd met, making each one sound like the greatest guy in the world. Many years later, Charles Jr., a linebacker, would play for Tulane, but he left the team after his freshman year. "The way Dad always talked about his teammates, it wasn't like that for me," he says. "He loved you guys like brothers; he had such respect for every one of you."

All three of Charles's sons played football at Archbishop Rummel, a Catholic high school in suburban New Orleans. When John Edward was a senior starter at offensive tackle, his girlfriend had a T-shirt made for him that said NOBODY WORKS HARDER THAN THE OFFENSIVE LINE. John was so proud, he hung it on the wall of his bedroom. "When Dad played, I think it meant a lot more to be an LSU football player than it does today," John says. "Now the players look at college as a step to the pros, but back then it was enough just to wear that uniform and be on the team."

We've been talking for more than an hour. Michael calls for a break and leads us into the kitchen for lunch. He places drinks and a tray of sandwiches on the table. Until now, Chris has contributed little to the conversation, and I wonder if his place in the family pecking order is the reason. He was only eleven when his father died. "I remember him, not long before he passed away, telling me about heaven," Chris says.

"Your dad told you about heaven?" I ask.

"He said there was one."

"Just out of the blue he told you this?"

"He said life was a test, and then you pass and go to heaven. Or something like that."

"Have you ever wondered if he talked to you about heaven because he'd had a premonition about his own death and he didn't want you to worry about him?"

Chris looks down at the sandwich on his plate. "Maybe. I just remember he told me that. He must've been thinking about it, anyway."

The brothers grow silent. I figure I should say something to drive the conversation forward. I remember my own father and what we talked about whenever the quiet between us became uncomfortable. If not for football, it occurs to me, there wouldn't be a word spoken in any home in this country where men gather together and are forced to look at each other across a kitchen table. "I remember your dad butting a guy with his helmet and knocking him to the ground," I say.

And Charles's sons, all three of them, sit up tall in their seats. I let some time pass, hoping to draw them in closer.

"Dad butted the guy?" Chris says finally.

"Yes, he did. Butted him right here." I point to a spot over my right ear, although I'm not completely sure about this detail. Maybe it was over the left ear. Or maybe it wasn't Charles who did it after all. Maybe it was one of the other linemen. Maybe I did it. Regardless of who was responsible, I feel compelled to give the boys something to replace what Charles's death took away from them, and at this moment, as his three sons sit staring at me, it doesn't matter if I have the details perfectly right. In the end, we were all one and the same anyway.

Michael gets up and walks to the refrigerator for a bottle of water. "Except at the stadium when they were younger," he says, "they haven't had the chance to meet people who knew their father back then or played with him. I'm sure they'd enjoy hearing any other stories about LSU you might be willing to tell them."

I understand now that they needed to see me today as much as I needed to see them. I consider telling them about the photo hanging in my closet at home and how for years I'd misread the image, seeing failure where there'd been the opposite. But then I revisit an old image of their father that requires less explanation. No camera was around to document it, but the story is as true as any I've ever told, and not one of the details is fudged.

"I remember this night when I saw him down at the end of the hall in the dormitory," I say. "All the overhead lights were out except for one, and he was standing under it wearing nothing but a jockstrap. He must've just finished working out in the weight room because he was all pumped up—ripped, you know?—and he was doing his poses. By that I mean his bodybuilding poses."

I stand up and imitate him, and Charles's sons begin to laugh.

"And so I yelled at him, 'McDuff, what the hell are you doing?'"

I shift to a different pose now, and I'm laughing too, although when I look across the table at them—when I look at those beautiful boys, men now—what I really want to do is cover my face and bawl.

"'What the hell are you doing, McDuff?' I called out. And your dad didn't say anything. He stayed under the light at the end of the hall. I can see him now. He just stood there posing."

IT'S SLOW IN ARRIVING, but finally the time comes when you don't get the questions anymore. Weeks, months, even years go by, and one day you're at a wedding reception and some kid with a smart mouth walks up. He might be twenty-two, still smells of the bathroom floor in the gentlemen's club where he consumed an entire tray of Jell-O shots the night before. You tell him to zip his pants. He thinks you're joking. "Hey, John Head. Go Tigers, right?"

You could break him to pieces, and yet the opportunity to talk about your football past excuses his impudence. "Yes, you're right, go Tigers. But that was a long time ago—half a lifetime, as a matter of fact."

Actually, it was longer than that, but the youth is too wasted to compute the error. "What was it like?" he asks.

"What was it like? Oh, it was great, what I can remember of it."

The smile grows larger. It's easy to see where he's leading you, and you suddenly wish you'd stayed home. "Did y'all wear leather helmets back then, John Head?"

"No, we didn't. The helmets weren't any different from today's helmets."

"What about face masks?"

"What about them?"

"Did the helmets have face masks when you played?"

He's a smart one, this kid in a rented tuxedo with a crushed boutonniere hanging sideways from his lapel. He laughs loudest when he has a crowd, and now he's attracted one. He grabs his crotch, stomps the ground, and runs off looking over his shoulder and pretending to be scared. "Take it easy on me, John Head. Oh, please, take it easy on me."

You later find him dancing with the most beautiful woman in the room, and it comes to you that she is the kind of girl you might've dated once. You wonder if you'd have been better off quitting that day in 1973 when you ran into Big Hamm and hurt your neck.

And yet, when you're home alone later and reach to turn off the light, the question comes back to you and you forgive the kid his thoughtlessness. So what was it like, John Head?

It's too bad no one's around. You might like to give an answer now.

A PRISON OFFICIAL leads me through the iron gates and down a long breezeway to the Unit-2 Callout Building. Past the guard gates and miles of cyclone fencing, blackbirds move in clouds that rise and fall in the bright winter sky. Their chatter is the only sound you hear. About fifty yards away, several dozen men wait in line outside the door of the low-slung mess hall, all wearing the same thing: shirts and pants made of denim and black, thick-soled shoes over white socks.

Hunt Correctional is a maximum-security prison situated in old plantation country near St. Gabriel, about twenty minutes southeast of Baton Rouge. I've come today for Ramsey Dardar, number 98 when he was my teammate at LSU, now Louisiana Department of Corrections inmate number 222823.

A guard mans the door to the Callout Building, another the inspection station inside. I'm escorted to a meeting area with a warren of conference rooms along one wall. Each room is about the size of a dressing closet and comes equipped with two chairs and a three-foot-square table. Acoustic tiles pad the walls. Hanging above one of the chairs is a hand-lettered sign that reads INMATES BEING INTERVIEWED SIT HERE.

Ramsey is one of two thousand and eighty-nine inmates assigned to the prison. On this day he is forty-six years old. He will be almost seventy-one before the state lets him out.

Even as I sit waiting in the hot, confined room, I struggle to believe that one of my teammates has ended up in such a place. It's true that Ramsey had a wild streak, but he was the kind of player coaches like to call "a good character guy," meaning he wasn't likely to let you down in the face of the temptation that came at us in a thousand different forms each day. By 1982, his senior year, he was one of the best defensive tackles in the country. At the peak of his NFL career, he had a contract worth four hundred and fifty thousand dollars. Now at Hunt, he labors as an orderly in the prison's educational building, making twelve cents an hour.

I met Ramsey when he reported for camp in August of 1979. Wearing faded bib overalls and a plaid short-sleeve shirt, he sat across the table from me in the dining hall, eating his first meal as an LSU player. I wondered what piece of backwater Charles Pevey had plucked him from, even as I admired Ramsey's stout, muscular form and the relish with which he devoured a huge cut of prime rib. His dark skin showed a blush of summer sunburn, the kind earned honestly from outdoor labor, and when I heard him speak, I felt an instant kinship. "Comment ça va, mon ami?" I said, responding to his accent. "Ça va bien, et tu?" he replied. He reached across the table for my hand, and I told him my name. "I'm Fontenot on my mother's side," I said.

Ramsey had grown up on a small farm in Cecilia, a town in the heart of Cajun country, about a forty-minute drive from Opelousas. In those days he identified himself as black, but his father, Murphy Dardar, was a mix of African-American, Native-American, and French ancestry. French was Ramsey's first language. As a matter of fact, he said he spoke little English until he entered first grade and his teachers forced him to learn it. His father spoke only a few words of English, Ramsey told me that day, and he couldn't read or write. When he wasn't farming, Ramsey's father worked as a laborer building the board roads that serviced derricks in the oil fields. His family owned a hundred and twenty acres, and they raised okra, cotton, corn, peppers, and sweet potatoes. They also grew hay and kept horses, hogs, and cows. Even though he came from rural Louisiana— and a fairly isolated part of the state at that—some of the best football schools in the country had managed to find Ramsey when he was a senior at Cecilia High. He wasn't interested. He was going to LSU.

In the spring of 1983, the St. Louis Cardinals selected Ramsey in the third round of the NFL draft. After three years with the club, he had short stints with the New York Giants and the Houston Oilers but didn't catch on with either team. Injuries and drug addiction forced him out of the game.

Without football to sustain him, Ramsey returned to Baton Rouge and started a career as a burglar. Stealing from garden sheds, uninhabited houses, and small businesses became the easiest way to finance his dependency on crack cocaine. He also approached old friends from school for money, as well as strangers he met on the street. One day he sought an audience with Dale Brown, the LSU basketball coach. The charismatic Brown had retired from coaching in 1997, but former Tiger athletes still went to him for help and advice. "When he came to me the first time," says Brown, "I told him, 'Ramsey, I'm telling you, you're going to get in serious trouble if you don't stop this.' Well, Ramsey got in trouble. Then he came to me a second time. 'You're going to get rapped, Ramsey. You're going to get rapped.' And this is exactly what happened. He got rapped."

Beginning in 1990, I followed Ramsey's criminal career in the *Advocate*, which chronicled his exploits under headlines so repetitive they read like reprints. EX-FOOTBALL STAR DARDAR ARRESTED IN BREAK-IN read one in November of 1997. FORMER LSU FOOTBALL PLAYER ARRESTED IN HOME BURGLARIES, read another six months later. In one stretch, Ramsey spent nearly six years in prison, only to return to his career as a thief eight months after being set free. He served two years in Angola, the penitentiary that houses many of the state's worst offenders. In one of his more colorful arrests, Ramsey ran from police and hid under a house. A dog was sent to flush him out. Ramsey fought the animal with a screwdriver. "The dog bit him fifty-six times and cut an artery in his leg," Ramsey's sister, Carmelita Alexander, tells me. "He had to go to Earl K. Long Hospital. It's true that he stabbed the dog and nearly killed it, but Ramsey was defending himself."

This incident was especially hard for me to imagine: the huge, powerful athlete stabbing a dog in the blackened crawl space under the floorboards of a house. Having faced Ramsey countless times in practice, I can tell you the animal didn't stand a chance.

During his playing days, Ramsey stood six-three and weighed two hundred and seventy pounds, but at the height of his addiction, he withered down to two-twelve. "He lived at my house in Baton Rouge for awhile," says Carmelita. "But he'd suddenly up and leave, and he wouldn't come back. One time he was gone for weeks, and I worried so much I got in my car and went looking for him. I went to a place in South Baton Rouge called the Bottom, and a man there told me Ramsey had moved to a house near Baton Rouge High. I found the place; it was an old, wood house. I stood at the door and looked inside. I could see a man counting piles of coins on the floor. There were coins scattered everywhere; some cash, too. I didn't know him. I said, 'I'm looking for Dardar.' The man said, 'That's me, Carma.'"

Ramsey invited her in. She could see the clear definition of his skull, the cheekbones sticking out. There was a crusty hole in the side of his head that he'd earned in a fight with a fellow crack addict. "It looked like they'd stabbed him there," says Carmelita. "He'd stolen coins from a car wash, and every one of those coins was precious to him. He needed every penny he could scavenge to buy crack. I said, 'Ramsey, later tonight I'm going to make a fish stew and fry some fish, and I want you to come eat.' But he said he couldn't wait, he needed food now."

She drove him to a fried chicken restaurant and spent twenty dollars on chicken, shrimp, mashed potatoes, slaw, biscuits, and hush puppies. Next they went to a general store for a bag of toiletries. "He was filthy dirty," she says. "He didn't even own a toothbrush."

Before Carmelita returned home, Ramsey talked her into lending him another twenty dollars. He promised not to spend it on crack, but when he failed to show up at her house that night, she knew he'd lied to her again. As she was sleeping, Carmelita felt a hand grab her ankle under the covers and give it a shake. A voice spoke in her ear, "Carmelita, wake up, baby. Wake up, Carmelita. You have to go find Ramsey." It was her mother, dead nearly fifteen months now.

"It put me in a cold sweat," Carmelita says. "I got up and went looking. I went to two or three corners where these men hang out. 'I'm looking for Dardar,' I told them. Everybody knew who he was, but no one had seen him. I got home at six in the morning and turned the TV on. There was a news story that former LSU football star Ramsey Dardar had been arrested again on burglary charges. The police arrested him at three in the morning, the time my mother came to me in my dream. I started shouting, 'Thank you, Jesus. Thank you, Jesus.' They were finally getting Ramsey off the street."

In June of 1998, prosecutors brought forty-three burglary counts against him. Had he not reached a plea agreement, admitting to eight of the charges, Ramsey might have faced more than a hundred years in prison. Instead, he got thirty-two flat years, meaning he had no chance for parole. The severity of the sentence angered Ramsey's family and left others mystified. "Murderers get off with lighter sentences," says Dale Brown. "I think it's ludicrous that he's going to be in for so long. It shows that our judicial system isn't keyed in properly. I can usually pick out a con artist, but I don't see this in Ramsey. I believe him when he says he regrets what he did. I believe a man like Ramsey can be rehabilitated, and I believe he's rehabilitated now, even though he's rotting away behind bars."

The prison official told me earlier that Ramsey was excited about my visit, and I can see it in his face when he comes striding toward me. He's wearing a smile, the same one from school, and holding his head back on his shoulders in such a way as to suggest immense pride. His shirt and pants are clean and neatly pressed, his shoes polished. He has a thin mustache, and his head is shaved clean. I've interviewed inmates for stories before, though never without a screen of metal or Plexiglas standing between us. Nor did I ever visit one who wasn't wearing shackles or handcuffs to restrain him. Ramsey has no such impediments. He enters the room and throws his arms around me. He does so without hesitation, confident that a guard won't stop him and that I'll welcome the embrace. "I can't believe you came to see me, John Ed," he says, wrapping me up.

"I'm here, man. Sorry it took so long."

The official moves another chair into the conference room and sits at the table with us. Ramsey takes the seat under the sign on the wall, leans back, and runs a hand over his scalp. "Have any of the guys come to see you?" I ask. "I'm not the only one, am I?"

"Coach Stovall came by about three weeks ago," he says. "We read the Bible, and he counseled me. Coach Brown has been by to see me. That man has been good to me, John Ed, better than anyone else from LSU. He gives me money every blue moon when I'm in a spot. He promises to keep working to get me out of here."

"But none of the guys, huh?"

"Well, I did see Greg LaFleur and Verge Ausberry. They were working for the athletic department at the time, and they came to the prison to give talks. Before he went off to prison himself, Lyman White came to see me. He was with Coach Brown. But there's been nobody else I can think of. Well, let me take that back. I did see Lawrence Williams."

"Lawrence, huh? He paid you a visit?"

"No, Lawrence was an inmate here. He got in trouble with drugs."

"You're kidding. Lawrence Williams?" Lawrence, a linebacker from Lake Charles, had been a member of Ramsey's class, another beautiful kid with a big smile beyond his face mask.

"I have to tell you, John Ed, it hurts me to talk about LSU. I'll get to remembering my old teammates, and I wonder what they must think of me. I feel shame like you can't believe. I can barely stand it sometimes. I let everybody down—all you guys and all those people who were good to me."

Inmates at Hunt often ask Ramsey about LSU and what it was like to play in Tiger Stadium. "I tell them it was the best time of my life," he says. "Because it was—there was nothing like it. Around here I get too much recognition sometimes. New people come through, and somebody points me out. 'See that guy? That's Dardar from LSU.' It embarrasses me, man."

"Why does that embarrass you?"

"Because well, it's not flattering, if that's what you're thinking. Look at where I am. I mean, I used to play football for LSU, and now here I am in prison. But I always greet people with a happy face, even when it's eating me up on the inside."

I tell Ramsey he doesn't look much different from the old days. He says he keeps in shape by running a lot and by playing in the prison basketball and football leagues. Hunt has a full-contact football club that includes four thirty-member teams. Ramsey, who says he weighs about two hundred and fifty-five pounds, plays defensive and offensive tackle for the Falcons. "The other teams are the Bucs, the Chargers, and the Rams," he says. "I played for the Saints for four years, but we were winning all the time, and the real Saints in New Orleans couldn't do a thing, so we changed our name to the Falcons. We play on Saturday, and while it's not Tiger Stadium, this prison does have some athletes—guys who could've been, you know what I mean?"

I hate to ask him about the drug addiction and crimes that put him behind bars, and when I do, a half-smile comes to his face, a smile of incredulity, as if he, even more than I, can't believe the nightmare he has made of his life. At LSU he smoked marijuana on "a social basis," he says, and experimented with cocaine. "But it wasn't bad until I got to the NFL. There was so much dope and so many parties. I was hanging out with wild guys, and next thing you know, I'm an addict. By the time I got to Houston, I was deeply involved in crack. The truth is, I try to forget what I went through. The only thing about the NFL that ever made me happy was the paycheck."

He pauses for a minute. I can tell he's struggling to share something else. "I married a woman named Lorraine, a beautiful woman."

"Yeah?"

"We had a family—three kids at the time I'm telling you about—and one day she and her friend went shopping for a car in Beaumont. My wife had my son with her, Ramsey Jr. She was talking to a salesman, and the friend was watching my little boy. Well, somehow he got away from her. He was two and a half years old, John Ed, and he was playing. He ran out toward this busy intersection, and the girl and my wife ran after him. My son was laughing, looking back over his shoulder. He thought it was a game, and he ran into traffic. This lady came along and hit him going sixty miles an hour."

"Come on, man."

"It's true. One of the back wheels of her car ran over him. All this happened while my wife was watching." Ramsey continues to look directly at me. He speaks calmly, without any apparent emotion, and I find it hard to return his gaze. "You could say that pushed me deeper into the drugs," he says. "People have a way—when you're an athlete and a big, strong guy, they somehow think you're invincible and you don't feel things the way they do. But we're like the normal man. We feel things like the normal man, don't we, John Ed?"

"God almighty, Ramsey. Your little boy."

"I was outside doing something, and the phone wouldn't stop ringing. It was my older sister's husband. It just kept ringing. I'm telling you, man, I was numb for a month. He'd be twenty-two now, Ramsey Jr."

"And your wife—you say she saw this, did she?"

"It messed her up, but I messed her up even worse. That's why you'll never hear me say anything bad about that woman. I put her through hell. You wouldn't believe what I put her through. I cried, man. I cried and I cried and I cried some more. And there has been many a time when I asked God to take my life, I was so fed up with myself. At night the dope kept calling me, calling and calling. I'm serious. It was calling like it wanted me. I'd have these conversations with myself. 'Ramsey, you were an LSU football player. You can't be doing this. You played in Tiger Stadium. Come on, man.' I knew what I was doing was wrong. My wife tried with me, man. She fought for me. Now she won't even take my calls. She won't write to me. She's off living in Atlanta, and she's got nothing to do with me."

"You can't blame her, Ramsey."

"No, I guess you can't. I went to other people for help, LSU people. They tried, but there was nothing they could do because I was so deep into it. Later, when I was arrested, some of the same people who'd cheered for me on Saturday night, I felt they didn't do right by me. Yes, I did those crimes. But the courts in Baton Rouge let me down; I didn't get the compassion I deserved. The people I called, they put me on standby. I was an embarrassment to them. I'm going to be an old man before those gates open and I walk out of here. You know what, John Ed? Sometimes I wonder if I'll ever see Tiger Stadium again."

I'm sure Ramsey's victims have suffered too, but I didn't play ball with them, and it's easy now to forgive him everything and to wish that I could do something to free him from both the prison and his long memory of mistakes. I consider telling him about the events in my own past that have swamped me in shame and self-loathing. I could share scenes from my years with Connie, tell him how my priorities were so screwed up I spent decades hiding from my coaches and teammates as if they'd done me some unforgivable wrong. But I know that my own failures would only sound trivial compared to his, and so I keep my mouth shut.

The prison promised us ninety minutes. I glance at my watch, and more than two hours has gone by. I look at the official and he nods, allowing us to continue. He seems as riveted by Ramsey's story as I am.

"This isn't me, John Ed," Ramsey says. "You know that, don't you? My family was a good family. Did I ever tell you I was the first person from my high school to get a scholarship? We only had four hundred students at that little school. I had three years of perfect attendance. I was named Best Personality and Most Likely to Succeed."

For some reason, this declaration is almost as difficult to hear as the story about his son, maybe because he seems to be pleading a case that was lost long ago, providing a character witness for a man who died the moment he smoked crack and stole from people for money to buy more.

I reach over and touch his arm. "Most Likely to Succeed? Is that what you said?"

"Yes."

"Can you tell me something, Ramsey? What are your chores here? What exactly does an orderly do?"

"I clean up. I'm like a janitor."

"Did you earn a degree from LSU?"

"No, I never finished."

"What did you study?"

"Sociology. Plus I had a minor in phys ed and coaching."

"When's the last time you went to the stadium?"

"I went to the Ole Miss game in 1997. We lost, and I got so upset I almost threw up. I get emotional anytime I get anywhere close to LSU. I could be driving in a car and see the stadium, and that's all it takes. I want to cry just looking at it."

The first time he played in a game, against Alabama in 1979, the All-American Dwight Stephenson was at center for the Crimson Tide. With our top two nose guards, George Atiyeh and Greg Bowser, sidelined with injuries and unable to take the field at one point, Coach Lynn LeBlanc ordered Ramsey in. "I was so scared," Ramsey says. "I tell you, I nearly peed my pants." Before the ball was snapped, Ramsey jumped offside in the gap between the center and the guard. "Stephenson and one of the guards double-teamed me. They lifted me off my feet and drove me all the way back to the safety, fifteen yards down the field. I came off the ground, and I could hear Coach LeBlanc yelling from the sideline. 'Get him out of there! Get him out of there!' I ran to the sideline, and he was yelling at me, 'Dardar, go sit your stupid ass at the end of the bench.' "

For the first time today, Ramsey lets out a laugh. He laughs so hard that after awhile it sounds peculiar, like a man at a funeral who can't hold back anymore. He uses his shirt to wipe his face.

"Some days I'll close my eyes and I'm there again," he says. "I'm not stuck here wasting away. I see the crowd, and we're down on the field. I play the game, every down. I start with the kickoff, and then the defense runs out on the field. We huddle, and I get in position waiting for the snap. I go as long as I can. You'd be surprised by how long that is."

The prison official looks at his watch. I take it as my cue to wrap things up. He stands, and I do too, but Ramsey waits half a minute longer before surrendering his seat. "I wish I could go back," he says. "You don't know how bad I wish I could go back."

We hug again, longer than before. I can think of no last words to tell him. "John Ed, you were good to come," he says.

Ramsey is smiling again, the same smile he flashed when he first came into the room, the one from when we were teammates. I'd bet it's the smile he'll be wearing twenty-four years from now, when they finally set him free.

He leaves, walking on the balls of his feet, shoulders held back in a show of pride, all the way down the hall to the guard who waits to take him away.

Chapter Eight

| BIG ED

ON SATURDAY, there was no escape. Coach Mac stationed monitors throughout the dorm, one at each exit. We called them monitors, but they really were guards hired to watch the doors and keep visitors out. He didn't want anyone bothering us. And he didn't want us to leave the building. Things could happen if we did. Gamblers could offer us bribes to throw the game. Girls could drag us into the bushes. A lightning bolt could come crashing down from the sky and kill us dead, even though the sky was blue. The monitors sat on cafeteria chairs in the open doorways, and if you tried to get past one, he stuck a leg out, planted it on the frame, and blocked your way. Meetings had ended at noon. We had to remain locked down in our rooms until the team meal at 4 p.m. Kickoff was seven hours away.

It was worse than prison, everybody complained. We were rodents in a cage without an exercise wheel to keep us from going crazy. And so we went crazy.

Did Mac want us crazy? I suspected he did. I suspected he wanted us as crazy as he could get us when we boarded the buses later in the afternoon for the half-mile drive to Tiger Stadium. Caution wasn't going to help us against USC. Caution would only get us spanked. Still and all, I was about to lose my mind. I couldn't stand the waiting. I wanted to hit somebody. It didn't matter who.

Big Ed Stanton and I didn't own a radio, and our little black-and-white television wasn't working because somebody had lost his temper earlier in the day and ripped the rabbit ears off the top. Okay, so what if I was this person? We had USC tonight, and the real wonder was how I'd kept from putting my foot in the thing when it failed to receive the local broadcast of ABC's *Game of the Week*. I liked to watch college football before I played college football, and all the set had given me was a haze of static. And so now I was left with only silence to contemplate before the biggest game of my life. I could've ripped a pit bull to pieces with my bare hands. Who invented rabbit ear antennae, anyway? He deserved a beating. Let me be the one who beat him.

Big Ed sat in his bunk with his back against the wall, drawing in a large spiral-bound sketchbook. He was a fine arts major, determined to make a career as an artist once football was done. But football would never be done, because this day would never be done—this Saturday like so many others when Mac condemned us all to two-man cells with only the game to think about.

"Can I see?" I asked Big Ed.

"It's not any good."

"Come on. Let me have a look."

He pulled the sketchbook up close to his chest.

Big Ed and John Ed. How corny was that? At least he was taking our imprisonment better than I was. He seemed calm, almost peaceful. His mind was on his work. He would show me his drawing when it was finished and he was ready and not a moment sooner. You had to be sensitive, even if it was Saturday and you were debating whether to carve the team logo into your thigh with one of Big Ed's X-Acto knives. No one was more vulnerable than the artist, Big Ed had taught me. Every time an artist showed you his work, he was really asking you a question, and the question was always the same: "Am I any good?"

Every half hour or so, I stuck my head out the door to check for activity in the hall. The showers and toilets had been going without a lull since noon, and you could hear the hyper electric whirr of blow dryers and the brittle insistent hum of electric razors. I usually let my whiskers grow out for a few days before each game because I thought the facial hair made me look like someone you didn't want to trifle with. I also liked the cushion it provided against my chinstrap, which could shred your jaw if you didn't wear it tight enough. In the hall, I smelled hair spray and cologne and baby powder and talcum powder. Why did everybody get so damned dolled-up before games? It made no sense. Before long, we would be in uniform tumbling in the grass, sweating and being sweated on, wetting our pants and bleeding from wounds, vomiting, leaking, and snorting out the stuff that kept us from breathing well. Maybe my teammates cleaned up because it gave them something to do. It gobbled time. Rinsing with mouthwash might take only twenty seconds, but this was an eternity on a Saturday afternoon in the dorm. If we were busy clipping toenails and trimming sideburns, we weren't thinking about running full speed down the hall and diving headlong into the guard at the door. We weren't thinking about spearing him under the chin, snapping his head back, and leaving him in a quivering, gelatinous puddle on the floor.

I took out a *Playboy* I'd stolen from one of my teammates, but it was hard to concentrate. Who cared about such things with the

Trojans in town? If the most beautiful woman in the world walked into the room, I'd want to drive my head into her sternum. I resisted an impulse to eat the magazine page by page to show Big Ed how miserable I was. But it was the August issue and Candy Loving was on the cover. Where was my *Sports Illustrated*? Better to eat that.

I looked at the clock. There were hours left to burn. I opened the door and checked the hall again. Frickin' monitors had bladders the size of Olympic swimming pools. I returned to my bunk and lay on my back. Big Ed had put his sketchbook away and turned on the light over his desk. He was propped up on a huddle of pillows reading the Bible.

I stared at him as he turned the page, willing him to put the book down and acknowledge my pain.

"You think USC is tough, John Ed?" he said finally.

"Do I *think* they're tough? No, I don't think it, Big Ed, I *know* it. You saw the film. They could probably beat half the teams in the NFL."

He shook his head. "You think it's tough playing against a nose guard like Ty Sperling, don't you? Well, try taking a blade from a spear in your ribcage. Try that, will you? Try hanging from a cross with nails driven into your palms and feet."

He reached up and turned the lamp off then lay in bed without moving. Against the white sheets, I could see the abrasions from his shoulder pads on his powerful upper body. I could see the helmet bruises on his neck and the yellow-green marks on his belly where weeks earlier an opponent had stepped on him with cleats and nearly ripped him open. He'd centered the Bible on his chest and fixed his eyes on a spot on the ceiling. He was praying, I knew. This was how he did it when there was something important to ask for.

"Say one for me," I whispered.

"What's that?"

"Pray for me, Big Ed. Just say a prayer for me."

He woke me up a few hours later, and I dressed and started for the cafeteria. The pregame meal was always the same: rib-eye steak, baked potato, green peas, and yellow cling peaches from a can. I knew better than to eat much; it would only have me running to the bathroom. And so I took a few bites and quietly sat awhile before I walked my tray to the slot in the wall. I took a seat on one of the red leather sofas in the lobby and waited until Coach Mac came by and handed me a mimeographed copy of the offensive roster, broken down by position. One of my duties as captain was to make sure everybody showed up on time. I checked the names off as the players filed past me one by one to board the first of two buses parked out on the circular drive. The lead bus was always for the offense.

"Anybody missing?" Coach Mac asked.

"No, sir."

I followed him onto the bus, the doors squeezed closed, and we started for the stadium, creeping along to avoid the fans who choked the streets and called out to us. A black-and-white police cruiser led the way, its lights revolving in slow circles. The late-afternoon sun drained in dusty streams through the magnolia trees that stood along Donahue Drive, coloring what was left of the day a wash of green and yellow and blue. I sat in the first row, window seat. Coach Mac took the seat next to me, his hand resting on my knee, staring straight ahead as cops on foot waved us onto Fieldhouse Drive, past the Indian Mounds, and deeper still into fans who slapped and punched the sides of the bus. We were moving into a mob, the route so narrow the driver had to ride his brakes and nose up close to the cruiser, the cops letting out blasts on bullhorns to get everyone back and let us through.

Big Ed sat to the left of Coach Mac on the other side of the aisle. I looked at him and nodded, and he smiled and nodded in reply. There was nothing left to say. Prayers wouldn't help us now. It was here, it was finally here, and it was time to be an animal again.

The bus stopped and the doors flapped open, letting in a roar that came with such force that it felt like a hammer blow to the chest. The people had surrounded us, thousands of them, leaving a narrow path for us to walk from the bus to the stadium.

"You ready to play, buddy?" Coach Mac asked. Before I could answer, he was outside, moving through a sea of hands reaching out to touch him.

THE ALMEDA ANTIQUE MALL was once an 84 Lumber. Old wooden furniture, vintage tools, and farm implements crowd what must've been the loading dock. A large, bald-headed man pushes through the glass doors of the building and stands at the top of the steps, hands thrust down deep in the pockets of his work pants. He looks at me for a moment, as if trying to place me, then comes walking in my direction, shuffling his shoes on the cement, moving like a kid who's been assigned a chore he'd rather not do. "That you, John Ed?"

"Yes, it is. How're you doing, Big Ed?"

I hop up on the dock and stride over to him, not sure whether to violate his natural reserve and throw my arms around him or offer him a handshake. I quickly come up with a compromise: I take his hand in one hand and pound his shoulder with the other. Big Ed does the same to me.

"Find us all right?" he asks.

"Found you fine," I answer.

Not long after the 1979 Tangerine Bowl, Big Ed married his girlfriend, Kerry. When they left for their honeymoon, I left for home, and I didn't speak to him again until January of 2006, when I looked his name up in the White Pages and gave him a call. Like me, Big Ed was undersized for his position, but at forty-eight, he fits the mold of the prototypical offensive tackle. That is to say, he looks like someone who's made an effort to stay fit without denying himself the pleasure of an occasional tub of ice cream. Almost as surprising is his lack of hair. Big Ed now shaves his head, much like Ramsey. Instead of the mustache he always wore, he has a thin, stubbly goatee, most of it gray.

"Find us all right?" he says again, apparently forgetting that he asked me the same question seconds before.

He's clearly as nervous as I am, and I'm glad. "It was pretty easy," I say. "You always did give good directions."

"I guess you think I've changed a lot?"

"I've changed a lot too. That's what happens to people when they get old."

"Come on in and look around," he says. "I know everybody'll be real happy to see you again, John Ed."

The antique mall, it turns out, is more than the metal structure that once housed a lumber company. Big Ed's family also owns the barn-size building on the adjacent lot and built a walkway joining the two spaces, filling both with antiques, junk, and collectibles, most of it belonging to vendors who rent space for things that otherwise would sit in attics and storage sheds. Big Ed's parents also own an outdoor flea market and several hundred storage units for boats and campers. He works for them full-time as the operations manager for the storage business, although he also takes on occasional odd jobs at the mall. Big Ed's mother, Jonel, is an authority on American art pottery, and her collections fill the vitrines and large glass cases.

"See these here," Big Ed says, only a minute after we've moved inside. "This is all Rookwood right here, and a lot of these vases are hand-painted. Each one is individually done, you see? I suppose that's why Rookwood is my favorite, why I like it more than the other potteries." He points to a glossy brown vase with a flower painted on the side. "An artist painted that. It's a painting, but it's also a vase."

"So it's a painting on a vase?"

"Yes, it is. That's it exactly."

We move to the next group of flower pots, and he tells me about his mother's McCoy, Weller, and Roseville finds, and I wonder why it's easier for Big Ed and me to look at animal figurines and talk about their value than it is to look at each other and talk about where life has taken us. For nearly an hour, we waste time walking from one side of the mall to the other, examining items that hold little interest for either of us: a ten-thousand-dollar rolltop desk, a Victorian bedroom suite, a Beatles poster, a pair of badly damaged Eames chairs, a stuffed baby alligator, a stuffed squirrel, and at least a thousand Beanie Babies, most of them complete with ear tags from the manufacturer. What I don't see are any paintings or drawings with Big Ed Stanton's signature on them.

I wait until we've left the mall to ask him what happened. We're on an interstate, driving south to a place called Bayou Vista, just north of Galveston and the Gulf of Mexico. Big Ed and Kerry recently bought a weekend house there. "Even after I graduated and left LSU I still wanted to be an artist," he says. "I painted and did a lot of drawing in those years. But then my father offered me a good-paying job to work with him, and our two children came along, and my responsibilities to my job and my family kept me from pursuing the career I'd dreamed about. At times this made me miserable, being unable to draw and paint. But I also went through periods when I wanted to paint and I had the time and I couldn't make myself do it. Something stopped me. I've been happy, John Ed, I want you to know that. You don't hear about too many families that work together the way we do. We all get along, which is unusual."

"Big Ed, you always got along with everybody."

"I'm not sure about that, but we really are close, and we do everything ourselves, where the business is concerned. Take the storage units, for instance. We put the roofs on ourselves. We drive the posts for the buildings and clean out the spaces that people abandon. We auction off the stuff they leave behind—we actually do the auctions, and sometimes we bid on items and buy them and put them for sale in the antique mall. I've always worked hard. Right now I'm in the process of replacing the metal on the buildings—I'm doing the labor myself—so I'm out in the hot sun all day. It isn't easy. There was a time not long ago when I began to wonder what I was doing. I took a room in the antique mall and turned it into a studio. I'd go in there and close the door and paint and draw for hours. I started believing I could make something of it, but then one day I decided it was time to lock the door and not go back in there. It's been locked now for four or five years. I've got my drawings and paintings in there, my art books, and a lot of things I've collected that once were important to me."

Big Ed's daughter, Kelly, is a sophomore at Texas A&M, and his seventeen-year-old son, Trey, is a senior at Friendswood High. Like their father, both were hometown sports stars. Six-foot-one Kelly received a full athletic scholarship to play volleyball for the Aggies, and six-foot-ten Trey, a forward on the Mustangs basketball team, had six schools recruiting him when he visited the Naval Academy in Annapolis, Maryland, felt an immediate kinship, and committed to play for the Midshipmen. Big Ed and

Kerry are waiting for Trey to leave for Annapolis before making Bayou Vista their full-time residence.

Big Ed pulls off the interstate and stops at a smokehouse for lunch. We order plates of barbecue and large iced teas and spend the next hour talking about our former teammates. I tell him about some of the success stories—Thad Minaldi, now a big-shot lawyer in Calcasieu Parish; Robert Dugas, the one-time team orthopedic surgeon for the Nebraska Cornhuskers; Tom Tully, a professor of avian medicine at the LSU vet school—but it's the players who suffered hardship that receive most of our attention. "It broke my heart when I learned that Charles McDuff was dead," Big Ed says. "Poor guy. I really liked him." I tick off the names of the teammates now in jail—the ones I know about, anyway—and he stares at me in disbelief. "Ramsey and George and Lyman went to prison? Can that be true?"

I thought I was alone in my efforts to remain estranged from LSU, but Big Ed knows even less than I do. We're almost done with the meal when he tells me he hasn't been back to Tiger Stadium since our last game there. "It's been easy for me to hide out here in Texas," he says. "Only a few old-timers even remember that I played football. But for years I'd dream about it and wake up feeling lost. In the worst dream I had, I was playing for LSU but I didn't know where I was. The coaches wanted me in the game, but for some reason I could never reach the field. I always woke up feeling sick, sort of haunted. The good dreams didn't make me feel any better. Like this one where I learn that it isn't really over. I still have a year of eligibility left. In my sleep it feels so real, and I'm happy and excited. I mean, I want it so much. But then I wake up and realize that my mind's tricked me again. Football's over and LSU's in the past. I can't tell you what a dreadful feeling that leaves me with."

Since moving from Baton Rouge in 1981, Big Ed and Kerry have returned to campus only once. Kelly and Trey were little, and Big Ed took them to the Indian Mounds and let them roll down the small, grassy hills. From where he stood, he could see Broussard Hall down past the trees at the end of the drive, and he felt something he hadn't expected. A kind of sadness, a yearning for what he could never have again. The kids were too young to understand, so he didn't say anything. He made no effort to look up any of our former teammates. He didn't want to impose on anyone.

Big Ed's closest friend at LSU was probably Barry Rubin, a fullback who transferred to Northwestern State in Natchitoches after our sophomore year. After college, Barry became a strength coach, mostly with the Green Bay Packers. Big Ed saw Barry a few times on television, standing on the sideline at Packer games. He sometimes watched Green Bay for the chance to see him again. He couldn't explain why he never called Barry or wrote him a letter. Something stopped him.

Several years ago, Big Ed was driving on Interstate 10 near Houston when he heard a horn in the lane next to him. He looked over and saw Sam McCage, a former tight end, who'd grown up in nearby Baytown. Sam had a young woman in the car with him; Big Ed assumed she was his wife. Sam and Big Ed waved to each other, and then Big Ed slowed down and let Sam move on. What was he supposed to do? he wondered. Pull over on the shoulder and strike up a conversation? No one had ever told him how to behave in such a situation.

Another time, Big Ed went to Lake Charles to visit Kerry's dad, who was in the hospital to have a kidney stone removed. Coach McCarty had become an insurance agent after he left LSU, and Big Ed looked him up and visited his office unannounced. He was nervous when he asked the woman behind the counter if Coach McCarty was in. The woman said he was away at lunch, and Big Ed walked back outside feeling as much relief as disappointment. He could've stopped by later; the woman said Coach McCarty would be back soon. Instead, Big Ed drove west into Texas, back home to Friendswood. He never tried to contact Coach McCarty again.

"So I'm the first guy you've seen in a long time?" I say, as we're leaving the smokehouse.

"Yes, I wish I'd gone to see Coach Mac before he died. But I wondered if he'd even remember me."

"I wondered the same thing, when I went. But he remembered me, Big Ed, and he surely would've remembered you."

"I don't know about that. But thanks for saying it." He reaches over and taps me on the arm. "John Ed, you ever think about the USC game? I mean, you ever remember what it was like?" Before I can answer, he says, "You know what I think about? It's a big regret of mine. We were playing them tough, the best team in the country, maybe the best team ever. We were threatening to score at the end of the game, and up to that point, we'd blocked so well, done so good. Well, I got excited and wasted all my energy screaming and hollering. I jumped around so much that I ran out of gas. I was exhausted, I had nothing left. If I'd just kept my composure, we probably would've scored and won the game. Instead, I'm out there acting like a cheerleader, and I'm supposed to be an offensive lineman—supposed to be disciplined and poised. A lineman takes it out on the other man. Not me. I've got to go and celebrate. I can't believe how stupid I was."

"Did you get beat or blow an assignment? Is that what bothers you?"

"I don't think I did. But I'd feel a lot better about myself if I hadn't behaved the way I did. I don't know why I had to be an idiot."

"Maybe you acted like an idiot because you saw me acting like one and thought it was the right thing to do."

"Are you trying to make me feel good?"

"No, it's true. Besides, Big Ed, that game was almost thirty years ago. And we lost. How can it still bother you that you celebrated too much?"

"I don't know, but it does. Every time I see pro players on television, every time I see linemen methodically going about their business, playing hard but keeping their heads, I wonder why I had to dance around like I did."

The house stands by a canal that flows into West Bay, which in turn joins Galveston Bay and the Gulf of Mexico. It's painted canary yellow and trimmed in white, and there's an eight-pole boathouse behind it with a deck on top and enough space under the roof to shelter Big Ed's fishing rig and a couple of Jet Skis. Inside the home, most of the furnishings come from resale and thrift shops; Kerry found them in her buying trips for the antique mall. Half a dozen large oil paintings hang on the walls, though none done by Big Ed's hand. "Something you might like to see," he says, leading me down to a garage. A golf cart sits in the darkened space. "I can never ride in that thing without thinking about Coach Mac," he says. "In fact, I see a golf cart anywhere and I think about him. He only invited me to ride in his cart with him one time—that was it, John Ed, just once—but I often think about what he told me. It seemed an odd thing to tell me at the time, because we'd just finished practice, but he said, 'Ed, the most important thing you can learn in your life is how to make adjustments. You want to be prepared to make changes for any situation that comes your way.' Then, in the next breath, he was telling me I should learn how to play golf. He said golf helps you get to know people. I was honored that he would let me ride with him and that he offered me advice, but I've never learned how to play golf. I have the cart because one of the fun things we do here is drive up and down the street. We feel the salt breeze, and we wave at people we don't even know, and we look at the pretty homes and the water."

Big Ed leads me to a clutter of lawn chairs by the canal, and we sit and watch ducks swim in pairs on the choppy black surface. A pelican swoops in low and completes a clumsy landing, splashing water. I glance over to see if Big Ed has been watching the bird. Instead I find that he's been staring at me. "What about you?" he says. "Why don't you tell me about your life, John Ed? You never married and had a family? How have your relationships gone for you?"

I shrug and turn back to the ducks. "It's been a disappointment, that part of things. I don't really like to talk about it."

I let the silence fall between us, hoping the moment will pass, but when I look back at him, he's still watching me.

"Tell me. You know you can talk to me."

"You can't want to hear it, Big Ed."

"But I do."

I lean forward in the chair, elbows on my knees. It's easier if I keep my eyes on the water. "Imagine you pursued your dream of being an artist," I say. "Going in, you knew the future offered no guarantees; the only real promise was struggle. This is what I thought awaited me when I left football and set out to be a writer. I had it in my head that I could take failure if I was alone. As a single man, I could take risks, and I'd be okay if they didn't work out. But I couldn't let down a wife and children who needed me. That was my biggest fear, and it's about crippled me, Big Ed. At times I have felt tremendous sadness that football is gone from my life, but the truth is it's just another hole in me. The others are every bit as hard to fill." I face him again. "If I'm certain of anything, it's that I'm guilty of dwelling on the loss of football because it's less painful than dwelling on my other losses."

I wait for him to laugh at me, but he doesn't. If three more decades pass before I see him again, we'll both be close to eighty. Do football players get that old? I can't name one who has. Suddenly there's something else I feel compelled to tell him.

"I always had such respect for you, Big Ed," I say. "I always thought you were as fine a guy as there was on the team. When I left LSU, I'd often think of you. I could be in a spot where I might be inclined to do the wrong thing, and I'd wonder what you'd do given the same situation. I'd remember our talks in Broussard, and how you'd pray before the games. You always seemed to know what to say to me. 'Do I want to do this?' I'd ask myself. 'Would Big Ed Stanton do this?'"

"When you were having that temptation, John Ed, I was having the same one. And I was asking myself the same questions and applying them to you. 'What would John Ed Bradley do?'"

"You mean it?"

He nods his head. "I feel a closeness to you that I can't explain. It started a long time ago, and it hasn't changed or gone away. This might be a cliché, but it really is like we went to war together. What we have is like what those servicemen have who spent time side by side in foxholes. They're brothers the rest of their lives. I don't talk about LSU football with anyone anymore. Oh, I could talk to my children about it. I could tell them all day long what it was like, but they still wouldn't understand. You and I were there."

He closes up the house, and we drive back to the antique mall. When we walk inside, his mother leads me over to the pottery cabinets and shows me some of her favorite pieces. I pick out a large Roseville jardiniere and a Shearwater goose to buy and take home with me. I suppose I spend too much time admiring an old piece of stoneware, because before I can object, Kerry has placed it in a box and walked out to put it in my truck.

If I want something to remember the trip by, I'll have more than pottery. Big Ed disappears minutes after we get back. I take a tour of both buildings before I find him. He's upstairs in the dark trying to open a door, but he can't make the combination lock cooperate. He tries several sequences then gives up, his face beading with sweat as he trudges past me without saying a thing. When he comes back, he's lugging a crowbar, brandishing it with such purpose that I wonder if he plans to beat the door down. Instead, he uses it to pop the lock off, and then he's inside, flipping a switch that drops light from a collection of fluorescent tubes high up on the ceiling. I'm watching him from about twenty feet away. Finally it comes to me what I'm seeing.

A step inside the room, set on an easel, there's a detailed portrait of Kerry, done in pencil. Big Ed's canvases are scattered here and there, some on the floor, others pinned to the wall. "John Ed, come on over here," he says. "I have something I want to show you."

Chapter Nine

COACH BRADLEY'S BOY

THAT MORNING, he took me downtown to Garbo's for a haircut, then to J.W. Low for a scoop of ice cream at the counter. Low's was the five-and-dime, and it was always crowded on Saturday. I liked the way people came up and talked to him about the team: "Y'all played 'em tough, Coach. Yes, indeed. Y'all sure played 'em tough." Old men in sweat-stained seersucker and porkpie hats, girls in tight cardigans and too much makeup, ladies who lightly placed a hand on his shoulder before walking off and claiming a stool. He nudged the side of my arm and asked me what I planned to wear that night. We were looking at each other in the mirror behind the fountains. I shrugged and spooned up a bite, and he said not to worry, he'd help me find something. I was only nine, and I'd never been to Tiger Stadium before.

He took me home, laid my Sunday shirts on the bed, and told me to choose one, then found the khakis with the sharpest creases in the legs. My shoes were dirty, so he brought them outside and gave them a shine. "I want you to know I'm jealous," he said. He was back in my room now, holding a shoe in each hand, the hands in the slots where you put your feet. "I wish somebody would invite me to Tiger Stadium."

"Have you ever met Coach Mac?"

"No, I haven't. But I understand he's a real fine person."

My friend William had gotten me the ticket. It came with a seat on one of the Greyhound charters that picked up passengers in the park in the early afternoon and drove them to Baton Rouge. Daddy took me to the lot where the buses were idling, the warm air inside fogging the windows. Because we were first to arrive, we waited in the shade of some pecan trees and looked out past the tall hurricane fence that surrounded Donald Gardner Stadium. The field where Daddy coached on Friday nights was in bad shape after the long season. A trough of dried mud ran down the middle from one goalpost to the other. The grass was sparse and stripped of color.

"Why do they take buses to the games?" I asked him.

"What do you mean?"

"They take buses. Don't they have cars they can drive?"

"Oh. Well, I guess it's because they like to socialize and have a good time on the way there and back." He gave me a look to make sure I was listening. "You might see some people from town behaving a little different from how you're used to seeing them. You be polite to them, you hear me?"

"Why will they be behaving different?"

"They get excited about the Tigers, and they have a highball or two. If they start doing things you're not used to seeing, just turn your head to the side and look out the window. Will you do that for me?"

"Yes, sir."

"Don't stare at anybody."

"I won't."

"You be a good boy, and don't disappoint me. I'll be here waiting for you when you get back later tonight."

I ate a chicken salad sandwich on the way. An old woman gave it to me. She was sitting across from me on the aisle, wearing a red dress and holding a red purse. Even her lipstick was red. She had cut the crust off the bread, but it was still a good sandwich. I also drank a Coca-Cola from a can, this too from the old woman. It was a real Coke, unlike the soft drinks we had on special occasions at home. The bus took us east on Highway 190 through cypress and tupelo swamps and farmland lush and green and little towns crowded with filling stations and bait shops and blinking traffic signals and dead armadillos on the side of the road. We slowed down to clear the speed traps, the men in dusty black-and-whites hiding in bushes growing untamed under billboards for a motor court or an all-you-can-eat catfish restaurant.

Most of the ladies on the bus were dressed in two-piece outfits decorated with corsages and spirit ribbons. They wore perfume that made you sneeze if you forgot to breathe through your mouth. The men wore black or gray suits and skinny neckties held in place with tie clips. They fiddled with binoculars and read from the sports page of the *Daily World*, sipping from monogrammed whiskey flasks made of dimpled pewter. Traffic was heavy on the old road, and almost two hours went by before we crossed the river and reached the stadium. Just as we were parking, the lady with the sandwich applied a fresh smear of lipstick with the aid of a compact. I watched her in the small, round mirror until her eyes darted right and met mine, and then I turned away and looked out the window, as my father had told me to do.

It was well before kickoff, and I followed William past the ticket takers and up the ramps to our seats. We climbed until the muscles in my thighs burned and my head was spinning. William knew where to go. He led me through a portal, and there, suddenly, the field lay stretched out before us, flat as a game board. On either end, players in uniform were doing exercise routines. They ran in zigzag patterns, tumbled on the ground, and popped up to their feet, running in place. They kicked and punted the ball great distances. Several balls flew in the air at once, and I was amazed at how they never seemed to touch the ground: Every one that went up found its mark upon coming back down, and its mark didn't drop it.

Standing at the center of it all was a man in a suit. He moved from one group of players to another, his mouth opening wide as he jawed at them, shouting orders. He slapped the players' helmets, shoulder pads, and rear ends. I had seen his picture before in the newspaper. It was Coach Mac.

Our seats were near the top of the south end zone—so high up you could barely make out the jersey numbers, but not so high that you couldn't tell one team from the other or follow the action without confusion. Daddy had given me money for food and a souvenir. I'd had the sandwich on the bus, so I used it to buy a game program and a bobblehead doll made to look like an LSU player.

The game was a rout. Midway through the third quarter, much of the stadium had cleared out. William and I waited until two minutes remained on the game clock before heading back to the bus, having to double-step down the ramps to keep up with the crowd. When we got there, everyone was waiting. "Don't let us keep you," somebody shouted from a seat in back.

Then there was another voice. "Isn't that Coach Bradley's boy?"

The driver sat at his wheel in the dark listening to the radio. A burst of noise came from the stadium, and I heard it seconds later on the broadcast in the bus, and I thought of my father back home in Opelousas, outside with his radio.

288

"Is that everybody?" the driver said. He walked the aisle counting heads. "Tell me if that's not everybody." As if the people who weren't yet onboard were somehow supposed to speak up or get left behind.

I slept most of the way home, the program in one hand, bobblehead in the other. Somewhere on the highway, down around the approach to the bridge that crosses the Atchafalaya and takes you into Krotz Springs, the old woman with the red lips reached across the aisle and tapped me on the shoulder. I could see her face illuminated by the track lights in the floor. "Is it true you're Coach Bradley's boy?"

"Yes, ma'am."

"John Jr.?"

"John Edmund Jr."

"You go by Junior?"

"No, ma'am. I go by John Ed." I looked at her awhile. "It's just the name they gave me. I don't like it at all."

"But it's such a nice name. And it's nice to meet you, John Ed. I'm Miss Marie Pavy." She pronounced her name *Pah-vee*. "I taught your daddy in school many years ago. He was one of my favorite students. Come to think of it, he's one of the finest young men I've ever known." She pulled the cellophane off another sandwich and held it out to me. The bread on that one didn't have any crust either. It looked like ham and cheese this time. "Aren't you hungry, John Ed?"

"No, ma'am."

"You didn't like the first sandwich I gave you?"

"I liked it."

"Here. Go ahead and try this one."

She seemed to enjoy watching me eat. When I was done, I rolled up the cellophane and placed it in her outstretched hand.

"You look just like your daddy," Miss Pavy said. She smiled, and I saw the lipstick smudges on her teeth. "Maybe when you grow up you can play football for LSU. You think you'd like to do that?"

I'd never be that old, never be that lucky, but the idea was a nice one, and it kept me awake and thinking the rest of the way.

Toward midnight, we pulled into the lot at Donald Gardner Stadium, and I could see him past the window. He was parked where he said he would be, down by the fence and the end zone, waiting by himself in the dark.

A FEW WEEKS after I saw Coach Mac for the last time, I bought a Plexiglas display box for my LSU helmet. The old yellow hat had been in closets since I left the team, much of that time in darkness under sheets. Now it's displayed on a fancy antique table in my living room, and sometimes when people come by to visit, I open the box and let them feel the long, jagged crack in the crown.

The scar on my chest is another matter. I'm still self-conscious about it, and I've actually let only a few people touch it, all of them women who must've prevailed on me at weak moments. I finally stopped inventing stories to explain how the thing got there. Somewhere along the way, I seemed to figure out that the story of how you receive a scar is rarely as interesting as the story of how you survive it. And in my case, anyway, it became easier to tell the truth. Now whenever anyone asks me about it, I simply say, "I hurt myself playing football a long time ago."

I'll go months without looking at it, and then one day I'll find myself back in front of the bathroom mirror, stripped down to my shorts and studying it with my face up close to the glass. It's flattened out over the years, and when you rub a finger over the flesh, it's not nearly as rough as it looks. As a matter of fact, it's as soft as a baby's bottom. No hair grows there, and I wonder if any will ever again. If archaeologists from the distant future dig up my grave and have a look inside the coffin, I hope there's still enough hide left on my bones to make them wonder at the life of the specimen. Was he a noble warrior, wounded by a weapon in battle? Or was he another kind of man, a victim of a violent time, shot in the chest while trying to foil a bank robbery? I could leave a handwritten message in the ground with me, explaining what had happened. But I'll spare them that. There's no bigger bore than an ex-ballplayer with a long memory and an audience to hear him out.

"Was it worth it?" my father asked me that day when I first realized that football had scarred me for life. It was just like him to ask a twenty-one-year-old a question that he'd still be trying to answer twenty-eight years after his last game.

There's something else my father told me that I remember now. "None of it matters, John Ed," he said. "Was I a good teammate? Did I do my best and give everything I had to help the team? These are the questions you need to be asking."

And they're questions I continue to ask myself today, even though I'm not sure why being a good teammate still matters to me. It ends for everybody, and then it starts all over again, in ways you never anticipated. Marty Dufrene sits in his wheelchair listening to the Tiger fight song to help him through a rough patch. Ramsey Dardar endures prison by playing the games over in his head, starting with the kickoff and moving play by play to the finish. Big Ed Stanton never took up the game of golf, and yet he rides the streets of Bayou Vista in a cart nearly identical to Coach Mac's, recalling the one time the old man invited him for a ride.

I haven't been back to Tiger Stadium since that night years ago when I left at halftime in the rain, but I now can watch the team on TV without feeling that I'll suffocate unless I go outside for air, and I no longer automatically give the dial a spin when I'm out driving on a Saturday night and an LSU game comes on the radio. There are things we never get over, and for me, football is one of them. Maybe the time will come when the memory fades and leaves me altogether and I'll wonder at my silliness for having loved those days so much. But more likely I'll still be remembering them at the end, the way Coach Mac did. The doorbell will ring, and my wife and daughter will rise to answer it. I'll hear footsteps in the hall, and then suddenly I'll see a friend from long ago. "Is that you?" I'll say and wave him over. He'll sit at my bedside, and I'll reach for his hand. "Do you remember the time the USC Trojans came to Baton Rouge?" Then we'll visit a night when it seemed we'd live forever.

I suppose I could seek out the rest of my teammates and make more apologies for the vanishing act, but, like me, most of them have elected to vanish too, moving into whatever roles the world had reserved for them. Last I heard, Greg Raymond had returned to New Orleans and was running his family's jewelry business. James Britt and Bob Weathersby were lawyers, and Leigh Shepard was teaching school. Hokie Gajan had transitioned from the field to the radio booth and now worked Saints games as a color analyst. And Jay Whitley, somebody told me, is an orthodontist, the father of four kids. If they're anything like their old man, they're stouthearted and fearless, and they eat linebackers for lunch.

On Saturdays, when the pregame prayer and pep talks were done, we filed out of the chute to the screams of people who were counting on us. The band began to play; up ahead, the cheerleaders were waiting. Under the crossbar of the goalpost we huddled, seniors in front. For the first few steps I kept a hand on the shoulder of the teammate next to me, so as not to lose my balance, arms pumping, knees lifted high. The heat felt like a dense, blistering weight in your lungs. If you looked up above the rim of the bowl, you couldn't see the stars; the light from the standards had washed out the sky.

Always in the back of your mind was the knowledge of your supreme good fortune. Everyone else would travel a similar course of human experience, but you were different.

And so, chinstraps buckled tight, we ran out onto the field as one, the gold and the white a single elongated blur, neatly trimmed in purple.

Acknowledgments

Since 1982, I've written occasional essays about my father, my hometown, and my years as a college football player. Some of the material in this book originally appeared, in different context and form, in The Washington Post, Esquire *and* Sports Illustrated, *and I'd like to acknowledge my former editors at those publications.*

Ben Bradlee, George Solomon, Leonard Shapiro, Jay Lovinger, and Jeanne McManus were especially good to me when I was a reporter for The Post. *I'd like to thank David Hirshey for publishing my work when he was at* Esquire. *And I'd like to thank Rob Fleder and Chris Hunt for being so generous to me over my fifteen years as a contributor at* Sports Illustrated. *Rob and Chris assigned the 2002 magazine article that inspired this book. I am forever indebted to them.*

I'm grateful to Esther Newberg for her loyalty and dedication. Esther's pep talks rank among the best I've heard, and without them I wouldn't have had the courage to tell this story.

Lastly, I wish to thank Chris Raymond of ESPN Books for his confidence in this project and commitment to seeing it done.